Fifty Things
You Need to Know About
British History

Fifty Things
You Need to Know About
British History

Hugh Williams

Collins

First published in 2008 by
Collins, an imprint of
HarperCollins Publishers
77–85 Fulham Palace Road
Hammersmith
London w6 8jb
www.collins.co.uk

A catalogue record for this book is
available from the British Library

ISBN 978-0-00-727841-1

Editor: Kate Johnson

Typeset by Rowland Phototypesetting Ltd, Bury St Edmunds, Suffolk
Printed and bound in Great Britain by Clays Ltd, St Ives plc

Mixed Sources
Product group from well-managed
forests and other controlled sources
www.fsc.org Cert no. SW-COC-1806
© 1996 Forest Stewardship Council

Contents

PART 5 Ingenuity: Britain's Innovations

Acknowledgements

I am not a professional historian. Much of the information contained in this book comes from authors I was encouraged to read in my childhood and at school – Macaulay, Trevelyan, G. M. Young and so on; from the historians I studied at university – Gibbon, Elton, Plumb, Namier and others; and the work of people like Simon Schama, Niall Ferguson, Andrew Roberts, Norman Davies, John Brewer and N. A. M. Rodger which I have read and admired as an adult. I have also read, browsed and scanned the work of many other writers: their knowledge has proved invaluable in preparing this book. These days the internet is an enormous source of useful information whose many historical websites, such as the Modern History Sourcebook, have proved very helpful in finding original documents easily. Cambridge University has recently made available online all of Charles Darwin's private papers, including the notes he made during his voyage on *HMS Beagle*. I have used these and other sites extensively.

I would like to thank Richard Melman, Channel Director of the History Channel in Britain, for agreeing to take up my idea in the first place and Taylor Downing, Managing Director of Flashback Television and Executive Producer of the television series, for his encouragement and help at all points during the production of the series and this book. Special thanks are due to my researcher, Caroline Harvey, who patiently listened to my opinions as she checked my work.

I would also like to thank my editor at HarperCollins, Denise

Bates, who saw the potential for this book and has supported it from the beginning, and my agent, Antony Topping, who introduced me to a world of which I knew little with masterly professionalism. I would like to thank all my family who have encouraged me in this, my first literary endeavour – with, as ever, a very large thank you to my wife, Sue, whom I abandoned to the washing up while I wrote and who cast her shrewd sub editor's eye over much of the finished work.

Introduction

Some years ago I was browsing in a bookshop in America. I've always liked American bookshops; much of what they sell reveals the differences between our two countries. So it proved on this occasion. On the history shelf I found a paperback called *What Every American Should Know About American History* by Alan Axelrod and Charles Phillips. Intrigued by the title, I bought it.

It turned out to be an intelligent and very readable canter through American history from the days of Viking exploration to the end of the Cold War. In all it covered 200 significant events, outlining the principal facts relating to each one. Enjoyable, unpretentious and above all, simple, it presented – in a take-it-or-leave-it sort of way – the story of the most powerful nation on earth. I enjoyed it immensely and felt my knowledge of American history had improved effortlessly. I also felt something else rather less heart-warming.

This book, I thought, could never be published in Britain. It was far too simplistic for all those sophisticated people who banged on about the Empire in a vague, unsympathetic way, or wrote off the whole of nineteenth-century Britain as a smoke-enveloped slum of exploitation and capitalist greed.

Disraeli once said that his wife could never remember which came first – the Greeks or the Romans. Lots of people I met didn't know whether Henry VIII came before or after Charles I; they couldn't put the battles of Bannockburn, Bosworth and Blenheim in a historical order; and they hadn't a clue about events of such fundamental importance to their country as the Glorious Revolution or the Great Reform Bill. They were all happy, well-connected, successful people, and these holes in their knowledge had not hampered their lives in any palpable way. Or had they? Wasn't that the whole point? In Britain, lack of knowledge of the country's past was becoming a badge of honour. All that mattered was now: look forward, never back. These people, I thought, would laugh at my American history book. They would dismiss it as an oddity, a typically American piece of patriotic fluff – quite unsuitable for the more refined British way of life. I kept the book by my bed and my thoughts to myself.

I also began work on my idea. As a television executive with experience in factual programmes including current affairs, history and the arts, I wanted to find a way to transfer the approach to history I'd found in that American book into a television series and a book about British history. They would have to run counter to current ingrained social attitudes. They would have more to do with the sort of history I read as a child – G. M. Trevelyan's *History of England*, or G. M. Young's *Portrait of an Age* – than the empathetic, judgemental, why-was-everyone-so beastly? school of history that seemed to be the preferred method of teaching it today. History should be straightforward, uncluttered and exciting. Above all, it should tell stories. The more I thought about it, the more I realised that the way to do this was to try to refine British history into a series of key events and explain the linkage between them. In this way I would be able to select the most interesting and exciting stories and put them into context, creating a framework so the readers and viewers would not only learn the details of a particular event, but also understand how it slotted into the progress of British history as a whole.

The idea was called 'Fifty Things You Need To Know About British History'. Its moment has now arrived. Why?

There are two main reasons. The first is the growing realisation among many academics and politicians that the way we have been teaching history in our schools is wrong. By moving away from narrative – the broad sweep of history – to concentrating on isolated episodes we have educated a whole generation who may know quite a lot about, say, Oliver Cromwell and the Battle of the Somme, but pretty much zero about everything that happened in between. That's not history.

Some distinguished historians have joined the debate about the way history is being taught in our schools. Simon Schama – no newcomer to television himself – argues for what he calls 'the three Cs': 'comprehensive chronological continuity'. Tristram Hunt, a Cambridge academic who presented a television series on the English Civil War says: 'What children need to learn first is a clear narrative. I'm all for empathy, but they can do that later.' Schama agrees: 'If empathy means weepily identifying with victims, it can be sentimental mush. The ability to put oneself in someone's shoes requires a lot of knowledge.'

The second, and perhaps more important reason, is the growing recognition that a proper knowledge of your country's history is an essential part of being a good citizen. Understanding a country's past helps to identify its strengths. Prime Minister Gordon Brown, in a speech in 2007, said 'Britain has a unique history.' British values have 'emerged from the long tidal flows of British history – from the 2,000 years of successive waves of invasion, immigration, assimilation and trading partnerships'. There is, he went on, 'a golden thread that runs through British history' from Magna Carta to the Bill of Rights of 1689 to the democratic reform acts of the nineteenth century. Knowing about these things builds a sense of being British, which 'helps unite and unify us'.

In other words, a knowledge of history is a badge of citizenship. Just as you would not call yourself a fan of a football club without knowing the history of its successes and defeats; or join a social club without knowing its rules, so you cannot call yourself a citizen without knowing how the country in which you live came to exist as it does today. If you have nothing to look back on, nothing to feel proud about, nothing to provide you with the understanding of where you came from and why, the present and the future stand without foundation and are therefore more prone to collapse. Human life is part of a continuum, not a vacuum. That's why our history is important.

At the same time, the *idea* of history continues to be very popular. Through watching television documentaries and historical dramas and by visiting famous landmarks many people begin to understand, and enjoy, aspects of history that were probably denied to them before. But it can also remain elusive. It may be around us everywhere all the time, but how it fits together is often much more difficult to grasp. Unless you've been lucky enough to be well taught, history can appear rather overwhelming – a dense mass of facts and dates that coalesce into an impenetrable fog. And nobody wants to set out into a fog if they can help it.

And so I have set out to provide a path through that fog. This book describes fifty key events in British history which, linked together, form an overview of our history. Those fifty events divide into five thematic chapters:

1. 'Roots: The Origins of Britain' describes where the British came from.
2. 'Struggle: The Battles for Britain' recounts some of Britain's greatest conflicts.
3. 'The Sea: Britain at Home and Abroad' tells the story of the growth of the British Empire.
4. 'Freedom: The Pursuit of Liberty' is about the fight for individual freedom and the development of British democracy.
5. 'Ingenuity: Britain's Innovations' lists some of the nation's most important scientific, cultural and social changes.

So why choose these fifty things in particular? The events in this book are not the only fifty things you need to know about British history. They are what I, and the producers of the television series, think are fifty of the most important things. Some people will say that we should have excluded some and included others. That's fine: history is not a perfect science and the differing judgements of individuals are just one of the things that make it interesting.

'History,' as the historian Hugh Trevor-Roper said, 'is too subtle a process to be firmly seized or summarily decided.'

This book is meant for everyone who is interested in history but is frightened of the fog. The 'Fifty Things' it describes will, I hope, provide a clear picture of the most important events in British history and how they fit together to create the nation we live in today.

Chronology

3100–2200 BC	Stonehenge
43 AD	The Roman invasion of Britain
597	Saint Augustine Arrives in Britain
871	Alfred the Great Becomes King of Wessex
1066	The Battle of Hastings
1215	Signing of Magna Carta
1381	The Peasants' Revolt
1387	Chaucer's *The Canterbury Tales*
1415	The Battle of Agincourt
1485	The Battle of Bosworth
1536	The Dissolution of the Monasteries
1564	The Birth of William Shakespeare
1577–1580	Sir Francis Drake and the Circumnavigation of the Globe
1588	The Spanish Armada
1605	The Gunpowder Plot
1611	The *Authorised Version* of the Bible is published
1620	The Voyage of the Pilgrim Fathers
1645	The Battle of Naseby
1649	The Execution of Charles I
1688–1689	The Glorious Revolution and the Bill of Rights
1694	The Foundation of the Bank of England
1704	The Battle of Blenheim
1707	The Act of Union
1711–1720	The South Sea Bubble
1714	The Longitude Act
1721	Sir Robert Walpole Becomes Prime Minister
1757	The Battle of Plassey
1769	James Watt Patents his Steam Engine Condenser
1776	Adam Smith's *The Wealth of Nations* is published
1781	The Surrender of the British Army at Yorktown, Virginia
1805	The Battle of Trafalgar
1815	The Battle of Waterloo
1829	The Metropolitan Police Act

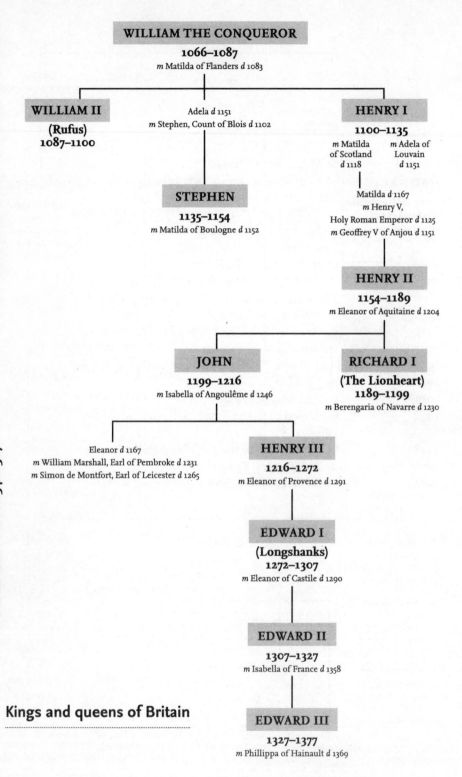

WILLIAM THE CONQUEROR

1066–1087
m Matilda of Flanders d 1083

WILLIAM II

(Rufus)
1087–1100

Adela d 1151
m Stephen, Count of Blois d 1102

HENRY I

1100–1135
m Matilda   m Adela of
of Scotland   Louvain
d 1118   d 1151

STEPHEN

1135–1154
m Matilda of Boulogne d 1152

Matilda d 1167
m Henry V,
Holy Roman Emperor d 1125
m Geoffrey V of Anjou d 1151

HENRY II

1154–1189
m Eleanor of Aquitaine d 1204

JOHN

1199–1216
m Isabella of Angoulême d 1246

RICHARD I

(The Lionheart)
1189–1199
m Berengaria of Navarre d 1230

Eleanor d 1167
m William Marshall, Earl of Pembroke d 1231
m Simon de Montfort, Earl of Leicester d 1265

HENRY III

1216–1272
m Eleanor of Provence d 1291

EDWARD I

(Longshanks)
1272–1307
m Eleanor of Castile d 1290

EDWARD II

1307–1327
m Isabella of France d 1358

Kings and queens of Britain

EDWARD III

1327–1377
m Phillippa of Hainault d 1369

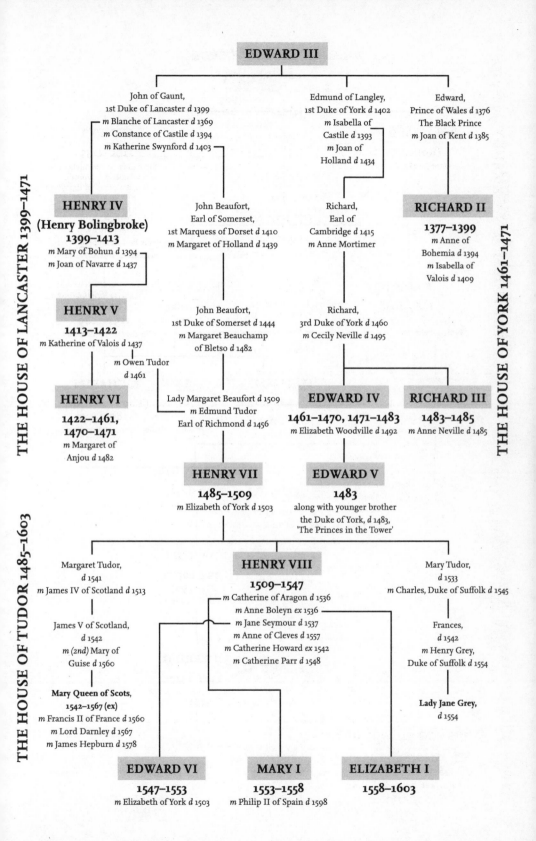

EDWARD III

John of Gaunt,
1st Duke of Lancaster *d* 1399
m Blanche of Lancaster *d* 1369
m Constance of Castile *d* 1394
m Katherine Swynford *d* 1403

Edmund of Langley,
1st Duke of York *d* 1402
m Isabella of
Castile *d* 1393
m Joan of
Holland *d* 1434

Edward,
Prince of Wales *d* 1376
The Black Prince
m Joan of Kent *d* 1385

THE HOUSE OF LANCASTER 1399–1471

HENRY IV
(Henry Bolingbroke)
1399–1413
m Mary of Bohun *d* 1394
m Joan of Navarre *d* 1437

John Beaufort,
Earl of Somerset,
1st Marquess of Dorset *d* 1410
m Margaret of Holland *d* 1439

Richard,
Earl of
Cambridge *d* 1415
m Anne Mortimer

RICHARD II
1377–1399
m Anne of
Bohemia *d* 1394
m Isabella of
Valois *d* 1409

THE HOUSE OF YORK 1461–1471

HENRY V
1413–1422
m Katherine of Valois *d* 1437

John Beaufort,
1st Duke of Somerset *d* 1444
m Margaret Beauchamp
of Bletso *d* 1482

m Owen Tudor
d 1461

Richard,
3rd Duke of York *d* 1460
m Cecily Neville *d* 1495

HENRY VI
1422–1461,
1470–1471
m Margaret of
Anjou *d* 1482

Lady Margaret Beaufort *d* 1509
m Edmund Tudor
Earl of Richmond *d* 1456

EDWARD IV
1461–1470, 1471–1483
m Elizabeth Woodville *d* 1492

RICHARD III
1483–1485
m Anne Neville *d* 1485

HENRY VII
1485–1509
m Elizabeth of York *d* 1503

EDWARD V
1483
along with younger brother
the Duke of York, *d* 1483,
'The Princes in the Tower'

THE HOUSE OF TUDOR 1485–1603

Margaret Tudor,
d 1541
m James IV of Scotland *d* 1513

James V of Scotland,
d 1542
m (2nd) Mary of
Guise *d* 1560

Mary Queen of Scots,
1542–1567 (ex)
m Francis II of France *d* 1560
m Lord Darnley *d* 1567
m James Hepburn *d* 1578

HENRY VIII
1509–1547
m Catherine of Aragon *d* 1536
m Anne Boleyn *ex* 1536
m Jane Seymour *d* 1537
m Anne of Cleves *d* 1557
m Catherine Howard *ex* 1542
m Catherine Parr *d* 1548

Mary Tudor,
d 1533
m Charles, Duke of Suffolk *d* 1545

Frances,
d 1542
m Henry Grey,
Duke of Suffolk *d* 1554

Lady Jane Grey,
d 1554

EDWARD VI
1547–1553
m Elizabeth of York *d* 1503

MARY I
1553–1558
m Philip II of Spain *d* 1598

ELIZABETH I
1558–1603

Mary Queen of Scots,

JAMES I

1603–1625
(James VI of Scotland)
1567–1625
m Anne of Denmark d 1619

CHARLES I

1625– ex 1649
m Henrietta Maria of France d 1669

Elizabeth, d 1662
m Frederick V,
Elector Palatine of the Rhine d 1632

JAMES II

1685–1688

m Mary of
Modena d 1718

Mary, d 1660
m William II,
Prince of Orange d 1650

m Anne Hyde
d 1671

**The Commonwealth,
Oliver Cromwell Lord Protector**

CHARLES II

1660–1685
m Catherine of Braganza d 1705

Sophia, d 1714
m Ernest Augustus,
Elector of Hanover d 1698

William   Mary

James,
The Old Pretender d 1766
m Mary Clementia Sobieski,
(granddaughter of John III,
King of Poland) d 1735

**WILLIAM III
& MARY II**

1689–1702
William III d 1702
Mary II d 1694

ANNE

1702–1714
m George of
Denmark d 1708

Charles,
The Young Pretender
'Bonnie Prince Charlie'
d 1788

GEORGE I

1714–1727
m Sophia Dorothea of Brunswick & Celle d 1726

GEORGE II

1727–1760
m Caroline of Brandenburg-Anspach d 1737

Frederick Lewis, Prince of Wales d 1751
m Augusta of Saxe-Gotha-Altenburg d 1772

GEORGE III

1760–1820
m Sophia Charlotte of Mecklenburg-Strelitz d 1818

GEORGE IV

1820–1830
m Caroline of Brunswick-
Wolfenbuttel d 1821

WILLIAM IV

1830–1837
m Adelaide of
Saxe-Meiningen d 1849

Edward,
Duke of Kent d 1820
m Victoria of Saxe-Coburg d 1861

VICTORIA

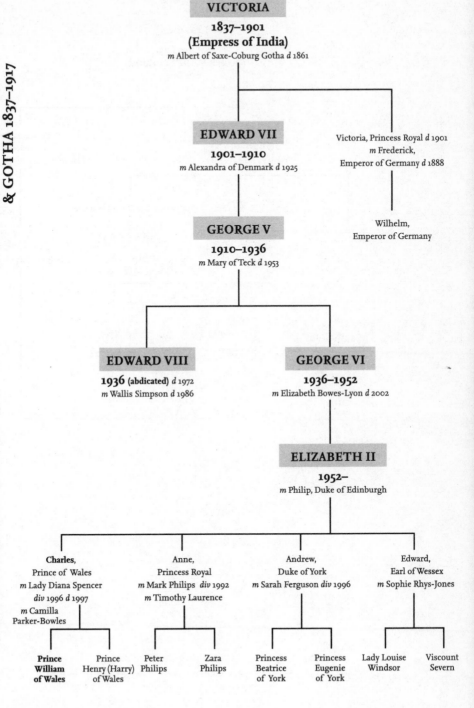

VICTORIA

1837–1901
(Empress of India)
m Albert of Saxe-Coburg Gotha d 1861

EDWARD VII

1901–1910
m Alexandra of Denmark d 1925

Victoria, Princess Royal d 1901
m Frederick,
Emperor of Germany d 1888

GEORGE V

1910–1936
m Mary of Teck d 1953

Wilhelm,
Emperor of Germany

EDWARD VIII

1936 (abdicated) d 1972
m Wallis Simpson d 1986

GEORGE VI

1936–1952
m Elizabeth Bowes-Lyon d 2002

ELIZABETH II

1952–
m Philip, Duke of Edinburgh

Charles,
Prince of Wales
m Lady Diana Spencer
div 1996 d 1997
m Camilla
Parker-Bowles

Anne,
Princess Royal
m Mark Philips div 1992
m Timothy Laurence

Andrew,
Duke of York
m Sarah Ferguson div 1996

Edward,
Earl of Wessex
m Sophie Rhys-Jones

**Prince
William
of Wales**

Prince
Henry (Harry)
of Wales

Peter
Philips

Zara
Philips

Princess
Beatrice
of York

Princess
Eugenie
of York

Lady Louise
Windsor

Viscount
Severn

1 Roots

The Origins of Britain

Introduction

When I was young we used to go on holiday to Anglesey, off the coast of North Wales. Our long drive would eventually take us across the Menai Bridge, Thomas Telford's great feat of engineering constructed between 1819 and 1826 to speed up the journey to the port of Holyhead. When it was built no suspension bridge had been designed on such a scale before. Today it is a 'World Heritage Site'. My father was Welsh and as we drove across he would recite a Welsh poem all about it. I cannot remember who it was by – probably the poet David Owen who wrote a number of poems about Menai – but I can remember that he tried to get my brother and me to recite it too. We never managed more than a few words. The Welsh language, despite our parentage, has remained a closed book to us. But sweeping across Telford's beautiful masterpiece high above the waters of the Menai Straits, my parents' ancient Austin looking forward like an exhausted horse to the end of the interminable drive, I felt a bit Welsh, a bit different and rather special. I felt I had roots. I was something more than just an ordinary little London schoolboy.

Over the past thirty years people in Britain have spent a lot of time returning to their roots. The fashion for devolution with the establishment of a parliament in Scotland and an assembly in Wales, combined with the long struggle to find political stability in Northern Ireland, have affected our sense of nationhood. Which comes first – our Britishness, our Scottishness, Welshness or Englishness? Meanwhile, beyond the shores of the

United Kingdom, our national interests are being absorbed into the common objectives of the European Union and constantly tempered by increasing globalisation. Outside we are hurrying to be part of a bigger world: at home, it seems, we want to be part of a smaller one. Who we are and where we come from have become increasingly important as a shrinking world seeks to suck our national identity out of us.

This chapter goes in search of who the British are and where they came from. It begins with Stonehenge, an enigmatic monument to the people who inhabited the country in its earliest times, and as good a place as any in which to invest our sense of history.

The Romans were the first people to give Britain shape. They occupied it for 400 years, but after they withdrew the order they had created collapsed into chaos. Slowly, very slowly, order began to return. It came first through the messages of the Christian missionaries, particularly Saint Augustine, who brought back the ideas of Rome, by then a Christian city, to the island which had been abandoned 200 years before. It was enlarged and developed by the Anglo-Saxon kings, the greatest of whom was Alfred the Great, King of Wessex.

Britain succumbed to invasion for the last time in 1066 when the Normans became its rulers, destroyed the Anglo-Saxon way of life and started to lay the foundations of the medieval state. The Catholic Church and the monarchy held the country in their grasp until the Reformation broke them apart. Henry VIII's dissolution of the monasteries in the sixteenth century was one of the most important acts in a process which would see the evolution of Britain into a nation state. Shakespeare helped give that nation its tongue.

In 1707 Britain joined with Scotland, but managed its relationship with its other neighbour, Ireland, far less successfully. The failure of the Home Rule movement in the nineteenth century would have disastrous consequences for both countries in the twentieth.

Today, in the twenty-first century, Britain is a part of Europe and shares its national aspirations with twenty-seven other countries. The island which carved its identity by withdrawing from the shifts and changes of a continent in turmoil has re-entered the arena from which it came. Once again Britain is replanting its roots.

CHAPTER 1

Stonehenge
3100 to 2200 BC

The huge and ancient stone monument known as
Stonehenge, in Wiltshire, is one of Britain's oldest
monuments. Its origins are uncertain. It is surrounded
by myth and legend. It belongs to the beginning of
Britain.

If you drive east to west across southern England you may well pass
Stonehenge. It stands just a few hundred yards back from the A303,
one of the country's busiest main roads taking traffic to and from
the West Country. Travelling westwards you are more than likely to
have time to get a good view of it
because it is here that the fast dual
carriageway funnels into a two-lane
road and the traffic queues can be
enormous. Stonehenge is an island
of antiquity stranded in a twenty-
first century melting pot. At this

*Stonehenge is an island of
antiquity stranded in a
twenty-first century
melting pot.*

point the journey west crosses a bridge of nearly 5,000 years of history as the achievements of the most ancient rites of man stare
stonily towards his most recent and most frenetic.

Stonehenge was built in different phases over many hundreds
of years. To begin with, in about 3100 BC, it was a circular ditch
with an internal bank and fifty-six holes around its perimeter.
A few hundred years later two circles of bluestone were erected.
Bluestone is not native to Wiltshire but comes from the Preseli
Hills in Pembrokeshire in West Wales. After that the bluestones
were dug up and rearranged and the familiar sarsen stones brought
to the site. These form Stonehenge's most famous image of the

pillars with lintels across the top. The sarsen stones came from Avebury, about 18 miles to the north. In the last phase, about 2200 BC, the bluestones were put back again to form a circle and a horseshoe inside the sarsen pillars. All these different arrangements took place over hundreds of years and leave many questions unanswered. What was Stonehenge for? Who built it? How did the bluestones get from Wales to Wiltshire? Throughout the history of Britain people have tried to answer these questions, adapting their answers to suit the age in which they live.

In the twelfth century Henry of Huntingdon wrote a history of the English people from the Roman invasion to the reign of Henry II. He described Stonehenge as one of the four wonders of Britain but declared that no one knew why it had been built, or by whom. His contemporary, Geoffrey of Monmouth, came up with a rather more colourful account. Stonehenge, he said, was constructed as a memorial to nobles who had been slain in battle by the Saxon chieftain, Hengist. He dates the origin of the monument to the time of Aurelius Ambrosius, who emerged from the chaos following the Romans' retreat to lead Britain in its war against the Saxons. According to legend, Ambrosius was the uncle of King Arthur and having decided to build the monument sought advice from the magician Merlin. Merlin told him of a stone circle in Ireland called the giants' dance. Ambrosius sent his men to fetch it and, with Merlin's help, they brought it back to Wiltshire. A sacred ceremony was held at Stonehenge where Ambrosius was crowned as king of his people: myth and ritual were even then part of its story.

In the seventeenth century, James I, always interested in scholarship, asked his Surveyor-General, Inigo Jones, to carry out an investigation into the reasons why Stonehenge was built. Inigo Jones was a great architect but a somewhat naive archaeologist. His love of classical antiquity influenced the design of the magnificent buildings he built for his king in London, but they got him off on the wrong foot as far as Stonehenge was concerned. He came to the conclusion that it was a Roman temple to the god Coelus. Once again the influences of the age, rather than historical accuracy, had been used to determine the origins of this ancient monument.

Later in the seventeenth century, another study of Stonehenge began to get a bit closer to the truth. John Aubrey was an antiquarian, biographer and gossip whose book, *Brief Lives*, is a highly entertaining account of many of the most distinguished people of the time. He was interested in objects as much as people and recorded his observations of Stonehenge in a book about British monuments. In particular he noticed the depressions or holes around the perimeter of the original ditch, which have since been called the 'Aubrey Holes' in his honour. He surmised correctly that Stonehenge belonged to an early British civilisation, but in trying to locate its origins more exactly he came up with the idea that it was a Druid temple. This thought fuelled the imagination of the eighteenth century. The concept of a mysterious ruin set in a quiet landscape, its eerie history of ceremony and sacrifice blending with the force of nature played perfectly into the romantic ideas of the time. Stonehenge obligingly fell in with fashion.

It was only in the twentieth century that Stonehenge started seriously to reveal at least a few of its secrets. Up until the end of the First World War it was privately owned. Back in the seventeenth century, when he had first seen it, James I had tried to acquire it but had been unsuccessful. In 1918 it belonged to a successful local livestock farmer and racehorse owner, Cecil Chubb, who had bought it on a whim for £6,600 three years earlier. He gave it to the nation and the Prime Minister, David Lloyd-George, made him a baronet as a token of thanks. After that, the monument began to be subjected to serious examination over an extended period of time. It became the responsibility of the Ministry of Works which, worried that the property it had inherited might be unsafe because of falling stones, asked an archaeologist, William Hawley, to carry out an extensive excavation. He would be the first person to take a prolonged look at Stonehenge for many years. He replaced stones that had fallen down and secured others that were in danger of toppling over. He found human remains which indicated that the monument might have been used as a site for funerals. Most importantly, he was the first person to realise that Stonehenge was not just one monument, but the result of different activity by different groups of people over many hundreds of years. In the 1950s and early 1960s, as further research revealed how Stonehenge probably looked when it was first built, other stones were put back in their original positions. The monument we see today is therefore to a certain extent a work of restoration. Previous ages had allowed it to suffer at the mercy of time and weather, leaving it to exist as a ruin in almost any form. It is only the meticulous knowledge of our own time that has let us see it as the early people who built it in the first place might have done.

With the work of restoration distinguished scientists, as well as archaeologists and historians, have turned their attention to Stonehenge. A theory developed that the monument was placed where it was as a temple to the sun and that the individual pillars and stones could predict eclipses of the sun and the moon. Computer science was used to try to substantiate this theory and other monuments were analysed to see whether they had similar characteristics. It established that there was every reason to believe that Stonehenge and other ancient places in Britain had astronomical connections and could have been used to interpret and predict the movement of the heavens. More extravagant theories have grown up alongside these purely scientific conclusions. Some people believe that ley lines connect places such as Stonehenge with other sites in Britain, emitting psychic or mystical energy. Their magical powers are part of an old religion that in a free and tolerant world can now be reborn to celebrate its rituals in the temples from which it was driven long ago. The earliest emblem of Britain's past still has a place in the life of the country today.

None of this of course provides final answers to the questions that still surround Stonehenge. It seems incredible, for instance, that the early inhabitants of Britain transported heavy bluestones – some of them weighing as much as 4 or 5 tons each – from Wales to Wiltshire. In 2001, a group of enthusiastic volunteers tried to see whether such a feat might be possible and, with £100,000 of lottery money behind them, constructed a replica of a Bronze Age raft with a piece of bluestone as cargo. It ended up at the bottom of the sea. A more prosaic explanation could be that the movements of glaciers carried the stones from the Preseli Hills to Salisbury Plain, but that will not prevent the invention of other notions about the origins of Stonehenge. In March 2008 archaeologists returned to the site to begin important new excavations. Their work was organised and funded by the BBC for a television programme and they were hoping to prove that ancient man transported the bluestones from the Preseli Hills in Pembrokeshire to Salisbury Plain because of their healing properties. The archaeologists broke through to a layer which once held smaller bluestones and unearthed fragments of pottery and artefacts. Stonehenge, they said, could have been a 'Neolithic Lourdes'. Britain's most ancient monument once again captured the spirit of the age as television went in search of its secrets.

At Stonehenge, ancient and modern will always coalesce. It belongs to a time when the evidence of history is nothing more than a silent landscape and a few fragmentary relics beneath our feet. We know very little about it or the people who built it, but its deep, forgotten past is where our history begins.

CHAPTER 2

The Roman Invasion of Britain
43 AD

In 43 AD, Roman forces under the command of the
Emperor Claudius invaded Britain and began what
became a complete conquest of the country. Britain
remained a province of the Roman Empire for
nearly 400 years.

In his famous novel, *I, Claudius*, Robert Graves gives us a striking
picture of the Emperor who conquered Britain. Hidden from
public view by a family ashamed of his stammer and slobbering, he
is dragged from hiding by the assassins who have murdered his
predecessor, the mad Caligula. They make him Emperor, confident
they can control him. What they do not realise is that Claudius's
behaviour is the result of illness, not foolishness: he will make a
better Emperor than they think.

Graves's portrait is based on the writings of the Roman historian, Suetonius, who described the activities of the first twelve
Roman Emperors in often lurid detail. According to him, corruption, a thirst for power and lust seemed to be the principal
characteristics of the men who ruled half the world. Their policies,
if they deserve such a description, were designed to keep them
in power by appeasing the people. The conquest of Britain fell
into this category. It began because a new Emperor needed to
consolidate his position: 400 years of Roman Britain started in
order to give Claudius the adulation he needed from the citizens
of Rome.

Claudius was not the first Roman leader to cross the Channel in
an attempt to incorporate Britain into Rome's vast foreign conquests. In 55 and 54 BC Julius Caesar, then master of all of Gaul,

decided to invade. His first expedition was on quite a small scale, but his second was much larger. In 54 BC he landed with five legions (about 25,000 men) and 2,000 cavalrymen somewhere near Deal on the Kent coast, and throughout the summer successfully fought his way north until he crossed the Thames, probably at Brentford in Middlesex. The purpose of this expedition is unclear. Some time before the end of the summer he decided to return to Gaul. He never went back to Britain although he recorded, as he did in many places where he fought, his impressions of the people. The men dyed their bodies with blue woad, he said, which made them look very frightening in battle; they wore their hair long, but shaved everywhere else apart from on the upper lip; and they shared their wives among them. These were the people that he had invaded, subdued and left behind. It would be nearly a hundred years before the Romans returned.

Claudius, aware that his survival as Emperor would require something more substantial than his reputation as a fool, turned to Britain as the place where he could demonstrate military prowess. It also made some strategic sense. Unless brought under Roman control, the island of Britain could have proved a useful base for the Empire's enemies to attack its possessions in Gaul. In May 43 AD, a large force of 40,000 men under the command of Aulus Plautius landed on the south coast, though not before their commander persuaded them to set sail in the first place. The soldiers did not like the idea of a journey into an unknown world. Once across the Channel, however, their campaign went well. They defeated the British chieftain, Caractacus, who fled to Wales, and by the autumn were ready to receive their Emperor so that he could enjoy his triumph. At Colchester eleven British tribal kings surrendered to Claudius, who was now able to return to Rome as warlord as well as Emperor. The Senate voted to build him a triumphal arch in recognition of his victory. The inscription on it read that he had 'brought barbarian peoples beyond the Ocean for the first time under the rule of Rome'. The Roman occupation of Britain had begun.

The Romans took Britain very seriously, grasping possession of their new province with ferocious speed. Within seven years of Claudius's triumph they had established a base at London, built a bridge across the Thames and begun to construct a road network throughout the south of England. Caractacus came out of Wales to confront them but was betrayed by a rival tribe and sent as a prisoner to Rome where Claudius pardoned him. Ten years later, Boudicca, the Queen of the Iceni in the east of England, attacked Colchester, London and St Albans. Apparently tall with long, red hair, Boudicca, and her army of tribesmen, succeeded in terrifying the Roman invaders. In 61 AD her vast troop of footsoldiers and charioteers, their women and children watching from wagons drawn up around them, faced a much smaller Roman force. The site of the battlefield is not known, but it is believed to be in the Midlands, possibly near what is now Wroxeter in Shropshire. Roman discipline utterly defeated British size. Tens of thousands of men, women and children were slaughtered by the victorious forces of the Empire and Boudicca herself died shortly afterwards, perhaps by her own hand.

By the end of the 70s AD most of England was under Roman control; however the Britons of Scotland remained unconquered. Agricola, who became Governor of Britain in 78 AD, decided to carry the fight into their territory and won a major victory at Mons Graupius near Aberdeen in 84 AD. He claimed that Scotland had been subdued, but in this he spoke prematurely.

At Mons Graupius the commander of the Britons made a speech to his troops in which, the Roman historian Tacitus tells us, he told his men that they were all loyal to one united race. The Roman troops, he cried, had no such glorious unity because they came from all over the world. His description of the Roman army's origins was quite accurate, although he was unwise to assume that this was a military weakness. The Roman Empire was by its very nature cosmopolitan and the men who fought for it came from many different backgrounds. Aulus Plautius, Claudius's commander, had been a provincial governor in Eastern Europe, in what is now Hungary and Austria. Suetonius Paulinus, the commander who defeated Boudicca, was the first Roman general to cross the Atlas Mountains in North Africa. Agricola, the victor at Mons Graupius – and, incidentally, Tacitus's father-in-law – was born in southern France, in what is now Provence. The conquest of Britain was carried out by men whose home was where duty took them. Wherever they were – in the African desert, the German forest, the English fen or the Scottish mountain – they rigorously applied their abilities to the cause of imperial victory.

Apart from Claudius, two other Emperors stand out as having an important part to play in the history of Roman Britain. The first, Hadrian, became Emperor on the death of Trajan in 117 AD. He turned out to be a highly competent ruler, conscientious and interested in learning about the territories he controlled. Like many Emperors of Rome, he had to watch his back: he had enemies everywhere. He therefore undertook long visits to the furthest outposts of the Empire to meet the troops who defended it. This was a wise strategy. It inspired loyalty in men who, separated from central government by long tours of duty in remote corners of the world, could become tempted into revolt. Hadrian seems to have enjoyed these expeditions, taking satisfaction from the task of securing his Empire's frontiers. In 122 AD he came to Britain at a time when, as far as we can tell, the northern part had been suffering from the invasion of barbarian tribes. Determined to put a stop to these – and to indulge in his love of building – the Emperor decided to construct a wall across Roman Britain's northern frontier. Picking the narrowest neck of territory that he thought suitable for the purpose, he built a great stone defence system from the estuary of the River Tyne in the east to the shores of Solway Firth in the west. This was Hadrian's Wall, 80 Roman miles long (73.5 in modern miles) with a small fort at one-mile intervals along the whole stretch of it. The size and shape of the wall changed as the Romans developed their thinking during its construction; most of it was completed within eight years. It was the biggest fortified frontier in the whole of the Roman Empire, a resolute emblem of its enormous power. After Hadrian died in 138 AD his successor, Antoninus Pius, who may have decided that he needed a military exploit to prove that he was not too mild-mannered, decided to reoccupy southern Scotland. He ordered his legions to move north and built another wall – the Antonine Wall – from the Firth of Forth to the Firth of Clyde. With an eye to economy he had it made out of turf. But the Pictish tribes of Scotland proved hard to subdue. When Antoninus's successor, Marcus Aurelius, came to power the Romans retreated to behind Hadrian's great edifice where they stayed until the time came for them to leave altogether. Marcus Aurelius is today remembered more for his writings as a stoic philosopher than as an Emperor, and in the rearrangement of Britain's northern defences he seems to have taken a leaf out of his own book: 'That which is not good for the bee-hive,' he wrote, 'cannot be good for the bees.'

The other great Roman Emperor inextricably caught up in the affairs of Britain was Constantine. In 305 AD he left the intrigues of the capital of the Empire behind to campaign with his father, Constantius, in Britain. Constantius was a Caesar, a junior emperor in charge of the northern provinces. Father and son fought against the Pictish tribes still untamed north of Hadrian's Wall, but in 306 Constantius died at York. His troops then proclaimed his son Emperor, even though the Praetorian Guard in Rome had nominated a rival, Maxentius. Some historians believe that Constantine built the great Roman walls around York at the time of his proclamation. Whatever the truth there is no doubt that at a crucial moment in the history of the whole Roman Empire, this ancient British city became the centre from which its future sprang. From there Constantine would go on to defeat his rival outside the gates of Rome and, as one of the greatest Emperors in the last century of Roman power, tolerate the rise of Christianity, create a new capital in Constantinople and die converted to the Christian religion.

The impact of the Roman occupation on Britain was profound. The country developed from a wild, barbarous land inhabited by fierce tribes into a unified self-governing province – Britannia. A network of roads linked all corners of the land; a single currency created a coherent market for trade; and the refinements of Roman civilisation brought fine buildings and magnificent fortifications to the towns and cities. Latin became the language of law and education. The British adopted the customs and attitudes of their governors: many of them wore togas. British metals were taken back to the heart of the Empire to be fashioned into weapons and armour, and wine and exotic fruits made their way northwards in return. Britain developed into what it would become again – a trading nation. But no empires last forever. By the end of the fourth century AD, Britain, like the rest of Rome's once indomitable possessions, was suffering from invasion on all sides. The

The country developed from a wild, barbarous land into a unified self-governing province – Britannia.

Empire had finally cracked in two with an eastern half based in Constantine's capital of Constantinople and a western part still trying desperately to cling to power in Rome. In 410 AD the last Emperor of the western Empire, Honorius, told the people of Britain that he had no legions left to defend them. Britannia, Rome's most northerly outpost, the troublesome island that had over four centuries succumbed to its power and become one of its most precious possessions, was abandoned. The unity of Roman Britain broke apart and the country surrendered to the tribal ambitions of foreign marauders. The Dark Ages had begun.

I remember once being involved in a documentary series for the BBC with the historian, John Roberts. It was called 'The Triumph of the West' and in it he explained how Western ideas and values had grown to be such a dominant force throughout the world. One sequence was filmed in the Forum in Rome. Roberts talked about Charlemagne, who in the late eighth century conquered a large part of Western Europe and tried to bring some sense of order to the chaos created by the wars of its different tribes. In 800 Charlemagne entered Rome where the Pope made him Holy Roman Emperor, a title that would exist in European history for centuries afterwards. Imagine, said Roberts, what it must have been like for Charlemagne, a man who could not write but who was struggling to tame the disruption all around him, to enter the Forum Romanum – a place which he had never seen before and of which he had no conception. He must have realised that the Roman Empire, although it had been extinguished four hundred years before, created a civilisation more advanced and more sophisticated than the one in which he was living.

For Britain, as for the rest of Europe, the collapse of the Roman Empire was an extraordinary period in its history. Nearly everything it had built – its language was one exception – was eventually demolished. It would be 600 years before anything remotely comparable emerged to replace it.

CHAPTER 3

Saint Augustine Arrives in Britain
597 AD

In 597 AD Saint Augustine landed in Kent as a
missionary from the Pope in Rome. At the same time
Celtic missionaries were at work in Ireland, Scotland
and the North of England. Britain's beginnings as a
Christian nation had begun.

The History of the Decline and Fall of the Roman Empire by Edward
Gibbon is one of the greatest works in British literature. Published
in six volumes over twelve years between 1776 and 1788 it surveys its
subject with effortless control, its elegant prose never distracted by
the mass of detail it seeks to describe. In the last chapter one short
sentence stands out. Summing up his colossal narrative Gibbon
wrote: 'I have described the triumph of barbarism and religion.' In
other words religion – Christianity – was for him as much a cause
of the collapse of the Roman Empire as was the rise of barbarism.
In the main part of the book he devoted two famous chapters to
Christianity in which he displayed the sceptical attitudes of the
Enlightenment of the eighteenth century. 'The clergy successfully
preached the doctrines of patience and pusillanimity,' he wrote;
'the active virtues of society were discouraged; and the last remains
of military spirit were buried in the cloister.' He is particularly
scathing about miracles: 'The lame walked, the blind saw, the sick
were healed, the dead were raised, demons were expelled, and the
laws of Nature were frequently suspended for the benefit of
the church.' There is much more in the same vein. For Gibbon,
Christianity sapped the strength of the Empire and so contributed
to its fall.

His views were undoubtedly harsh – the barbarians would

probably have sacked Rome with or without Christianity – but in today's secular age Gibbon's disenchantment with organised religion must still sound appealing to a lot of people. Whether or not one takes his view, the fact remains that from the start of the seventh century to the middle of the nineteenth, the history of Britain is as much about the history of religion as anything else. Today we may have abandoned Christian teaching in favour of scientific instruction, and prefer a society built on civic concepts of liberty rather than any thoughts of a duty before God, but we were not always like that. Saint Augustine's mission ensured that Britain was eventually drawn into Europe's Catholic Church. The Emperors might have gone, but Rome remained a powerful force in the life of Britain.

We know very little about the development of Christianity in Britain during its early years. Rumour has it that Joseph of Arimathea, the man who gave up his prepared tomb for the body of Jesus, visited Glastonbury many years after the Crucifixion, but there is no evidence for this. As Christianity developed, its organisation spread all through the provinces of the Roman Empire and by the middle of the second century AD had become established in Britain. The religion prospered as the Empire tottered. In the third century, when Rome was under threat from Asia as well as Northern Europe, Christians were able to evade prosecution as their persecutors turned their attention to more pressing matters. By the beginning of the fourth century they had strengthened sufficiently to become tolerated; by the end of it theirs was the official religion.

The history of Britain is as much about the history of religion as anything else.

The British took on the role of independent thinking even at this very early stage of Christian development. A man called Pelagius, who came from Britain, began to teach a doctrine that denied the idea of Original Sin, and the bishops of Gaul became so worried about its effects that in the early fifth century they sent

Saint Germanus to meet with British Christians and explain the errors of their ways. During his visit Germanus went to pay homage at the shrine of Saint Alban, a martyr who had been executed during one of the last crackdowns on Christianity in the middle of the third or possibly at the beginning of the fourth century.

Before Augustine reached Britain, Celtic missionaries had begun their work, starting in Ireland, which was never part of the Roman Empire. Saint Patrick, who in his youth had been captured by raiders and taken to Ireland as a slave, seems to have carried out missions around the early part or middle of the fifth century. Much later Saint Columba travelled from Ireland to Scotland, and had founded the monastery on the Western Isle of Iona by the time Saint Augustine arrived in Kent. Christianity had successfully survived the Roman withdrawal and was continuing its work among the people of Britain. Up until the end of the sixth century, however, this work had been concentrated in Celtic areas, among the people who had previously fled west and north when German and Scandinavian tribes invaded in the wake of the Romans' departure. It had not yet penetrated the lives of these new arrivals who were masters of Britain's central areas. The decision to try to convert them was the most important in the whole history of Christianity in Britain.

The man responsible for Augustine's mission was Pope Gregory. The story goes that some years before, while still an abbot, he was walking in the Forum when he saw some English slave boys for sale. Intrigued by their blond hair he asked the slave owner where they came from. 'They are Angles,' he was told. 'Not Angles, but angels,' he is reported to have replied, 'and should be co-heirs with the angels in heaven.' On becoming Pontiff Gregory, remembering the Saxon children he had seen in the Forum, he decided to put into action a plan to convert them and chose Augustine for the task. Augustine collected a group of monks to help him and set off. They travelled from Rome, through southern France, and stopped to rest at a monastery on the island of Lérins off the coast of Provence. Here in the pleasant surroundings of the Mediterranean they began to hear frightening stories of the dangers of travelling through Gaul, as well as being treated to tales of the Saxons and their murderous ways in the untamed country to the north. They asked Gregory if they could come home, but the Pope refused. 'It is better not to begin a good work at all, than to begin it and then turn back,' he told them in a letter. Suitably reprimanded, the little band pressed on. They travelled up the Rhône valley, spent the winter in Paris and in 597 AD crossed the Channel landing at Thanet in Kent. Their whole expedition had been carefully planned. They chose Kent because its king, Ethelbert, whose territory extended as far north as the Humber, was married to a Christian.

The mission was a great success. Ethelbert was converted and by December of that year over 10,000 of his people had been baptised. The missionaries found the ruins of an old Romano-British church in Canterbury which they rebuilt. By the end of the seventh century it had become the spiritual headquarters of the leader of the Christian Church in England – and remains so to this day. Pope Gregory sent Augustine reinforcements from Rome and with them letters explaining how he saw Christianity spreading through the country. He laid out in considerable detail the future organisation of the Church, recommending that the country be split into two halves, north and south, as it had been in Roman times, with the northern section based in York. Augustine failed to complete this part of his task, mainly because the Celtic bishops refused to cooperate with him. Augustine had been less than tactful in his second important meeting with the Celts, refusing to rise from his chair when they approached him. They were naturally suspicious of him and his Roman ways: this sort of behaviour convinced them that he was not to be trusted. The Christian religion had its divisions then as now. But the planning and care with which Augustine approached his task ensured that Roman ideas prospered, and eventually triumphed, in the way in which the English Church was organised. Pope Gregory was a wise guide. He knew how easy it was to lose people after they had been converted: they needed your constant attention. He urged Augustine not to abandon the old pagan rituals completely, but to incorporate them into new forms of worship. The heathen midwinter solstice, for instance, was slotted in to coincide with the birth of Christ. Old temples were consecrated as new churches, and Christianity embraced rather than uprooted the practices it intended to replace.

Early in the sixth century, long before Pope Gregory planned Augustine's mission to England, a monk called Saint Benedict wrote a rule book for the monastic life. He described a monastery as 'a school for the Lord's service', and set out the qualities a monk needed to have. 'Idleness,' he said, 'is the enemy of the soul.' Work, obedience and humility were essential to a life of devotion. Monks should own nothing and share everything. Saint Benedict told them what they should eat, what they should drink, what they should wear and when they should worship. His book became the basis upon which monasteries all over Western Europe were run: the discipline of the early Christian monks made them a powerful force capable not only of putting down deep roots in a single place, but also going out into the world as the persuasive agents of conversion. In Britain the growth of monasteries proved to be an important part of the country's submission to the Christian message. Lindisfarne, founded by Saint Aidan in 635, became the centre for wresting Northumbria – which in those days made up the whole of the North of England – from pagan worship.

The date of Augustine's death is not known but he seems to have died very early in the seventh century, probably around 604 AD. The English Church prospered but arguments continued about the proper days for feasts and important celebrations. In 664 AD the King of Northumbria, Oswy, called a synod at the abbey in Whitby to resolve the disputes between the Celtic and Roman Churches. The southern kingdoms of Wessex, Kent and Essex were following ritual according to the teachings of Rome, but the north preferred the Celtic way that had been taught them by Saint Columba and his missionaries from Iona. Oswy, influenced as much by a desire to form political alliances with his fellow princes in the south as he was by religious convictions, listened to the debate and pronounced in favour of Rome. 'Peter is the guardian of the gates of Heaven, and I shall not contradict him,' he is supposed to have said and, mindful of his own salvation, added: 'otherwise, when I come to the gates of Heaven, he who holds the keys may not be willing to open them.' All bishops and monasteries were brought under the authority of the Archbishop in Canterbury where Saint Augustine had built his church nearly seventy years before. The mission sent from Rome had finally triumphed and the long, troubled history of the Catholic Church in Britain had begun.

CHAPTER 4

Alfred the Great Becomes King of Wessex
871 AD

Alfred the Great was the most important Anglo-Saxon king to rule in Britain between the fall of the Roman Empire and the Norman invasion of 1066. By protecting his kingdom against conquest by the Vikings, he ensured the survival of the English language and English laws.

'Rule Britannia!' is one of Britain's favourite patriotic songs. Even those who find its expressions of national superiority a little hard to take can find themselves jolted into acquiescence when it is belted out with gusto at events like the Last Night of the Proms. It has been a hit ever since it was first performed in the grounds of Cliveden House in Buckinghamshire in 1740 where it was the last, rousing number in a masque composed by Thomas Arne for the daughter of Frederick, Prince of Wales. The masque tells the story of a wise, brave king who has fled from his enemies to live anonymously in exile among his people. He is visited by a spirit who tells him not to despair. He rallies, rounds up his troops and leads them to victory. The plot ends as the King's son announces that British values have triumphed – 'See liberty, virtue and honour appearing' – and then comes the song that tells us 'Britons never will be slaves.' The masque is called *Alfred*.

Alfred was a good subject for Thomas Arne's entertainment. The Prince of Wales was the centre of opposition to the King's prime minister, Robert Walpole. He and his followers called themselves 'patriots' – so it suited their purposes to make a connection between their beliefs and those of Alfred, the patriot king who had saved his country from the tyranny of the Viking invaders. In the early eighteenth century, Alfred came to be seen as the perfect representation of British liberty and justice. The gardens at Stowe House in Buckinghamshire, one of the great ornaments of the English landscape, contain a 'Temple of British Worthies' designed in 1734 by William Kent in which King Alfred is described as the 'mildest, justest, most beneficient of kings'. He 'crush'd corruption, guarded liberty and was the founder of the English constitution'. He is the only king in British history to be called 'Great'. He looms out of the Dark Ages like a beacon of safety. He is seen as an image of courage and common sense around which the British can build the continuity of their history. Without Alfred all might have been lost. He is the link to our true past.

By the beginning of the ninth century Britain was broadly divided into the Celtic areas of Wales, Scotland and Cornwall and the Anglo-Saxon kingdoms of Northumbria, Mercia and Wessex. The highly successful King of Mercia, Offa, who ruled in the second half of the eighth century, had built a fortification along the length of his boundary with the Celtic tribes to the west. Offa's Dyke effectively created the outline of the country which has been known as Wales ever since. The Anglo-Saxon kingdoms had emerged through battle and conquest between rival warlords. Since the middle of the seventh century they had fallen under the command of the Roman Church and their monks and clergy held enormous power. The Church was divided into parishes which supervised the needs of the people in their immediate vicinity. The abbots and monks could read and write, but many of the people to whom they preached could not. The clergy became the administrators of many aspects of everyday life, making wills and apportioning land. Superstitious kings, anxious to save their souls, were often only too happy to grant estates to the abbeys and monasteries that were growing up everywhere, and the Church was equally happy to benefit from this need for spiritual insurance.

Already the very early signs of feudal society were beginning to emerge, a world in which each man had his place and was expected to keep to it. The Anglo-Saxons were farmers and woodsmen. They lived in clusters in small townships or in groups alone in the forest. They were suspicious of each other and did not take kindly to strangers. Then, into this quiet, inward-looking, agricultural world came the Vikings.

The Vikings were seafarers: the Anglo-Saxons were landsmen. Towards the end of the eighth century and into the beginning of the ninth, Viking sailors began to cross the North Sea from Denmark and Norway to loot monasteries and churches positioned on the British coast. Throughout the ninth century the Vikings fanned out all over Europe in search of treasure to steal and land to conquer and some went further afield, across the Atlantic to the coast of North America. The British invasions came mainly from Denmark. Great armies of Danes, different bands of warriors who had agreed to unite behind a single leader for the purpose of carrying out a raid, landed on the shores of Northumbria, Mercia and Wessex. Their numbers grew as they learned more about the prizes Britain had to offer. By the end of the ninth century they had created 'Danelaw', the rule of Vikings over Anglo-Saxons, across the whole of Northumbria, Mercia and most of Wessex. Only the western end of Wessex, Somerset and Devon, the furthest point in England from their Danish base, had not yet fallen under Viking control.

Alfred became King of Wessex in 871. He had the foresight to get a friend and confidant of his, Bishop Asser, to write his biography and much of what we know about him comes from this. His four elder brothers, three of whom had served as Kings of Wessex for a brief period of time, had died, perhaps killed in fights against the Danes. He was only twenty-one when he succeeded to the throne but experience of fighting the Vikings meant that he was an ideal choice to take over. He was not in good health and his natural temperament seems to have been for scholarship rather than war. He was a devout Christian.

In 878 the Danes mounted a surprise attack. Alfred was nearly captured and had to retreat into the Somerset marshes. The apocryphal story of his burning the cakes probably stems from this period: the lonely, troubled King so lost in thought while he shelters amidst his people that he forgets to watch the cakes before the fire as the farmer's wife has told him. We have no evidence for this incident. What we do know is that this was a time of crisis for him. 'King Alfred, with a few of his nobles and some knights and men of his household, was in great distress leading an unquiet life in the woods and marshes of Somerset,' Bishop Asser tells us. 'He had no means of support except what he took in frequent raids by stealth or openly from the pagans, or indeed from Christians who had submitted to pagan rule.' From this position he managed to regroup and defeat the Danish leader, Guthrum, at Edington in Wiltshire. This decisive victory led to the Treaty of Wedmore in 878 in which Guthrum agreed to be baptised and to withdraw to behind the lines of existing Danelaw, leaving Wessex free. Alfred consolidated this victory eight years later when he recaptured London from the Vikings, and succeeded in beating them off when they attacked again in the mid-890s AD. This was a heroic achievement. The wars against the Vikings had left the Saxons demoralised and recalcitrant. They often resented royal orders and sometimes deserted to the other side. Alfred must have displayed impressive qualities of leadership to maintain an army capable of defeating the Danes. He knew he had no choice: it was the Vikings' custom to kill the leaders of the forces they defeated in battle.

Alfred's victory against Guthrum temporarily preserved the Anglo-Saxon tradition in a foreign world, but it might not have lasted had the victorious King not then demonstrated that he was as good a governor as he was a general. He ruled Wessex for another twenty-one years after the Treaty of Wedmore, a period in which he set about trying to improve the standards of education at his court. He recruited scholars from across the Channel where, following the civilising efforts of Charlemagne at the end of the eighth century, standards of literacy were higher. He was determined to resist the encroachments of the pagan Vikings and encouraged his clergy to improve both their teachings and writings. Most significantly he translated books from Latin into Anglo-Saxon, including Pope Gregory's *Pastoral Care* and Bede's *Ecclesiastical History of the English People*. He also introduced the *Anglo-Saxon Chronicle*, the first record of historical events to be written in English.

He also turned to the administration of his kingdom laying out laws, as other Anglo-Saxon kings had done, in his *Doom Book*. He wanted to protect weaker members of his disheartened country pronouncing: 'Any judgement should be even, not one judgement for the wealthy and another for the poor.' He provided a structure for rents and taxes, regulating how much people had to pay and to whom. He also introduced a system of fines – *wergild* – the money to be paid by those who committed crimes. Women enjoyed greater rights in Alfred's Anglo-Saxon world than they would for many years to come under other rulers of Britain. They could own land in their own name; there was no natural right for a first-born son to inherit; no woman could be sold or forced into marriage; and wives were entitled to divorce their husbands.

Women enjoyed greater rights in Alfred's Anglo-Saxon world than they would for many years to come.

Alongside all of this Alfred strengthened his country's defences, copying the earthwork forts which the Danish used very successfully. He built a strong administrative system and, aware of how vulnerable his kingdom had been from attacks from the sea, created a fleet. Taken together these things gave his people a primitive nationhood. Alfred knew they needed an army for protection, and laws for their administration, but he also realised that these on their own would not be enough to keep them safe forever. To survive Wessex needed things that it believed in, that were worth fighting for. Alfred wanted his people to understand the value of their own history and the importance of their Christian learning. The importance of their past was their best defence against the uncertainties of their future. The little nation of Wessex was an embryo from which grew ideas and methods which would heavily influence the future course of British history.

In 1693 an Anglo-Saxon jewel was found in Somerset, not far from Athelney where Alfred hid before his successful counter-attack against the Danes. It is made of gold and enamel and covered with a piece of rock crystal. The purpose of the jewel is unclear, but some believe it to be an *aestel*, a book pointer, which Alfred intended to send to his bishops with his translation of Pope Gregory's *Pastoral Care*. Another theory is that it might have been a symbol of office for Alfred himself, or for one of his officials. The face of the jewel has a figure on it which may be Christ representing the incarnate 'Wisdom of God', or possibly the spirit of Sight. Whatever its use might have been, it is a beautiful relic from a time more than eleven hundred years ago when the Anglo-Saxon people of England faced the possibility of virtual extermination at the hands of a savage enemy. The jewel, now in the Ashmolean Museum in Oxford, bears the inscription, in Anglo-Saxon: 'Alfred ordered me to be made.'

Alfred died at the age of about fifty in 899 AD. In the biography that he commissioned from Bishop Asser he comes across almost as a saint, and succeeding ages have not demurred from that opinion of him. It was not only the eighteenth century that held him up as an icon of liberty. In the next century Charles Dickens in *A Child's History of England* called him 'the noble king ... whom misfortune could not subdue, whom prosperity could not spoil, whose perseverance nothing could shake'. Today we tend to take a more objective view. Alfred's achievements were momentous, though we probably feel they fell short of sainthood. But then a man does not need to be a saint to inspire affection or gratitude. When we think of the plight of Wessex in the second half of the ninth century and reflect on the King who rose out of the marshes of Somerset to rebuild his kingdom in such an extraordinary way, we realise that, saint or not, we owe a great deal to Alfred, the Anglo-Saxon King, and for the things he did. We might even say: 'Alfred ordered me to be made.'

CHAPTER 5

The Battle of Hastings
1066

The Battle of Hastings represented the start of the
last great foreign invasion of Britain. The Norman
Conquest unified the country under a powerful
monarchy and provided it with the foundations
of the medieval state.

In the centuries leading up to the Norman Conquest of Britain,
the future of Europe turned on the ambitions of individual men.
The continent was in turmoil as peoples from its different parts
travelled from their homelands in search of opportunity elsewhere.
Powerful men grabbed land and held on to it during their life-
times, but their successors were likely to lose it if they did not
display the same aggressive qualities. Anglo-Saxon England might
have been extinguished if Alfred had not turned the tide against the
Danish invaders in 878 AD. Nearly two hundred years later the
future of Britain and Europe might have evolved in a very different
way if King Canute had reigned for longer. He was a Dane who
became Emperor of Denmark, Norway and England. In England
the successive Viking invasions had brought Anglo-Saxon and
Danish cultures together, and Canute consolidated this process
allowing both to prosper. However, when he died in 1036 his great
empire broke up and England was once again ruled by Anglo-Saxon
kings. But their survival depended entirely on their individual
strengths and weaknesses. The country was eyed greedily by
the Vikings, who by now had rivals to the south. In France the
Normans were looking for new territory into which they could
expand.

The Normans were, in fact, descendants of Vikings who had

originally moved into France in the early part of the tenth century. By the time of the Norman Conquest they had become French-speaking Christians, but they had not lost the Viking taste for adventure and war. By 1066 they had already invaded Italy where they were the rulers of lands throughout the south. Only five years before the Battle of Hastings, in 1061, Roger, 'the Great Count', was with his brother Robert, organising the invasion of Sicily, which would eventually provide the Normans with a powerful Mediterranean base. They were an energetic and fierce race described by one contemporary chronicler, Geoffrey Malaterra, as 'altogether unbridled unless firmly held down by the yoke of justice. They were enduring of toil, hunger and cold ... given to hunting and hawking, delighting in the pleasures of horses, and of all the weapons and garb of war.' These were the people who were about to capture all of Britain.

To a certain extent the Normans, like their Viking predecessors, were pushing at an open door in their plans to invade Britain. Edward the Confessor became King of England in 1042. He was a grandson of Richard, Duke of Normandy, through his father's marriage to Richard's daughter, Emma. His father, Ethelred, had been a disastrous King who failed to protect his people from the predatory Vikings and his marriage to Emma, who brought to his court a train of Norman followers, only increased his unpopularity. After Ethelred died, Canute succeeded him and Edward fled to Normandy, returning to the throne a few years after Canute's death. By this time he had developed Norman tastes.

Edward the Confessor, as his name implies, was as much a priest as a king, adopting the ideal of chastity even though he was married. His religious activities earned him sainthood, but his political incompetence at a time of national danger prepared the way for the final collapse of Anglo-Saxon England. His enjoyment of Norman ways caused resentment among his Anglo-Saxon subjects, particularly Earl Godwin of Wessex who was at one point driven into exile in Flanders, but returned to secure his place in the kingdom with popular support. By 1066, when Edward the

Confessor died, England once again looked like a prize worth taking. It was unsettled – the Anglo-Saxons resented the power and influence that had been given to Norman intruders; it was un-governed – Edward had not passed any laws or concerned himself unduly with the management of his country; and it had no heir – Edward's devotion to chastity had seen to that.

There was no precise formula for the succession of a new king in Anglo-Saxon England. The nearest blood relation to Edward was a boy called Edgar the Atheling, but the Witan, the assembly that chose the next monarch, rejected him in favour of Godwin's son, Harold of Wessex. England's enemies saw their chance. The King of Norway, Harald Hardrada, declared himself the true successor, and attacked, supported in his claim by Harold of Wessex's brother, Tostig. William, Duke of Normandy, announced that Edward had promised him the throne and prepared to attack as well. Harold, the last King of Wessex, heir to Anglo-Saxon England's last brief surge of glory, was trapped. While he waited and watched for William to arrive along the south coast of England he heard news that Harald Hardrada had landed in the north-east and had defeated the north-ern earls. Turning away from his southern watch he marched north and at the end of September 1066 met his Viking enemy at Stamford Bridge in Yorkshire. The story goes that before the battle Harold rode out to meet his disaffected brother, Tostig, who was now his mortal enemy. He offered him a third of his kingdom and his own life if he would desert the Norwegian king. Tostig asked him if there was anything he was prepared to give to Harald Hardrada. Harold of Wessex replied: 'Seven feet of ground or as much more as he is taller than other men.' Tostig then said: 'We are united in our aim. Either to die with honour, or else conquer England.' A furious battle then took place. Harald Hardrada fought like a man possessed but was slain. Eventually the whole of his army was destroyed: his men were cut down and killed as they ran for their boats to get home. Harold of Wessex had won a huge victory. As he led his exhausted forces back towards York he heard news that William had arrived off the south coast.

After a four-day ride, Harold reached London. Much of his army followed him on foot and had not arrived by the time William had landed and begun to carry out raids in the immediate vicinity. Harold rounded up what troops he could to reinforce the exhausted victors of Stamford Bridge and on 14th October took up his position on Senlac Hill in Hastings. Harold and his army fought to the last against the Norman invaders but the Norman cavalry supported by their archers proved too strong for them. Harold was killed and his army scattered. The last Anglo-Saxon King of England had held power for only a few months, but he had held it bravely. His country was lost forever. A band of invaders probably not much more than 10,000 in number had captured the country. The Norman Conquest had begun.

William the Conqueror was shrewd. He made sure that he had papal blessing for his English excursion and he could now proclaim that his victory was ordained by God. He also had other advantages of a rather more practical kind. His principal rival, the King of Norway, had been killed. He had a strong, loyal force of experienced knights and a Church that was well organised and international in its approach. On Christmas Day 1066, he was crowned King of England in London and within two years had brought all of the south under Norman control. The north took a while longer to subdue. Two northern earls, Edwin and Morcar, supported by another Danish invasion, took up arms against the new King but their rebellion was suppressed with fierce savagery. This was a new time in Britain. The confused society that had arisen from the uneasy partnership between Anglo-Saxons and Danes was now ripped away. North and south were united and the country fortified with stone castles: the Normans were great builders.

Towards the end of his reign, in 1085, William ordered a survey of his newly conquered kingdom and by the following year had received its first draft. 'The Domesday Book' is an extraordinarily detailed document about all the land lying south of the rivers Ribble and Tees, which at that time formed the border with

Scotland. 'No single hide nor a yard of land, nor indeed one ox nor one cow nor one pig ... was left out', according to one account of its compilation – an indication of what an exacting master William the Conqueror was. Everything he needed to know for the purpose of raising money, or controlling the population, was in there. Landholders, tenants, slaves, freemen, woodlands, rivers, meadows, ploughs, fish, cattle, churches and mills are all meticulously recorded. It is a unique document about the British state at a crucial point in its development: for William it must have represented a very satisfying inventory of conquest.

William died in 1087 before the book was completed, but by that time far-seeing changes to the way the country was run had taken place. He confiscated land from its previous owners and redistributed it among his loyal aristocratic followers. Poaching deer was forbidden and punishable by mutilation and, later, death. The new landowners could now keep the poor at bay and under their control. The grant of land came with the obligation to raise soldiers for the King whenever necessary: the lord gave some of his property to knights who in return had to supply forty days of military service as required. William also carried out Church reforms, separating Church and lay courts and enforcing celibacy on the priesthood. These great changes created a feudal structure that would remain at the heart of British society throughout the Middle Ages. The country's language changed too. The Normans spoke French and this began to permeate existing Anglo-Saxon.

The battle marked the moment when Britain emerged from the Dark and Early Middle Ages into the Medieval Period.

Human beings tend to adapt. History is as much about evolution as it is about sudden, transforming events. The Battle of Hastings was a single episode of momentous significance. Without doubt it marked the moment when Britain emerged from the Dark and Early Middle Ages into the Medieval Period. The country was united and its systems of government and administration integrated into a single machine. But William the Conqueror used what he found: he retained, for instance, many features of the Anglo-Saxon legal system, albeit converted to suit Norman purposes. Like the Romans a thousand years before, or the German tribes who flooded across Britain in the wake of their departure; like the Anglo-Saxons and the Danes who fought each other and lived side by side in the centuries that followed, the Normans made sure that Britain gave to them at the same time as they gave to it. The success of the Norman Conquest lay in its flexibility as much as in its rigour.

The population of England in 1066 was about 1.5 million. The whole country collapsed before a Norman force of a few thousand men. For a thousand years it had suffered conquest and intrusion, an island which was as much a prison as a fortress. After 1066 things began to change. The people became increasingly integrated. They began to look outwards. Their island became their greatest protection and, unaware of the significance of what they were doing, they began to put together the first tiny pieces of a European nation.

Some examples of British food through the ages

Roman Britain: Dormice fattened in jars of nuts

Norman Britain: Suckling pigs' trotters and ears in onion sauce

Tudor Britain: Roasted peacock served in its feathers, with a gilded beak

Eighteenth century: Udders stuffed with veal

Nineteenth century: Roasted ortolans (tiny songbirds), eaten whole

Second World War rationing: 'Apricot' flan, made from carrot, jam and mashed potato

CHAPTER 6

The Dissolution of the Monasteries 1536

Between 1536 and 1541 Henry VIII set about destroying the power of the Catholic Church in England by closing down its monasteries. The process was one of the most important acts of the English Reformation. It created the biggest social and political change in Britain since the Norman Conquest.

Thomas Cromwell was the epitome of Tudor success. He was born in Putney in about 1485, the son of a brewer and blacksmith, and rose to become the King's Chief Minister and Earl of Essex. He was one of the new men of sixteenth-century Britain. In his youth he seems to have fallen out with his father and worked abroad, perhaps as a soldier for a while, visiting Venice, Florence and Antwerp. On his return he found work with Cardinal Wolsey, Henry VIII's Lord Chancellor, who may have recognised similar qualities as his own in his young employee because they came from similar social backgrounds: he himself was the son of a butcher from Ipswich. When Wolsey fell, Cromwell survived, and a few years later he became Secretary to Henry VIII, a position which made him the political architect of the King's break with Rome. There is a famous Holbein portrait of Cromwell at the height of his career – a great bulk of power with a broad, fleshy face, his eyes narrowed and watchful. Tough, clever and cosmopolitan he was the man who drove through the administrative and ecclesiastical reforms that broke the power of the Church and strengthened the Tudor monarchy. They profoundly changed the future course of British history. They were, in their way, a revolution.

The court of Henry VIII must have been a bewildering place.

The King himself was a man of virulent energy. He loved music and learning as well as physical pastimes such as hunting, tennis – and the pursuit of women. This energy was controllable while it was confined to the enhancement of his social life, but once it spilled over into the affairs of state it was violently disruptive. Henry was self-willed. He did not make nice distinctions between his own wishes and the wider policy of the state: as far as he was concerned they often amounted to the same thing. By the late 1520s he had decided that he needed to divorce his wife, Catherine of Aragon. She had failed to produce a son which he felt the Tudor dynasty would need if it were to survive and anyway he wanted to marry his mistress Anne Boleyn. He asked the Pope, Clement VII, to annul his marriage. The Pope refused, but his reasons were as much pragmatic as moral. He was under the control of the Holy Roman Emperor, Charles V, whose mutinous troops had sacked Rome in 1527. Charles was Catherine of Aragon's nephew and the Pope dared not offend him by granting Henry's wish. Henry became impatient. He dismissed his Lord Chancellor, Cardinal Wolsey, for failing to persuade the Pope of his requirements – Wolsey died before he could be brought to trial and almost certainly executed – and, under the influence of Thomas Cromwell and his newly appointed archbishop, Thomas Cranmer, began to organise a break with the Roman Catholic Church.

These events took place against a background of great religious change in Europe. The attack on the corruption of the Roman Catholic Church led by reformers such as Martin Luther and John Calvin had taken root and Protestantism was developing fast as a new, coherent form of religious worship. Henry's attack on papal authority was seen in Britain as a natural part of this process, but it was not at this stage a Protestant movement: far from it. The ideas of Luther and his followers were increasing in popularity, but they were still a long way short of demolishing people's belief in the Roman Catholic Church which had been at the centre of their lives for centuries. After he dismissed Cardinal Wolsey, Henry turned to Sir Thomas More to be his Lord Chancellor. More was a devout

Catholic. He disapproved of Lutheran teachings which he regarded as heresy – he ordered Lutheran preachers to be burnt at the stake during his time in office – and he wanted to suppress Protestant translations of the Bible into English. Henry VIII was supportive of More's policies: for him the issue of the power of Rome was a matter of state business, not religious controversy.

What the Protestant reformers had succeeded in doing was to generate strong antipathy against the Church and clergy in general. It was the priesthood as much as Catholicism which was disliked. The Church at the beginning of the sixteenth century enjoyed extensive powers, and had the right to exact money from ordinary men and women through its own courts. It was also enormously rich. People eyed its splendid churches and beautiful abbeys with envy and resented its ownership of the vast lands it had been able to acquire during the long period of clerical expansion during the Middle Ages. The fact that their King could not get his way because the Pope was embroiled with a hostile foreign power only served to intensify these feelings. The Church was a nuisance. It interfered with the smooth running of the British state. It was too wealthy and too powerful: it needed to be brought under control.

The Church was a nuisance. It interfered with the smooth running of the British state.

In 1531 Henry VIII announced that he wished to be recognised as the Supreme Head and Sole Protector of the Church in England. Parliament acquiesced. Three years later in 1534 it passed the Act of Supremacy proclaiming that he was 'the only supreme head on earth of the Church in England' and that the English crown was now due 'all honours, dignities, preeminences, jurisdictions, privileges, authorities, immunities, profits and commodities to the said dignity'. Henry, having achieved the power he wanted, then proceeded to exercise it and began his attack on the Church's land and property. By this time Thomas Cromwell was his principal lieutenant. He was a brilliant administrator, mercilessly efficient in his management of the state's affairs. During his time as Henry's chief minister, the machinery of government was tuned to a higher level of performance than before. Cromwell gathered around him a small council of administrators loyal in their service to their crown. They were bureaucrats – a sort of very early, primitive prototype of the civil service – and they provided the monarchy with the means to get things done. The Tudors developed as a powerful dynasty because they took full control of all aspects of the affairs of state. To do this they worked with strong, capable advisors and, to a large extent, through Parliament. As a result the growth in their power was accompanied by a growth in the power of the country as a whole: in sixteenth-century Britain dynastic ambition and nationhood went hand in hand.

The attack on the Church's property was devastating. The abbeys, monasteries and nunneries of Britain were suppressed, their land confiscated and their inhabitants thrown out. The monks on the whole seem to have been well treated – many took livings as local priests, or were given pensions – although some who resisted were executed. The dissolution of the monasteries was a ruthless operation, but its real effects were felt, not in terms of individual human misery, but in the wholesale change to land ownership which it created. For those with money, the dissolution was a bonanza. Henry decided to sell confiscated property to raise money for the Exchequer. In the space of a few years he brought on to the market estates and buildings which had been out of the public domain for centuries. Many of the buyers were gentry and merchants whose families had grown wealthy in the stable climate of early Tudor Britain. A new landowning class began to appear, proud men of property whose successors would have a profound effect on the future direction of the country. This was one of the unforeseen side effects of the English Reformation. The destruction of the power of the Catholic Church encouraged new freedom of thought. The confiscation of its land empowered a new class of men.

The assault on the Church met with little opposition because in many places the strict discipline of the monastic life had long ago softened into pleasant, well-fed ritual. The monks were often poor managers of their land; they had given up the hardships of manual labour; and they had abandoned their habits of study and learning. But they did still own great libraries and works of art which were broken up and sold in the feeding frenzy that accompanied the destruction of the buildings in which they were kept. The loss of these treasures was an inevitable part of the surge of change which was being driven through the country. Spiritual matters were not entirely forgotten either. The English Bible, which a few years earlier had been outlawed, was allowed back into circulation. The money-making medieval superstitions of relic-worship and selling pardons were suppressed.

Henry VIII, having unleashed great change, fell prey to his conscience. Always restless, rarely consistent, he decided in 1539 that matters had perhaps moved a bit further than he intended. He introduced the Act of Six Articles – otherwise known as 'An Act Abolishing Diversity in Opinions' – which upheld basic Catholic teaching as the basis of faith for the English Church and reinforced laws against heresy. The flood of opportunity which had accompanied the break with Rome was suddenly checked. Henry was not ready to watch the country desert the principles of faith which had supported it since the establishment of the Christian Church in Britain a thousand years before. He might have made himself head of the Church, but he was still a Catholic. The Act of 1539 provides a good example of the confused world created by Henry's dispute with Rome – a confusion which would bedevil the country for another hundred and fifty years as the ideas, hopes and attitudes it spawned seeped into every part of it. It was not possible for Henry VIII, as he might have thought, to simply transfer power from Rome to London and put himself in charge of the British division of the Catholic Church. The transfer required far greater change than that – the creation, in effect, of a whole new Church whose doctrine and beliefs became the source of ceaseless debate and conflict.

A year after the Act of Six Articles was passed, Thomas Cromwell suffered the same fate as many other loyal servants of Henry VIII. The mood of the King had changed. Having enjoyed his glorious exercise of power, he was beginning to worry about his soul. Cromwell promoted the King's marriage to Anne of Cleves, a German whom he thought would help strengthen Britain's relationship with countries hostile to the papacy. The marriage was a disaster: Henry took one look at his intended bride, decided he did not like her, and told Cromwell to try to find a way out of the marriage. None could be found, and the marriage went ahead. For Henry this was further evidence that change had gone too far. On 9th July 1540 he told Anne of Cleves that their marriage was to be annulled on the grounds of non-consummation. She received a generous pension and Anne Boleyn's old home of Hever Castle in Kent. She would remain in England for the rest of her life. Thomas Cromwell was less fortunate. He was executed nearly three weeks later, on 28th July.

At the beginning of the seventeenth century the poet Michael Drayton, who rejoiced in the title of 'England's Ovid', wrote a historical poem about him called 'The Legend of Thomas Cromwell'. Drayton was no Ovid, but his poem captures the tension of those feverish times when great power created great change, and everything turned on the mood of a prince.

> But whilst we strive too suddenly to rise,
> By flatt'ring princes with a servile tongue,
> And being soothers to their tyrannies,
> Work on much woes by what doth many wrong,
> And unto others tending injuries,
> Unto ourselves it hap'ning oft among,
> In our snares unluckily are caught
> Whilst our attempts fall instantly to naught.

The Elizabethan Religious Settlement 1559

Elizabeth I did not want, she said, 'to make windows into men's souls'. When she became Queen in 1558, men's souls had been put through a considerable amount of agony. Her father, Henry VIII, had wrenched the Church away from Rome, but her sister, Mary, who had reigned for five years before her, had unleashed a vigorous Catholic counter-offensive. Elizabeth, whose own position was precarious, needed to find a solution that would establish her authority over a divided nation. She did so with her customary skill.

The Act of Supremacy of 1559 made Elizabeth Supreme Governor of the Church of England, rather than the more contentious Supreme Head, which was the title Henry VIII had taken. All public officials had to swear an oath of allegiance to the monarch or risk being barred from office. The heresy laws were repealed. The Act of Uniformity, passed at the same time as the Act of Supremacy, made attendance at church compulsory, but introduced some alterations to the form of service to make it more acceptable to Catholics and required the use of an adapted version of the Book of Common Prayer.

Elizabeth I knew her people well. She recognised that their passions were always streaked with pragmatism, and her solution provided the country with remarkable stability for more than fifty years.

CHAPTER 7

The Birth of William Shakespeare
1564

Shakespeare is the greatest writer Britain has ever
produced. He lifted the English language to new
heights and gave us words and phrases we still
use today.

When I was a small boy I was taken by my parents to see a production of *Henry IV, Part I*, at the school where my father was headmaster. I was greatly impressed by the character of Falstaff who
in my childish innocence I thought seemed rather like Father
Christmas. When towards the end of the play I thought he had been
killed at the Battle of Shrewsbury I was very upset. My relief when
he revealed he had been pretending and struggled to his feet again
was highly audible. My yelp of delight made the audience laugh
almost as much as the actor's performance. Shakespeare has always
been part of my life – as he has for thousands of British men
and women. He rose out of one of the most vivid and exciting
periods in our history – the Elizabethan Age – and then surpassed
it, moving forward with each succeeding period. We still use his
words and phrases. His characters still live with us. Perhaps most
importantly of all, we feel proud of him because we share his
genius with the world. The Prince of Wales, speaking at the Shakespeare Birthday Lecture in Stratford-upon-Avon in 1991, used
language that is very familiar when the British talk about him.
'Shakespeare's message is the universal, timeless one, yet clad in
the garments of his time. He is not just our poet, but the world's.
Yet his roots are ours, his language is ours, his culture is ours.'

Our knowledge of Shakespeare's life is incomplete. He was
born in Stratford-upon-Avon in 1564, the son of a prosperous wool

merchant. He went to the local grammar school where, among other things, he studied Latin and at the age of eighteen married a local girl eight years his senior called Anne Hathaway. She was pregnant at the time. Towards the end of the 1580s he seems to have become an actor with the Queen's Men and began writing plays. By the middle of the 1590s he had teamed up with the Lord Chamberlain's Men, a group of actors who came together after London's theatres had been closed because of a plague epidemic, and stayed with them for the rest of his career. He died in 1616 and was buried in his home town of Stratford.

Shakespeare's life had many modern qualities about it. He was a well-educated, middle-class man from a provincial town who did well and got rich in London's bustling, fast-moving media world. His was the first generation to enjoy the theatre as a full-blooded form of general entertainment. In the years before his time plays tended to be based on religious themes but by the end of the sixteenth century they were tackling all sorts of subjects – romance, comedy and history – holding, in Shakespeare's own phrase 'the mirror up to nature'. Theatre was fashionable. It attracted sponsorship from wealthy courtiers. It was rivalrous, catty and scandalous. A female fan of Richard Burbage, one of the most famous actors of the day, was so enraptured by his performance as Richard III that she asked him to come and visit her dressed as the villainous king. Shakespeare – so the story goes – got wind of this and managed to seduce her before Burbage arrived. As they were lying in bed together the actor appeared, announcing that Richard III had arrived, to which Shakespeare is supposed to have responded that William the Conqueror came before Richard III. The world of the stage was just as heady and exciting in Elizabethan London as it is today.

Shakespeare was good at his chosen profession – head and shoulders above his contemporaries. In a time that produced a great number of fine writers, he produced the best work. Christopher Marlowe wrote beautiful, heroic verse and Ben Jonson had a clever, satirical wit but neither of these could match Shakespeare in his ability to write about anything to which he turned his hand. He sometimes collaborated with other writers in the town but his greatest plays and poems, the work for which he is remembered and revered, was all his own. He knew what made people tick, he knew what made them laugh and he knew how to make them feel patriotic and proud; he understood politics; and he knew how the world was opening up through voyages of exploration. All of this understanding he brought into his plays. His words and phrases were unlike anything that had been written in the English language before. They gave it dynamism: the power to express everything. The people with whom he worked knew this. When the *First Folio* of Shakespeare's plays was published in 1623, several writers contributed introductory poems praising his talent and recognising the immortality of his work. Leonard Digges ended his piece with:

> *Be sure, our Shakespeare, thou canst never die,*
> *But crowned with laurel, live eternally.*

And Ben Jonson, while joshing that his old rival 'hadst small Latin and less Greek', wrote:

> *Triumph, my Britain, thou hast one to show*
> *To whom all scenes of Europe homage owe.*
> *He was not of an age, but for all time.*

Digges and Jonson were right. They may just have intended to help the publisher sell their former colleague's work and so indulged in a little hyperbole, but they must also have realised that Shakespeare had been something special. They sensed even then that his work was ageless.

Twenty-five years after Shakespeare died Britain was engulfed by the Civil War and the Puritan Revolution. Plays and play-going were frowned upon and the lively brilliance of the Elizabethan stage was forgotten as more sober matters preoccupied the rulers of the nation. After the Restoration in 1660, Shakespeare once more found himself admirers, although he had to take his place among

Shakespeare's language

Shakespeare's influence on the English language can still be heard or read today. Here are fifty expressions still in use after he first used them in his plays 400 years ago.

'A sorry sight' – Macbeth, *Macbeth*
'All that glisters is not gold' – Prince of Morocco, *The Merchant of Venice*
'All's well that ends well' – Helena, *All's Well That Ends Well*
'At one fell swoop' – Macduff, *Macbeth*
'Bated breath' – Shylock, *The Merchant of Venice*
'The 'be-all and end-all'' – Macbeth, *Macbeth*
'Be cruel ... to be kind' – Hamlet, *Hamlet*
'Brave new world' – Miranda, *The Tempest*
'A charmed life' – Macbeth, *Macbeth*
'Come full circle' – Edmund, *King Lear*
'Dog will have its day' – Hamlet, *Hamlet*
'Eaten me out of house and home' – Hostess Quickly, *Henry IV, Part 2*
'Elbow room' – John, *King John*
'Fair play' – Hector, *Troilus and Cressida*
'For ever and a day' – Biondello, *The Taming of the Shrew*
'Foregone conclusion' – Othello, *Othello*
'Foul play' – Gloucester, *King Lear*
'The game is up' – Belarius, *Cymbeline*
'Good men and true' – Dogberry, *Much Ado About Nothing*
'Good riddance' – Patroclus, *Troilus and Cressida*
'Greek to me' – Casca, *Julius Caesar*
'Green-eyed monster' – Iago, *Othello*
'Heart's content' – Henry, *Henry VI, Part 2*
'I have not slept one wink' – Pisanio, *Cymbeline*
'In my heart of heart' – Hamlet, *Hamlet*

'I will wear my heart upon my sleeve' – Iago, *Othello*
'Into thin air' – Prospero, *The Tempest*
'The lady doth protest too much' – Gertrude, *Hamlet*
'Lay it on 'with a trowel' – Celia, *As You Like It*
'Love is blind' – Jessica, *The Merchant of Venice*
'Milk of human kindness' – Lady Macbeth, *Macbeth*
'More fool you' – Bianca, *The Taming of the Shrew*
'Murder most foul' – Ghost, *Hamlet*
'My own flesh and blood' – Shylock, *The Merchant of Venice*
'My salad days' – Cleopatra, *Antony and Cleopatra*
'Pomp and Circumstance' – Othello, *Othello*
'Pound of flesh' – Shylock, *The Merchant of Venice*
'Seal up your lips and give no words but mum' (giving us the saying 'Mum's the word') – Hume, *Henry VI, Part 2*
'Send him packing' – Falstaff, *Henry IV, Part 1*
'The short and the long of it' – Mistress Quickly, *The Merry Wives of Windsor*
'Short shrift' – Ratcliff, *Richard III*
'Sorry sight' – Macbeth, *Macbeth*
'Of sterner stuff' – Mark Antony, *Julius Caesar*
'Strange bed-fellows' – Trinculo, *The Tempest*
'Such stuff as dreams are made on' – Prospero, *The Tempest*
'To the manner born' – Hamlet, *Hamlet*
'Though this be madness, yet there is a method in't' (giving us the saying 'There's method in his madness') – Polonius, *Hamlet*
'Truth will out' – Launcelot, *The Merchant of Venice*
'Wild goose chase' – Mercutio, *Romeo and Juliet*
'The world's mine oyster' – Pistol, *The Merry Wives of Windsor*

the new writers who were jostling for favour in a London which was coming back to life once more. The theatre had come under the influence of classical convention. Aristotle's 'three unities' of time, place and action were brought back into fashion: a play should have only one plot and should take place over twenty-four hours in the same place. That was hardly Shakespeare. His huge imagination was incapable of being bound by rules. John Dryden, one of the greatest writers in Britain at the end of the seventeenth century, spotted this and acknowledged Shakespeare's pre-eminence, although he also wrote entirely new versions of some of his plays, constructed along classical lines. *All For Love, or The World Well Lost* is his take on Shakespeare's *Antony and Cleopatra*. Less capable hands than Dryden's also tinkered with Shakespeare's work. In 1681 Nahum Tate – the author of, among other things, the words of the carol 'While Shepherds Watched Their Flocks by Night' – produced a version of *King Lear* with a happy ending: Edgar and Cordelia get married and the old king is restored to his throne. In the London of Charles II nothing was allowed to get in the way of a good time.

Shakespeare survived these upheavals to emerge by the middle of the eighteenth century as Britain's supreme dramatist and poet. The theatre had changed enormously since his time. The open air spaces of the Elizabethan stage had been enclosed and Londoners crowded into places like the carefully lit auditorium of the Theatre Royal in Drury Lane. The building itself had been designed by Sir Christopher Wren in 1674 but under the management of its latest impresario, David Garrick, had introduced many new features. There was a clear division between actors and audience. The auditorium was darker and the stage brighter, with footlights and other effects to enhance the action. Before these innovations members of the audience had been allowed to sit on the stage where they could prove troublesome, particularly if the production was not to their liking. In this environment David Garrick set about building his reputation as the finest actor-manager of his time. Many of his productions were boisterous pieces of popular fun, but he never lost sight of Shakespeare and wanted to be identified as a great interpreter of his roles. He played all the great parts – Hamlet, King Lear and Macbeth among them – but his most popular performances were as Richard III and Benedick in *Much Ado About Nothing*. In 1769 he organised a jubilee at Stratford-upon-Avon to celebrate the 150th anniversary of Shakespeare's death. It was three years late, but nobody minded. Garrick gave the public a splendid festival of entertainment, including snippets from his Shakespearean performances and his very own 'Ode to Shakespeare':

> *Untouch'd and sacred be thy shrine,*
> *Avonian Willy, Bard divine.*

No wonder Garrick's friend and mentor, Samuel Johnson, described his death as having eclipsed 'the gaiety of nations'.

Shakespeare's international reputation began to grow in the nineteenth century. The rapid expansion of the British Empire brought with it British ideas and British culture, with Shakespeare at the helm. The first performance of a Shakespeare play in India was in Bombay, in 1770. Ten years later, in Calcutta, the capital of British India, *Othello* was performed at Christmas with many other Shakespeare productions following after that. By the middle of the nineteenth century his plays began to be translated and performed in Indian languages. In South Africa the African Theatre in Cape Town staged *Henry IV, Part I*, in 1801, with a notice in the *Cape Town Gazette* announcing that this was 'the customary honour paid to our Immortal Bard'.

But it was not in the Empire but in a part of Europe where in the early nineteenth century Shakespeare achieved his most remarkable success. His work appealed naturally to the romantic imagination which was then the strongest cultural force in all branches of the arts. In Germany two of the principal exponents of romanticism were the brothers Friedrich and August Schlegel. Friedrich was a philosopher, but August was a writer and poet and in the early 1800s he began to translate Shakespeare into German. The results were outstanding. His understanding of Shakespeare combined with his own talents as a poet gave his translations a vitality all their own. Edited and amended by his fellow poet and critic, Ludwig Tieck, they became important works of literature in their own right. Today in Germany Shakespeare is revered almost as highly as the great masters of German literature, Goethe and Schiller: he has become almost German.

A nation needs inspiration. It may have been created out of purely pragmatic considerations, but it needs ideas to survive. Shakespeare helped to give the British the ability to express themselves, to look inwards with imagination and outwards with confidence. Ever since he first entertained the boisterous crowds in the theatres of London at the end of the sixteenth century, he has been, and will remain, Britain's big idea, a vital stream of thought and ideas forever sustaining 'This blessed plot, this earth, this realm, this England.'

> *Shakespeare helped to give the British the ability to express themselves.*

CHAPTER 8

The Act of Union
1707

In 1707 England and Scotland were united in the Act of Union. The two countries had had the same monarch for more than a century. The Act of Union gave them the same parliament and the same government, but it was by no means the end of their long, complicated relationship.

Scotland, too, once had a dream of an empire all its own. At the end of the seventeenth century it was in an unhappy state. In the years immediately following the dethronement of James II in 1688 the Catholics of the Scottish Highlands had risen up in his defence only to be defeated by their countrymen of the Lowlands, loyal to the new joint monarchy of William and Mary. The most shocking episode in this internal war had been the massacre at Glencoe in February 1692 when members of the Clan MacDonald were murdered by a division of Lowland soldiers to whom they had offered hospitality. The troops had been staying with their victims for nearly two weeks before they turned on them, killing in the early hours of the morning those they had been eating and playing cards with the previous night. 'You are hereby ordered to fall upon the Rebels, the McDonalds of Glencoe, and putt all to the sword under seventy,' said the orders sent to the commanding officer of the soldiers who carried out the massacre. 'This is by the Kings speciall command, for the good and safty of the country.' The bitter treachery of Glencoe, sanctioned by government at the highest level, was followed by terrible weather and famine. Divided and hungry, Scotland looked abroad for ideas for its salvation.

William Paterson had founded the Bank of England in 1694 by

proposing that a company was created to lend the cash-strapped British government £1.2 million (see pages 331–336). Having fallen out with his fellow directors he returned to his native Scotland where he came up with a new money-making scheme. He proposed to start a Scottish colony in Darien on the isthmus of Panama. His idea, in principle, was perfectly sound. He argued that long journeys around Cape Horn at the tip of South America, or the Cape of Good Hope in South Africa, were hampering Europe's trade with Asia. He proposed the formation of a colony on the narrow strip of land between the Atlantic and Pacific Oceans, where a profitable trading post could be established to ferry goods across land, speeding up the lengthy sea voyages. Nearly 200 years later his ideas were actually put into practice with the building of the Panama Canal, but in the 1690s the problems facing the Scottish colonists proved insurmountable. New Caledonia, as the colony was to be called, never rose as an imperial beacon of Scottish enterprise. It sank into oblivion, extinguished by the rigours of the terrible journey to reach it, the poor quality of its land and the hostility of the existing commercial empires of England and Spain. More than 2,000 men and women lost their lives: just as many lost all their money. Scotland, it seemed, could not survive in the rapidly expanding world of commerce and exploration on its own. It needed to be amalgamated with England, and it was in this climate that the two countries became one.

The uneasy relationship between England and Scotland stretched back for centuries. By the end of the eleventh century, after the Norman Conquest, Scotland's territory looked very similar to how it does today, but the Scottish kings still hankered after expansion into Northumbria and Cumbria. The line of the border – from the Solway Firth in the west to the mouth of the Tweed in the east – was not actually finally settled until the Treaty of York in 1237 between the Scottish King, Alexander II, and Henry III. At the end of the thirteenth century civil war in Scotland played into the hands of the English monarchy. Edward I agreed to support John Balliol's claim to the throne in return for being acknowledged as

Scotland's overlord, but Balliol lost control of the situation and his barons formed a council which signed an alliance with the French. Edward defeated the Scots at Dunbar in 1296 and suppressed the uprising of William Wallace at Falkirk in 1298 – although not before Wallace's band of rebels had shocked the English by winning a surprising victory at Stirling the year before.

England's control of Scotland was not tolerated for long. In 1314 Robert the Bruce won a devastating victory over Edward II at the Battle of Bannockburn: 6,000 Scotsmen massacred an English army of 15,000 men. Robert the Bruce was declared King of Scotland by the Declaration of Arbroath in 1320 – as proud and defiant a defence of liberty as any in British history: 'As long as a hundred of us remain alive, we shall never on any conditions be subjected to English rule. It is not for glory, nor riches, nor honours that we fight, but for freedom alone, which no honest man gives up except with his life.' England acknowledged Robert the Bruce's sovereignty in the Treaty of Edinburgh of 1328, by which time the boy king, Edward III, had succeeded to the English throne.

The two countries were not destined to be friends. At the centre of their hostility was Scotland's relationship with England's historic rival, France. 'The Auld Alliance' led the Scots to invade England on more than one occasion – most disastrously in 1513. The Scottish king, James IV, believing the English army to be preoccupied with Henry VIII's expedition against the French, marched across the border and was killed with many of his nobles at the Battle of Flodden Field. Scotland, constantly beset by internal warfare and always under threat from its more powerful southern neighbour, struggled after the reign of Robert the Bruce to build itself into a significant independent power.

Its moment came when the last of the Tudors, Elizabeth I, died without leaving an heir. The main political aim of James VI of Scotland was to make sure he succeeded to the throne of England in 1603. In achieving this he gave Scotland position and prestige, as well as an opportunity for its nobility to get its hands on the more affluent lifestyle which London offered. It seemed as though the quarrelsome difficulties of the past might finally disappear as the new King attempted to create a new, integrated country – Great Britain. In this he and his successors throughout the seventeenth century were unsuccessful. Scottish hostility and rivalry continued and, inevitably, worsened during the period of the Civil War when the two countries divided not along national, but on religious lines. Scottish Calvinists were the natural allies of English Puritans, while the Catholic Royalists of the Scottish Highlands remained on the whole loyal to their Stuart king. In the end hard political reality drove the two countries together. England could not afford to let Scotland go its own way again, and used its greater muscle to coerce the Scots into full union.

When in 1702, James II's younger daughter, Anne, became Queen of England, it was quite clear that she was not going to produce an heir. Four of her children had died in infancy – only a son had lived until he was eleven – and she had suffered several miscarriages. Securing her succession became the most important domestic political issue of her reign. The British government wanted the Protestant Hanoverians to take over the throne, but the country's powerful enemy, Louis XIV of France, had sheltered the exiled Stuart king, James II, and was now harbouring his son. Scotland was the Stuarts' power base: it could not be allowed to make its own arrangements for royal succession. The Scottish Parliament was pushed into acquiescence. Weakened by famine and the disastrous Darien expedition, the shame of the inevitable sweetened a little by the odd judicious bribe to members of the Scottish nobility, it agreed to abolish its institution of 157 seats in return for forty-five places in the Westminster House of Commons and sixteen elected peers. The act proclaimed that there would be 'one United Kingdom by the name of Great Britain'. The nation's one ruler would be Protestant: it had one legislature

Scotland had judged survival more important than sovereignty, and cut a deal.

and one system of free trade. Scotland's losses incurred in its colonial adventure were repaid; the Scottish Kirk kept its independence; and the two country's systems of law and education remained separate. Scotland had judged survival more important than sovereignty, and cut a deal.

If Scotland had failed to build an empire of its own, it more than made up for this disappointment in the years following the Act of Union. The Scottish contribution to the growth of the British Empire was immense. The East India Company, the engine of Britain's worldwide growth, was full of Scots. In 1731, John Drummond, a director of the company, reported that 'all the East India Company ships have either Scots Surgeons or Surgeon's mates'. A hundred and thirty years later the Liberal politician, Sir Charles Dilke, who travelled throughout the Empire, wrote that 'for every Englishman that you meet who has worked himself up from small beginnings, without external aid, you find ten Scotchmen'. Half of the first six governors of New South Wales were Scottish. Scots dominated the China trade: they owned and ran many of the prosperous merchant houses of Canada, India and the Far East. Scotland may have assimilated its new opportunities with gusto, but for some this exciting commercial expansion came at a price. The nineteenth century adoption of all things Scottish, thanks in large part to the enormous success of the novels of Sir Walter Scott, brought about an image of Scotland which was criticised in some quarters for being unreal and romantic. In particular Scott helped introduce the wearing of the tartan to Lowland Scotland, of which it had never been part, and his stories, often adapted into melodramatic operas by Italian composers like Rossini and Donizetti, only served to reinforce an image of Scotland as a medieval tableau of long-dead heroics. While the Scottish people blazed a trail of enterprise abroad, or worked and suffered in the grinding difficulties of the Industrial Revolution, the world was fed a picture of Scottishness far removed from reality. Perhaps: but perhaps, too, Sir Walter Scott was just another example of Scottish skill and ingenuity, one of the world's first examples of an international best-selling novelist, many of whose books remain classics of the English language.

The Act of Union combined Scotland's future with England's but it could not subdue its aspirations for a separate identity. In 1745 the Young Pretender, Charles Edward Stuart, landed in the Hebrides, raised his standard in the Highlands, defeated a British army at Prestonpans east of Edinburgh and was halfway to London before England roused itself to confront him. 'Bonnie Prince Charlie' was confident that he could win back his family's throne, but his military advisors, worried that his army would find itself isolated in the south of England, persuaded him to turn back to Scotland. The support in the countryside was far less than they hoped and the French fleet they expected had failed to materialise. The Scots rebels were pursued by the King's son, the Duke of Cumberland. He caught up with them at Culloden in 1746 and cut them to pieces with frightening savagery. He returned to London to rapturous renditions of the popular song 'God Save The Queen'. Bonnie Prince Charlie escaped to Europe disguised as an Irish maid, for a life of heavy drinking and ever-changing female companionship.

The post of Scottish Secretary was abolished after the rebellion of 1745 and responsibility for managing Scotland's affairs was given to the Lord Advocate, the King's advisor on Scottish matters. In the early nineteenth century it was passed to the Home Office, but in 1885 the post of Secretary of State for Scotland was created. Its powers were increased considerably in 1926, but pressure for greater devolution continued. In 1979 proposals to establish a Scottish Assembly were put to referendum in Scotland, but failed to win sufficient support. In 1995 the Scottish Constitutional Convention, which had been set up a few years before, finally brought forward proposals which, this time supported by a referendum, led to the creation of a separate Scottish parliament in 1999. Similar devolved powers were granted to assemblies in Wales and, ultimately, in Northern Ireland as well. The Scottish Parliament was given powers to elect a separate executive which enjoys complete

The Union Jack

In 1606, three years after James I became King of both Scotland and England, a new flag was invented to celebrate the union of the two monarchies. It was to be used solely at sea. A royal decree proclaimed that Britain's ships 'shall beare in their Mainetoppe the Red Crosse, commonly called St Georges Crosse, and the White Crosse, commonly called St Andrewes Crosse, joyned together according to a forme made by our Heralds'.

The square blue cross of St Andrew was used as a background with a white border separating the blue bits from the red, as required by the rules of heraldry. The third element of the flag, the red diagonal cross of St Patrick, was added in 1801 after the Act of Union with Ireland. The Welsh flag does not feature in the design at all because Wales was considered to be a principality of England.

The flag was not used during Cromwell's time as Lord Protector because a new design incorporating the St George and St Andrew crosses, together with a golden harp and Cromwell's white lion on a black shield, was introduced. The original version was reinstated after the restoration of the monarchy in 1660. The term 'Jack' may derive from protective jerkins known as 'jacks' or 'jacques' which sometimes bore saints' emblems, although there is also a theory that it refers to King James whose name in Latin is 'Jacobus'.

The Union Jack became an emblem of the Empire. More than a hundred nations, colonies, dominions or protectorates have included it on their flags at one time or another. Today it can be seen on the flags of Australia, New Zealand, Fiji, Tuvalu and Hawaii.

jurisdiction over a number of issues such as health, justice, education, the environment and economic development. No change was made to the number of MPs which Scotland sends to Westminster.

The creation of a parliament gave back to Scotland some of the sovereignty it had lost in 1707, but tensions with England remained. In 2008 the Scottish National Party, which advocates complete independence for Scotland, secured enough votes to form the minority administration of the Scottish Executive. Meanwhile voices in England were beginning to say that it was unfair for Scotland to return MPs to Westminster who then had a say in English affairs, while the House of Commons had no jurisdiction over most internal issues relating to Scotland. Their concerns were framed in a question that had been asked in the House of Commons thirty years before. 'For how long will English constituencies and English Honourable Members tolerate,' asked the MP, Tam Dalyell, 'Honourable Members from Scotland, Wales and Northern Ireland exercising an important, and probably often decisive, effect on British politics while they themselves have no say in the same matters in Scotland, Wales and Northern Ireland?'

The question stands unanswered. When the Chancellor of Scotland, James Ogilvy, Earl of Seafield, signed the Act of Union in 1707 he remarked wistfully: 'There's *ane* end of *ane* auld song.' Two hundred years later echoes of the old song can still be heard in Scotland: perhaps his lordship spoke too soon.

CHAPTER 9

The Irish Home Rule Bill
1886

In 1886 the British Prime Minister, William Gladstone, introduced a bill to the House of Commons proposing Home Rule for Ireland. It was defeated. Gladstone's failure to solve the problems of Britain's relationship with Ireland would lead directly to the bitter troubles of the twentieth century.

'My mission,' said William Gladstone when he first became Prime Minister in 1868, 'is to pacify Ireland.' Gladstone was the political colossus of the Victorian Age. He was Prime Minister four times. Although he started his career as a Conservative he graduated to become the greatest Liberal leader of the nineteenth century, a constant advocate of individual liberty and free trade. He was complex, energetic and determined and during his periods of office introduced or proposed an enormous amount of reforming legislation. His arguments were sometimes a bit difficult to follow, and he was prone to outbursts of rather histrionic moral indignation, but he loomed over the political scene of nineteenth-century Britain like a great headmaster trying to drum a sense of responsibility into his pupils. But he did not succeed in his mission towards Ireland. In this he was not alone.

The great invasions which affected the early development of Britain never got as far as Ireland. The Romans never settled there. The Vikings managed to establish a strong presence in the ninth and tenth centuries but never on the same scale as they did in England. Norman barons invaded the country in 1166 at the invitation of the Irish King of Leinster, Diarmuid MacMurrough, who enlisted their help in trying to win his throne back from his local enemies. Their success disturbed the King of England, Henry II, who was worried about a rival Norman power base being created close to his own territory. As a result, England gained control of much of the country after the Pope – in fact the only English Pope, Adrian IV – granted him permission to invade, ostensibly to sort out the abuses of the Irish Church. Henry was the first King of England to set foot in Ireland and in 1175 signed the Treaty of Windsor with the Irish leader, Rory O'Connor. O'Connor was recognised as High King on condition that he accepted Henry as his overlord. From this moment on English monarchs would always lay claim to Ireland. Their hold on the country weakened in the fourteenth century, mainly because they were preoccupied with wars in France, but the Tudor dynasty set about recapturing lands which their predecessors had lost. In 1494, Sir Edward Poyning, Henry VII's Lord Deputy in Ireland, introduced an act which stated that the Irish Parliament was subservient to the English, and in 1541 Henry VIII declared himself King of Ireland. By the end of the sixteenth century the English were beginning to send settlers over to Ireland to manage land which had been confiscated from their Irish owners. The deliberate Anglicisation of Ireland had begun.

At the end of the sixteenth century the Irish rebelled against their English masters. Hugh O'Neill, the Earl of Tyrone, led a nine years' war against the forces of Elizabeth I. Her favourite, the Earl of Essex, failed completely to halt the rebels' advance and it was not until the year she died, in 1603, that they were defeated. At the Battle of Kinsale the army of O'Neill and his Spanish allies was utterly destroyed, but in the peace that followed he and his fellow Irish nobles were not treated particularly harshly, although they did lose a substantial amount of land. Eventually in 1607, reduced and disaffected by the Protestant policies of the new English government, O'Neill and some of his companions fled the country. They never returned, and their country was left to the mercy of its English rulers.

Ireland was and is predominantly a Catholic country. The

majority of its people never accepted the teachings of the Reformation. As a result, from the beginning of the seventeenth century until Catholic emancipation in 1829, the British ruled a country which they were bound to regard with suspicion and hostility. Oliver Cromwell's Protectorate, the Glorious Revolution and the Bill of Rights had all established Protestantism and the Protestant succession on the English throne as fundamental principles of the nation's constitution. But in the country which it governed across the Irish Sea most of the people believed in something else altogether. Despite all its efforts to settle Protestants on the land and to impose the Anglican Church upon its people, successive British governments failed to convert the majority of Irish to its religious views. In such circumstances, however enlightened in their individual attitudes or however scrupulous and fair they tried to be in their administration, they operated a system which was intrinsically unjust. At the same time, by encouraging and giving power to a minority of Protestants in order to maintain control, they created a society which was divided along sectarian lines. This was 'the Irish problem'.

Injustice encourages different forces to combine against it. In 1798 it was a Protestant, Wolfe Tone, who persuaded the government of revolutionary France, the Directory, to organise a naval attack on Ireland. The French fleet was defeated and Tone was sentenced to be hanged. He died before his execution took place – possibly by committing suicide. Tone's rebellion convinced the British government that it needed even greater control of Irish affairs and it drove through the Act of Union of 1801 which abolished the Irish Parliament altogether in exchange for a hundred MPs at Westminster. Rebellion had destroyed the dream of independence: Ireland had become a full part of the United Kingdom for the first time in its history.

Between 1845 and 1849 Ireland was struck by famine. A potato blight destroyed its crops: the population was reduced by a quarter as 2 million people either died or emigrated to places such as America to start new lives. In 1846 a letter by a Cork magistrate

The plantation of Ulster

Britain treated Ireland as a colony. After the Irish rebellion was suppressed in the early years of the reign of James I, it set about the business of colonisation in a ruthlessly well-organised way. Six Ulster colonies were divided up and given to government supporters on condition that they settled them with Protestant English and Scottish immigrants. The people who received the land were families who had opposed Hugh O'Neill, the principal leader of the revolt against the British, or British government officials. The established Church and Trinity College, Dublin were also granted estates. So were wealthy companies: the Corporation of London received the town of Derry – and promptly added the prefix 'London' to its name. Derry and Armagh were planted with English settlers; Tyrone and Donegal were planted with Scottish; and Fermanagh and Cavan were opened up to both.

The Plantation of Ulster not only enforced a complete change of land ownership, it introduced a social revolution as families arrived from Scotland and England to farm their new possessions. By the late 1630s about 40,000 settlers had arrived in Ulster. But despite the large numbers of new arrivals they remained in a minority, often resented and viewed with suspicion. The plantation would never succeed in its purpose of trying to turn Ireland into a compliant offshoot of Britain.

was published in *The Times*. He described what he had seen in the village of Skibbereen:

... the scenes were such as no tongue or pen can convey the slightest idea of ... six famished and ghastly skeletons, to all appearances dead, were huddled in a corner ... in a few minutes I was surrounded by at least 200 such phantoms, such frightful spectres as no words can describe ... The same morning the police opened a house ... which was observed shut for many days, and two frozen corpses were found, lying upon the mud floor, half devoured by rats.

It seemed to many people in Ireland as if their country, owned by absentee landlords and ruled by a government that had no knowledge of its problems, had been abandoned to its fate. The cause of independence, born out of resentment, was now imbued with hatred.

Gladstone had already carried out some Irish reforms by the time he presented his Home Rule Bill in 1886. In his first administration between 1868 and 1874 he had disestablished the Irish Church, abolishing the taxes people had to pay to a Church they did not believe in and redistributing much of its wealth to the Poor Law Board to provide relief for the impoverished. He had also tried to improve conditions for Irish tenant farmers by introducing legislation to protect them against being charged excessive rents by their landlords, but this had not been particularly effective. Home Rule was a far bigger step and one where Gladstone, among British politicians, was very much on his own. The Irish Parliamentary Party led by Charles Stewart Parnell, a Protestant Anglo-Irishman converted to the cause of Irish independence, had been campaigning for self-government since the 1870s, and helped convince Gladstone of the need to do something. Parnell did not much like the bill Gladstone proposed – in his view it did not go far enough – but he decided to support it because it seemed to be better than nothing. It gave Ireland its own assembly through which it could legislate on its own affairs, but matters of foreign policy and trade would continue to reside with Britain whose Lord Lieutenant retained executive power. It was more devolution than Home Rule – but for the time in which it was presented it was still radical. Gladstone, by now seventy-six years old, defended it in one of the greatest speeches of his long career: 'Go into the length and breadth of the world, ransack the literature of all countries, find, if you can, a single voice, a single book ... in which the conduct of England towards Ireland is anywhere treated except with profound and bitter condemnation.' Finishing with a passionate flourish, he declared: 'Think, I beseech you, think well, think wisely, think, not for the moment, but for the years that are to come, before you reject this bill.' History is what it is: it does not allow for hindsight. But anyone surveying Britain's relations with Ireland from the end of the nineteenth century to the present day and then reading Gladstone's words in defence of Home Rule would be forgiven for sighing 'If only', or wondering 'What if?'

Gladstone's bill was rejected by thirty votes. In the election that followed his government was defeated. He came back to power in 1892 when once again he brought a Home Rule Bill before Parliament. This time he won a majority in the House of Commons, but the House of Lords threw it out. Gladstone was by this time eighty-three. In 1894 he retired from politics and died four years later. Parnell, the leader of the Irish Parliamentary Party, died in 1891: his health deteriorated after he was forced out of power following a scandal in which he was cited as co-respondent in a divorce case. Home Rule had lost its boldest and most energetic evangelists. Caution tempered by misgiving was now its guide: the result for Britain and Ireland was disastrous.

'find, if you can, a single voice, a single book ... in which the conduct of England towards Ireland is anywhere treated except with profound and bitter condemnation'

The Liberals were in government again from 1906 until the outbreak of the First World War. They did not possess the same vision for Home Rule as Gladstone but they were grateful for the support of the Irish Parliamentary Party in their battle with the Conservative House of Lords. In 1911 they brought forward a Home Rule Bill very similar to the one Gladstone had proposed eighteen years before. This time it was not just Conservative opposition they faced. The Ulster Protestants, led by Sir Edward Carson, set their face against any notion of separation from Britain. Carson was a leading lawyer who had prosecuted Oscar Wilde in 1895 with, in Wilde's phrase, 'all the added bitterness of an old friend'. (The two men had been at Trinity College, Dublin together.) Carson led Protestant opposition to Home Rule. In 1912 he organised the signing of the 'Ulster Covenant' by half a million men and women, which declared they would 'use all means which may be found necessary to defeat the present conspiracy to set up a Home Rule Parliament in Ireland'. All means necessary appeared to include force: Carson founded a militia group called the Ulster Volunteer Force in 1912.

The Liberal Prime Minister, Herbert Asquith, dithered and then compromised. As war began in Europe in 1914 a Home Rule Bill received royal assent – but with two significant amendments. The first was that Ulster was to be temporarily excluded from the agreement: its final position was to be decided at a later stage. The second – and in the end most significant – was that the whole bill was not to be enacted for at least a year when the confident politicians of early twentieth-century Britain expected the war to be over. John Redmond, the leader of the Irish Parliamentary Party, encouraged Irishmen to join Britain and its allies in the fight against Germany. There was not long to wait before Ireland would be free and the war would be won.

While Britain's warlike optimism died in the trenches of the Western Front, Ireland's dreams of peace were killed on the streets of Dublin. At Easter 1916, a group of Irish republicans staged a rebellion against British rule. It was suppressed and its leaders executed, but an armed struggle against British occupation had begun. In 1921 the British government agreed to the creation of an Irish Free State, but the six counties of Northern Ireland were allowed to secede and remain part of the United Kingdom. Ireland had been partitioned and divided along sectarian lines. This was something which all those who had fought for Home Rule, both Catholic and Protestant, and many of the Ulstermen who had opposed it, including Edward Carson, had never wanted and never envisaged.

Today, in 2008, a power-sharing assembly with devolved powers administers the affairs of Northern Ireland. After thirty years of dissension and bloodshed peace has returned to Ulster.

The Good Friday Agreement 1998

Attempts to end 'The Troubles' in Northern Ireland have had many false starts. In 1997, the British Prime Minister, Tony Blair, anxious to bring them to an end once and for all, announced the beginning of a new series of all-party talks. They started in September 1997 and ended the following Easter with the Good Friday Agreement.

The Good Friday Agreement of 10th April 1998 was an important turning point in the modern history of Ireland. It announced the introduction of devolved government to Northern Ireland on what it called a 'stable and inclusive basis' and created human rights and equality commissions. It agreed to the early release of terrorist prisoners. It demanded the decommissioning of paramilitary weapons. It promised reforms of the criminal justice system and the police. The government of the Republic of Ireland was brought into the process through a formal 'ministerial conference' in which it would meet regularly and formally with members of the Northern Ireland administration.

The Agreement was ratified by two referendums – one in the North, in which 71 per cent of the people agreed to it, the other in the South when more than 94 per cent agreed. There was one further significant terrorist incident. A group calling itself the 'Real IRA' set off a bomb in Omagh in August 1998, killing twenty-nine people. Failure to agree on the process for decommissioning weapons delayed final agreement even further, but in May 2007, following local elections, the Northern Ireland Assembly resumed its administration of the province on a power-sharing basis.

'The Troubles', as they are called, began in the late 1960s when the Catholic minority in Northern Ireland began to protest against what they believed to be discrimination by the Protestant majority. Their grievances developed into violent civil unrest. The Catholic cause was supported by the Provisional Irish Republican Army, 'the Provos', whose members saw themselves as the direct descendants of those who had first fought on the streets of Dublin in 1916. The Protestants had their own militia, the Ulster Volunteer Force, which took its name, although not its organisation, from the group formed to defend the Union in 1912. In Ireland, north and south, history is only just below the surface. Perhaps as Ulster's old enemies, now partners in peace, set about building the future they will sometimes care to look back to Gladstone, the Grand Old Man of Victorian politics who wanted, but failed, to pacify Ireland. Perhaps they will sigh 'If only'. Perhaps they will ask 'What if?'

CHAPTER 10

Britain Signs the Treaty of Rome
1973

In 1973 Britain joined the European Economic
Community by signing the Treaty of Rome. It agreed
to relinquish certain aspects of its national sovereignty
in return for the benefits of cooperation with other
European powers.

In 1910 a newspaper headline caught the eye of the comic poet,
Harry Graham. 'The Kaiser,' it said, 'spoke at length with the Baron
de Haulleville, Director of the Congo Museum, in French, German,
and English.' Graham decided to celebrate this multi-lingual
occasion as follows:

> *Guten morgen, mon ami,*
> *Heute ist es schones Wetter!*
> *Charmé de vous voir ici!*
> *Never saw you looking better!*

Another verse reads:

> *Und die Kinder, how are they?*
> *Ont-ils eu la rougeole* [measles] *lately?*
> *Sind sie avec vous today?*
> *J'aimerais les treffen greatly.*

This piece of fun, written nearly a hundred years ago, can still raise
a smile today. In fact it feels quite modern. It displays a certain
relevance to the integrated European world in which we live – a
continent without borders, sharing for the most part a common
currency, which has turned its back on the conflicts of the past to
sink its hopes in a united vision of prosperity and peace.

Harry Graham's poem was written before the First World War devastated the hopes of Britain and its Empire, before the long depressions of the inter-war years and the fight to the death against Nazi Germany. It is no wonder that after nearly forty years of conflict and decline the tottering nations of Europe decided to grasp each other for support and to build something between them that might prevent the outbreak of war again. The European Union of today was created out of the ashes of war, and the greatest of the wartime leaders, Winston Churchill, was one of its first proponents. Speaking in Zurich in 1946 he said: 'We must build a kind of United States of Europe.' Quoting William Gladstone in his famous defence of Home Rule for Ireland he called for what the nineteenth-century Prime Minister had called 'the blessed act of oblivion' and added: 'We must all turn our backs on the horrors of the past and we must look to the future.'

The European Union of today was created out of the ashes of war.

Most importantly, and presciently, he said there 'must be a partnership between France and Germany'. He thought this was more important than Britain's involvement and ended his speech with this: 'If at first all the States of Europe are not willing or able to join a union we must nevertheless proceed to assemble and combine those who will and those who can.' In the event this is what happened. The European state which was not willing or able turned out to be Britain.

In May 1950 the French Foreign Minister, Robert Schuman, announced that the French and German governments were going to create a common 'High Authority' to regulate and control the production of coal and steel within the two countries. Other countries in Europe would be invited to participate in the plan which would 'make it plain that any war between France and Germany becomes not merely unthinkable, but materially impossible'. The British government was given only a few hours' notice of Schuman's announcement, and its reaction was one of dismay. The nation still felt itself to be a world power. It was not like the other countries of

Europe. It did not need to be pushed or chivvied into schemes it had not helped to invent. Furthermore it had just completed the nationalisation of its coal industry and was not inclined to unpick this to please some new, European dream.

In fact Schuman and the planning brains behind the Franco-German idea, Jean Monnet, were prepared to let Britain join their partnership even though its coal industry was nationalised, but the British government under the re-elected Labour leader, Clement Attlee, declined. The country had a strong trading relationship with the Commonwealth and a political alliance with America – although America was very much in favour of seeing Britain absorbed into the European alliance. In 1952 the Treaty of Paris created the European Coal and Steel Community, made up of France, West Germany, Italy, Holland, Belgium and Luxembourg. Five years later, in 1957, the Treaty of Rome took it one stage further and established the European Economic Community. Britain could only watch these developments from the sidelines. It had decided to stay out, following the approach laid down by Winston Churchill who, although he had eloquently defended the idea of European integration in 1947, told his cabinet four years later: 'We help, we dedicate, we play a part, but we are not merged and do not forfeit our insular or Commonwealth character.'

By the 1960s the realities of international commerce were beginning to filter into the minds of British politicians. In 1960 Britain joined an organisation called the European Free Trade Area, or EFTA, whose other members were Denmark, Norway, Sweden, Austria, Switzerland and Portugal. This was simply a trading association without the same political apparatus of the European Community. A year later, the British Prime Minister, Harold Macmillan, told the House of Commons that Britain was tendering a formal application to join the Common Market on condition that its obligations to the Commonwealth could be met. He was, he said, 'not confident, but hopeful' of success. Neither confidence nor hope would prove enough. The French President, Charles de Gaulle, sceptical of Britain's commitment to the European idea, exercised his veto on two occasions, in 1963 and 1967, to prevent it from joining. In 1967 he loftily declared that Britain would need to accomplish 'a profound economic and political transformation' before it could become a member. Only in 1973, with the first enlargement of the original six-nation membership, was Britain allowed into Europe, along with Denmark and Ireland.

Britain today, in 2008, has been part of the European idea for thirty-five years. The EEC has become the European Union. The collapse of the Soviet Union's control of the countries of Eastern Europe in the late 1980s, combined with the reunification of Germany in 1990, has fuelled its expansion on an unexpected scale. There are twenty-seven members with three more waiting to join. One of these is Turkey whose candidacy is highly controversial: a former French President, Valery Giscard d'Estaing, declared that Turkey was 'not a European country' and that its membership of the EU would mean 'the end of Europe'. Meanwhile the member states have committed, under the Treaty of Lisbon of 2007, to strengthen the organisation and institutions of the Union, giving more power to its parliament, appointing a new President of the European Council and extending its activities to include defence. In Britain, and in some other countries, there has been strong opposition to these reforms being introduced without ordinary people approving them through a popular vote. The idea of the war-torn nations of Europe embracing one another in an act of self-protective friendship has grown into a vast multi-national conglomerate. It has turned European history on its head; the historic rivalries of individual sovereign states have been abandoned in a surge of democratic optimism; 'Europe' is as influential in the life of the modern British citizen as Britain itself.

Britain has always been a bit unsure about its feelings towards the rest of Europe. It grew out of it and then away from it: its real power came ultimately from an empire which had few roots in the European continent. It also came to believe that its political development was different from its continental neighbours. The Victorian historian Macaulay, for instance, argued that Britain had

The French view of Britain

In March 2008 the President of France, Nicolas Sarkozy, paid a state visit to Britain. He was a President in a new mould, very different from the sort of men who had held power in France since the end of the Second World War. To many British eyes the main thing that set him apart from his predecessors was his glamorous Italian wife, a former model and singer, whom he had recently married after his second divorce. But if they had eyes only for his wife, their ears burned with what he had to say about the relationship between France and Britain. In a speech to the combined Houses of Parliament on 26th March, Nicolas Sarkozy spoke in a way no other French President had done before. Ever since Charles de Gaulle had refused to allow British entry into the Common Market, the leaders of France had always displayed a certain *froideur* in their dealings with Britain – friendly but invariably slightly cool. Sarkozy's approach was completely different.

The son of a Hungarian immigrant who fled from his homeland to France as the Red Army marched westwards in 1945, the new President instinctively recognised Britain's wartime achievements, and had no trouble in talking about them. 'I want to say something on behalf of the French people,' he said. 'France won't forget. France will never forget that when she was verging on annihilation it was Britain who was at France's side ... We haven't forgotten because we haven't the right to forget what young Britons did for the freedom of the French people ... France will never forget the British people's heroic resistance, without which all would have been lost.'

With a few passionate words, President Sarkozy sought to blow away the diffidence that had been the hallmark of Franco-British relations for sixty years. Ironically, it was exactly two years to the day since his predecessor, Jacques Chirac, marched out of a European Union summit meeting in disgust after a fellow Frenchman insisted in making a presentation in English because, he said, it was 'the language of business'. In the European Union, unity has often been a fragile affair: Nicolas Sarkozy's speech gave new and unusual strength to Britain's relationship with France.

Charles I, seen here in this picture by Anthony van Dyck, with his wife, Henrietta Maria and his two eldest children, Charles (later Charles II) and Mary, the first daughter of a king to be given the title Princess Royal. Charles I was tried for high treason and executed in 1649.

Top: Following his discovery of the Victoria Falls in 1855, David Livingstone was given a paddle-steamer to continue his exploration of the Zambesi River. Built by the Merseyside firm belonging to John Laird (later to become Cammell Laird) the African natives called it the *Ma-Robert* in honour of Livingstone's wife whose eldest child was called Robert. Livingstone's discoveries opened up central and eastern Africa to colonisation in the second half of the nineteenth century.

Bottom: Mahatma Gandhi on his famous March to the Sea in 1930 to make salt, in defiance of the British salt monopoly.

Major-General Robert Clive, 1st Baron Clive of Plassey, also known as Clive of India (1725-1774). Clive's victory over Indian forces at the Battle of Plassey in 1757 laid the foundations for the creation of the British Raj in India.

Above: Sir Francis Drake was the first sea captain to circumnavigate the globe between 1577 and 1580.

Above right: A country gentleman with strong Protestant beliefs, Oliver Cromwell rose to command the army that overthrew Charles I. He went on to become Lord Protector of England in 1653.

Right: In the eighteenth century British slave ships carried human cargo from Africa to work as slaves. Conditions were appalling: the slaves were crammed into the hold and chained together. Surviving records suggest that up until 1750, 20 per cent of them died on board.

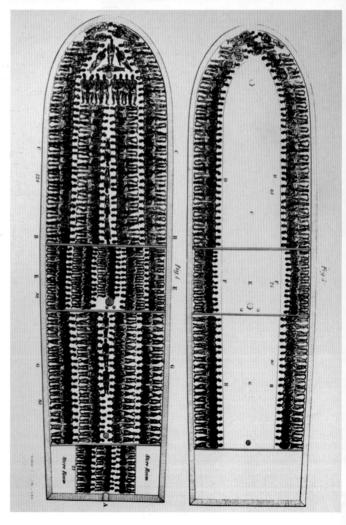

22nd June 1948: the ex-troopship *Empire Windrush* arrives at Tilbury Docks from Jamaica. On board – 482 West Indians arriving to start a new life in Britain.

Top: Laurence Olivier as
Henry V in the 1944 film of
Shakespeare's play. The film was
in part intended to boost
morale in wartime Britain.

Bottom: The Battle of Trafalgar painted by Joseph Mallord William
Turner (1775-1851). Turner researched the events of the battle very
carefully. This picture depicts the action from the mizzen starboard
of *HMS Victory* and was first exhibited a year after the battle in 1806.

nd June 1982: captured Argentinian soldiers are guarded by a British Royal Marine at Goose Green in he Falkland Islands. 712 Argentines, 255 Britons and three islanders were killed in the war which lasted o weeks.

Top: A suburban house in south-west London after it had been hit by a bomb in 1940.

Bottom: 'The Battle of Orgreave' 1984: the police line in the confrontation with miners trying to prevent coal reaching a British Steel coking plant.

avoided the upheavals of the revolutions which affected several European nations in 1848 because it possessed a constitution founded on precepts of liberty. 'All around us,' he wrote in his *History of England*, 'the world is convulsed by the agonies of great nations ... It is because we had a preserving revolution in the seventeenth century that we have not had a destroying revolution in the nineteenth. It is because we had freedom in the midst of servitude that we have order in the midst of anarchy.' Macaulay believed the history of England to be a history of progress – beneficial progress at that. In the twentieth century his views fell out of fashion but today they are being reconsidered. Britain did not succumb to either communism or fascism: does this not tell us that an innate belief in liberty lies deep in its roots?

By the end of the nineteenth century, secure in the wealth of Empire, Britain preferred isolation to involvement. In the twentieth it fought against German militarism and saved Europe from tyranny. But it still harboured suspicion of the motives of some European countries long after that fight was over. Margaret Thatcher, to date Britain's longest-serving post-war Prime Minister, was determined to prevent 'a European super state exercising a new dominance from Brussels'. Today 'Europe' is still a place which for many British people means 'somewhere else'.

If the European Union is to succeed it will have to convince not only the people of Britain, but those of other countries too, that they are better off relinquishing some of their sovereignty in return for the benefits of being part of something bigger. To the kings, queens, politicians, writers, artists and historians who helped build the British nation from the beginning of the sixteenth century to the middle of the twentieth, the notion of losing national status would have been unthinkable. They devoted their energies to the idea of a Britain which was proud, independent and free. But if you go further back, to the days of Henry II, or William the Conqueror, or even Alfred the Great, it does not seem so incredible. In those days Europe's regional borders were altogether more flexible. The nation state as we understand it today did not exist. Places and peoples were merged as required under the authority of victorious kings. The European Union marks another great turn in the wheel of history: nobody yet knows to where it might roll.

2 Struggle

The Battles for Britain

Introduction

Each evening at precisely 8 o'clock, three, sometimes four, members of the volunteer fire brigade in the town of Ypres in Belgium pick up their silver bugles and sound 'The Last Post' at the Menin Gate. The Gate is a memorial to the soldiers who lost their lives in the Battle of the Somme in 1916 and whose bodies were never found. I filmed this ceremony for the BBC some years ago. To stand in front of the memorial listening to the plaintive sound of 'The Last Post' as your eyes scan the names of nearly 55,000 soldiers who have no grave is an intensely moving experience. A small Belgian town, a great memorial and a simple ceremony combine to express the colossal sadness of war.

Human beings can probably make no greater sacrifice than to die for their country, however wrongheaded the conflict in which they find themselves might be. In the history of Britain, millions of men and women have died in this way. Sometimes they have died in acts of aggression, sometimes in acts of defence; sometimes they have fought for national salvation, sometimes they have found themselves caught up in futile power struggles. Whatever the reason, their deaths were part of British history. The story of the battles in which they died is a central part of the story of who we, the British, are.

This chapter starts in 1415 with one of the most famous battles of the Middle Ages, the Battle of Agincourt, which began the last phase of the so-called Hundred Years' War against France. Britain's ambitions to rule France declined after Agincourt and domestic problems became more significant. The Battle of Bosworth in 1485 ended years of internal conflict and ushered in the powerful Tudor dynasty.

It fell to the Tudors' greatest monarch, Elizabeth I, to defend the country against the Spanish Armada in 1588. She was also very successful at holding the nation together but her successors were less so. The Battle of Naseby in 1645 saw Charles I having to defend his throne against the forces of parliamentary opposition.

By the end of the seventeenth century stability had begun to return to the nation but it had powerful enemies abroad. The next three battles were fought against France, which had once again become its greatest European rival. The Battle of Blenheim in 1704 held in check the imperial ambitions of the French king, Louis XIV. The Battles of Trafalgar in 1805 and Waterloo in 1815 first disrupted and then defeated the Emperor Napoleon's attempts to dominate the continent of Europe.

Comparative peace in Europe followed the victory at Waterloo, but this was shattered by the outbreak of the First World War, which saw many terrible battles. The Somme in 1916 was one of its worst.

The heavy price that Germany was forced to pay at the end of the First World War led directly to the Second World War just over twenty years later and Britain had to fight for its life in the Battle of Britain in 1940.

The last battle of the chapter, the Battle of Goose Green in the Falklands War of 1982, marks the moment when Britain rallied from a long period of post-war decline to tackle important problems both abroad – and at home.

These ten battles against enemies within and without are an important part of the British story. Britain has had to fight, fight – and fight again – to become the nation it is today.

CHAPTER 1

The Battle of Agincourt
1415

In 1415 an English army under Henry V defeated the French at the Battle of Agincourt in northern France. The battle was a central event in the last phase of the Hundred Years' War between England and France.

Henry V won the Battle of Agincourt but it was Shakespeare who made his victory live forever. Shakespeare was not only the finest poet and dramatist Britain has ever produced, he was also a skilful propagandist. In *Henry V* he gives us an account of a brave and noble English king sacrificing everything to win – against all the odds – a monumental battle against a far greater power. Shakespeare's play appeared in London right at the end of the sixteenth century, about ten years after England had repulsed the invasion by the Spanish Armada. Elizabeth I was nearing the end of her long, careful reign. Her little country had a new-found confidence and had begun to flex its muscles as it struck out to explore new territories abroad. Shakespeare provided it with the images to support its developing strengths. He was so good at it, and his ideas so enduring, that his play would be used for pretty much the same purposes nearly three hundred and fifty years after it was written. Laurence Olivier's film was produced in 1944 as a morale booster for a Britain once again at war and the government provided some of the money to make it:

> *We few, we happy few, we band of brothers;*
> *For he today that sheds his blood with me*
> *Shall be my brother; be he ne'er so vile,*
> *This day shall gentle his condition;*

And gentlemen in England now a-bed
Shall think themselves accurs'd they were not here ...

In those six lines alone are contained some of the most famous phrases about men and battles in any piece of literature anywhere in the world. 'We happy few', 'band of brothers', 'gentlemen in England now a-bed' – these marvellous words have remained an inspiration for men and women in adversity since the day they were written. As far as the British are concerned they tell the story of Agincourt.

Henry V became King of England two years before Agincourt. His father, Henry Bolingbroke, had seized the throne from his cousin Richard II in 1399 and had then ruled as Henry IV. Richard was imprisoned in Pontefract Castle in Yorkshire where he died in 1400, some say murdered on the orders of the man who had taken his throne. Henry IV's reign had been about as troublesome as any mediaeval monarch's could be. His barons constantly jostled for power and he faced a rebellion from Henry Percy, the Earl of Northumberland, known to all lovers of Shakespeare as Harry Hotspur. The Welsh too were in revolt: their leader, Owain Glyndwr, declared himself the true Prince of Wales and led an army against the English King. In fighting off these uprisings Henry IV came to rely increasingly on his son. The young prince fought against Hotspur and Glyndwr and by the time his father died was already well blooded in the business of military leadership, as well as the management of political affairs. He put this experience into practice as soon as he ascended the throne.

Henry V had known Richard II well. Richard had banished Henry's father from the kingdom and taken his inherited lands away from him – one of the main reasons why Bolingbroke had rebelled against him. Richard had no quarrel with Bolingbroke's son and had befriended him while the young man's father was in exile. When Henry V became king thirteen years after Richard had died at Pontefract, he ordered that Richard's body be reburied at Westminster Abbey. His motives perhaps had as much as to do with a need to calm rebel spirits as to demonstrate an act of friend-ship – but they had the right effect. By honouring the memory of Richard, Henry V showed that he was rather more than just his father's son. He also knew that gestures of this kind would not on their own be enough. He needed something else and in searching for it he looked towards France.

The concept of the nation state as we understand it today did not exist in the Middle Ages. Rulers owned and controlled lands through war and conquest. Their approach was to a certain extent as much tribal as it was national: they sought to capture territory in the name of their families and to pass it on to their successors. The Normans, the most successful of the conquering tribes of the medieval period, had added Britain to their tally in 1066 – and from this time on the Kings of England began to own lands on both sides of the Channel. When Henry II, one of the greatest of the medieval kings, died in 1189 the English monarchy owned territory throughout western France, but bit by bit his successors managed to lose a great deal of it. In 1327, another powerful English monarch, Edward III, came to the throne. He ruled for fifty years – and spent much of his reign trying to reassert England's claim to France. He had considerable success, winning great battles at Crécy in 1346 and Poitiers in 1356. He was the king who started the Hundred Years' War – a war that Henry V, his great grandson, decided he would continue. He declared himself King of France and began to prepare to recapture Normandy for the English crown.

Henry V was a warrior king. At the beginning of the fifteenth century it was customary, as it had been in the centuries before, for a king to lead his troops into battle. Henry supervised and managed all aspects of his expedition to France – guns, artillery, weaponry for breaching city walls, scaling ladders and food supplies. Most important of all, he also had to raise the army itself and find the men at arms whom he would lead into war. This was the most difficult part of the operation. All his noblemen were expected to take part – but Henry had to help foot the bill by raising loans on his royal jewellery. The final size of Henry's army is not

The Hundred Years' War

1337	Philip VI of France confiscates Aquitaine from Edward III of England
1338	Edward III lands in Antwerp with an army
1340	Edward III assumes the title King of France; English naval victory at Battle of Sluys
1346	Battle of Crécy; the severely outnumbered English win a resounding victory, partly thanks to the use of longbows
1347	Calais captured by the English
1348	Edward III establishes the Order of the Garter
1356	Edward the Black Prince defeats the French at the Battle of Poitiers; John II of France captured
1360	Treaty of Brétigny signed; Edward III obtains much of Aquitaine and a huge ransom for King John
1369	Fighting resumes and the French gradually win back almost all lost territory
1415	Henry V of England renews the English claim to the French throne; Harfleur captured; English victory at Battle of Agincourt
1417–19	English conquest of Normandy
1420	The Treaty of Troyes makes Henry heir to the French throne
1422	Deaths of Henry V in August and of Charles VI of France in October; Henry's infant son succeeds to the thrones of England and France
1429	Joan of Arc breaks siege of Orléans; the Dauphin crowned King of France at Reims
1431	Joan of Arc burned at the stake
1435	Congress of Arras: the Duke of Burgundy switches allegiance to the French
1450	The French successfully retake Normandy
1453	English defeat at the Battle of Castillon; the French win back Bordeaux; England left only with Calais, which is finally won back by France in 1558

known for sure but it is believed that he eventually led 12,000 men across the Channel to France. They sailed in a fleet of 1,500 ships – not just soldiers, but horses, grooms, blacksmiths, tent makers and carpenters. The royal household went too, including the King's minstrels. The whole panoply of medieval government set sail for war.

The English invaders landed at Harfleur where for over a month they laid siege to the town. It was well fortified and surrounded by water ditches that had to be filled in to enable Henry's forces to bring their guns close enough for attack. The conditions were difficult: many English soldiers died from dysentery. 'Once more unto the breach, dear friends, once more/ Or close the wall up with our English dead,' cries Shakespeare's Henry in his famous speech during the siege. The stirring words are eerily prophetic. Five hundred years almost exactly separate the Battle of Agincourt from the Battle of the Somme fought in the same area in 1916: five hundred years between one wall of English dead and another. In both cases ultimate victory came at a high price.

Once Henry had captured Harfleur he set up a garrison there and prepared to march deeper into France. First, though, he issued a challenge to the Dauphin, the King's son, to meet him in a duel. The French King, Charles VI, was mad: his son, then eighteen years old, rather fat. The Dauphin declined. Henry wanted to go north towards Calais but he was forced to strike inland because the French had destroyed all means of crossing the Somme river. Supplies ran out and a contemporary account reports that the troops were 'made faint by great weariness and weak from lack of food'. Discipline was harsh: one Englishman caught stealing from a French church was hanged as an example to other would-be looters.

On 19th October 1415, the English army finally succeeded in crossing the Somme: five days later they came in sight of the main French army. Henry ordered his army to pitch camp, stay silent and wait. He had learned from some French prisoners that the enemy planned to use cavalry against his archers and, according to one chronicler, issued an instruction during the march 'that every archer was to prepare and fashion for himself a stake or staff, either square or round, but six feet long ... and sharpened at both ends'. These hastily prepared defences were to be driven into the ground on the battlefield to impale horses and riders as they charged at the English longbowmen. It had been raining hard and the field where the battle would take place was a quagmire.

As far as Henry was concerned, it was now or never. His army was exhausted by its march to Agincourt and was being constantly depleted by illness and death. On 25th October, the English attacked. The conditions were in their favour. The French men-at-arms were weighed down by their cumbersome armour and their horses became lanced by the archers' staves. The longbowmen did their work, sending volleys of arrows into the advancing cavalry, disrupting the attack and driving the French into the soggy mud. When they ran out of arrows they picked up anything they could find – axes, mallets, swords and spears – and waded into the fight, hacking at the oncoming enemy. After three hours, 5–10,000 Frenchmen had been killed, but the English army was still remarkably intact. Within the space of a morning, a group of exhausted Englishmen a quarter of the size of their enemy had renewed their country's claim to territory across the Channel and heightened its reputation in the eyes of the world around it. No wonder Shakespeare chose their victory as the subject of his great pageant: it was a story to stir the blood of anyone with an ounce of patriotism in him.

Agincourt was a glorious memory, a historical legend and a Shakespearian dream.

Henry continued his campaigns in France throughout his reign. He captured Caen in 1417 and Rouen two years later: Normandy fell into English hands for the first time in 200 years. He married the French King's daughter, Katherine, and was declared heir to the French throne and Regent of France. In 1420 he entered Paris. The noble families of France did not intend to stand by and watch their country handed over to an Englishman, and Henry would have to keep on fighting if he wanted to secure these great victories. In 1422 he died suddenly following the siege of Meaux just outside Paris. He was only thirty-four.

In a reign of nine years, Henry V had restarted the Hundred Years' War and put England back in the ascendancy. His successes were short-lived. His infant son, Henry VI, was crowned King of England and France, but he turned out to be more priest than soldier. In 1429, seven years after Henry V's death, the British were defeated at Orléans, thanks in part to the inspiration that the French received from a young visionary called Joan of Arc. Long before Henry VI's reign was over, most of the land that his father had conquered was returned to France. Agincourt was a glorious memory, a historical legend and a Shakespearian dream.

CHAPTER 2

The Battle of Bosworth
1485

In 1485, Henry Tudor defeated King Richard III at the
Battle of Bosworth in Leicestershire. The battle marks a
turning point in English history. The instability created
by the Wars of the Roses came to an end and England
began to be governed by a new, powerful dynasty –
the Tudors.

The murder of the princes in the tower is one of the most famous
mysteries of British history. The two princes were the sons of
Edward IV. When he died in 1483, his elder son was proclaimed
Edward V and the younger became Duke of York. Their uncle,
Richard, Duke of Gloucester, was made Protector. As the new King
made his way to London, he was met by Richard who lodged him
in the tower in order, he said, to protect him. He was joined there
by his brother a while later. The two boys were never seen again. It
is generally believed that Richard, who declared the boys' claim to
the throne illegitimate and made himself King in their place, was
their murderer. There is no absolute evidence for this. In 1951, the
writer Josephine Tey wrote a novel called *The Daughter of Time* in
which her detective hero set out to prove that the real villain of the
piece was not Richard III, but his successor Henry VII. Winston
Churchill disagreed. In his *A History of the English Speaking Peoples*
he remarked: 'It will take many ingenious books to raise this issue
to the dignity of a historical controversy.' His dismissal of
Josephine Tey's theory did just that. The murder of the princes is,
and will remain, a historical controversy.

The story of the princes captures very well the condition of
England at the end of the fifteenth century. Throughout the reigns

of Henry VI and his successor, Edward IV, the country had suffered civil war as rival families fought for their competing claims to the throne. For thirty years, from 1455 to the Battle of Bosworth in 1485, the two divisions of England's ruling Plantaganet family, the Yorkists, symbolised by a white rose, and the Lancastrians, symbolised by a red, fought each other for the crown. In 1461 Edward, Duke of York, seized the throne from Henry VI whose mild manners and mental instability meant that he was dominated completely by his fierce wife, Margaret of Anjou. Edward had to fight hard to defend his position and was briefly deposed in 1470 when his former ally, the Earl of Warwick, changed sides and led an army that successfully reinstated Henry for less than a year. Edward fought back and at the Battle of Tewkesbury in 1471 succeeded in destroying the Lancastrian army. Old Henry VI was murdered and for twelve years Edward managed to rule again in comparative peace. His death in 1483 and the antics of his brother Richard, Duke of Gloucester, was the beginning of the end of the Wars of the Roses.

Even without having the little princes murdered, Richard III's position as King of England would have been fragile. His seizure of the throne was a coup d'etat, an act of personal ambition that was bound to create envy and resentment. His former ally, the Duke of Buckingham, rebelled against him, but his uprising was quashed and he was executed. The Lancastrian claim had by this time passed to Henry Tudor whose right to the throne was in fact extremely tenuous. He was a grandson of John of Gaunt by John's third wife whom he had married after she had borne him several children. The children born before they were legitimised, and their heirs, of which Henry was one, were barred from becoming monarchs. Such niceties did not deter Henry Tudor: for fourteen years he had been exiled in France. As Richard's hold on power weakened, he determined that the time had come to return.

In 1485 Henry sailed from Harfleur to the Pembrokeshire coast where he landed on 7th August. He made his way through Wales, recruiting support as he went. Two weeks later, on 22nd, his army faced Richard III's at Bosworth. He had the smaller force – around 5,000 men. Richard's army was about 12,000 strong, but in the event 3,000 men under the command of Lord Stanley changed sides and fought with the Lancastrians. Lord Stanley had managed to pick his way through the turbulent years preceding Bosworth with great success and he was not about to jeopardise his position at the moment when the King might lose his crown. However, he had to act with care. His son, Lord Strange, was being held by Richard and he was frightened he would be killed if he acted too rashly. In the event he stayed out of the battle until the very last moment, although his younger brother, Sir William Stanley, did eventually join the attack on Henry's side. Deserted by his supporters, a leader all alone, Richard led the final attack against Henry and his body-guard himself. He almost succeeded in breaking through but was killed in the attempt, the last King of England to die on the battlefield. His naked, mutilated body was slung across a horse and taken to Leicester where it was put on public view as evidence of his death. He never received a proper burial. His crown, so the story goes, was retrieved from a hawthorn bush on the battlefield and placed on Henry's head by Lord Stanley. His Lordship had played his cards well. Henry made him Earl of Derby, thus founding an English political dynasty that would last until the height of the nineteenth century when the 14th Earl became Prime Minister. The humble hawthorn bush took its place in history too: from 1485 it would always have a place in Tudor propaganda, appearing in books and architecture commissioned by the new King.

Henry VII attempted to cement his entitlement to the mon-archy by marrying Elizabeth of York, the Yorkist heiress, but the marriage had less dynastic importance than it might have done in earlier years. He used his victory at Bosworth to secure his power in other ways too. Like his predecessors he also faced opposition but the rebels who challenged him were of a different breed alto-gether – impostors such as Lambert Simnel and Perkin Warbeck who concocted claims to the throne, but were defeated by a new, powerful King.

For the first time since the death of Edward III in 1377, the throne was unusually secure. The nobility, weakened by years of squabbles, were not for the moment in a position to challenge Henry's authority. They stayed quiet. He took the opportunity to strengthen the machinery of government and to make sure that power was concentrated where he wanted it – in his own hands. He deliberately excluded the aristocracy from this process, but he was careful not to subvert the traditional methods of governing the country. He knew the English were averse to change and hostile to signs of despotism. He was a king with modern methods in a medieval world, and his success lay in achieving what he wanted without appearing to disrupt established forms and processes. The King's Council, for instance, had sat in the Star Chamber – a room with a ceiling decorated with stars – since the reign of Edward II. Henry created a special tribunal within it to deal with complaints, particularly against the nobility. A group of hand-picked men were thus able to dispense the King's justice with speed and efficiency. The old form of government had been preserved, but its methods and results were rather different. He enforced acts such as the Statute of Liveries that prevented the nobility from keeping large groups of retainers that were, in effect, private armies. When he went to visit the Earl of Oxford, one of the House of Lancaster's strongest supporters, two long lines of liveried retainers were wheeled out to greet him. 'I thank you for your good cheer, my Lord,' said Henry when the time came to go, 'but I may not endure to have my laws broken in my sight. My attorney must speak with you.' The earl was fined £10,000. Henry also greatly strengthened the numbers of justices of the peace. The statute of 1489 that increased their numbers and set out their powers claimed that for the King nothing is 'more joyous than to know his subjects live peaceably under his laws and to increase in wealth and prosperity'.

In *The Daughter of Time*, Josephine Tey's detective comes to the conclusion that Henry VII was a more likely murderer of the princes in the tower than Richard III. Certainly Henry's claim to the throne was the weaker of the two and if the boys had survived

Richard's reign they would have represented a threat to his survival. Henry had to work hard to make sure that he did not lose his crown in the way so many of his predecessors had done, but he seems to have been able to manage this without royal murder. A long period of exile had taught him self-preservation and he had a natural preference for peace rather than war. He liked money and he knew how important commerce was to the success of his country. One of his most distinguished servants was John Morton, Archbishop of Canterbury and Lord Chancellor, who devised the infamous 'Morton's Fork' – a crafty tax-raising theory that argued that if people were rich they could obviously afford to pay, and if they were not, they were probably just hiding their money and should be taxed anyway. Many of the men he found to do his bidding tended not to come from the old landed families, although as the Tudor dynasty grew their descendants would begin to receive aristocratic titles. Henry VII built his kingdom in his own image, clever, mean and risk-averse.

Henry VII built his kingdom in his own image, clever, mean and risk-averse.

More happened at the Battle of Bosworth than any of its participants realised. On 22nd August 1485 it may have seemed that yet another chapter in the long dynastic battles for the throne of England had taken place, precursor most likely of many more to come. It had all the usual ingredients – an incumbent from one family, a challenger from another, two armies hastily raised and turncoats ready to throw in their lot at the last moment with the side they thought would win. This time these factors produced an altogether different result. They brought to the throne a man who understood in a way that his predecessors had not that the strength of the monarchy lay in its detail. All kings had needed to raise money or levy taxes – but none before him put in place the methods for doing this as successfully as Henry VII. All kings had to control the aristocracy, the power brokers in the land, but none organised their management as skilfully as the first Tudor.

The England that Henry VII governed was still medieval in the one central concept of a king and his people. All power flowed through the King and it was he who held the country together. By improving the methods through which this could be done, Henry began the process of allowing the country to begin to feel itself as something separate and different from the King himself. By the time his granddaughter Elizabeth came to the throne in 1558, England had started to develop as a nation in its own right: the people began to enjoy their own identity, their own sense of nationhood. Many things would happen that would make this possible – things that Henry, as he began the task of ruling after Bosworth, could never have imagined. As the defeated army ran from the field, as the naked body of a dead king was paraded around the streets of Leicester, and as a royal crown was picked from a hawthorn bush, England made a small but significant step towards becoming a very different place from that which it had been before.

CHAPTER 3

The Spanish Armada
1588

In 1588 the King of Spain sent a fleet of ships to
invade England and seize the throne from Elizabeth I.
Its defeat was one of the most stirring events in
British history.

In nearly a thousand years of history, since the Battle of Hastings in
1066, Britain has never been invaded by a foreign power. There have
been three occasions when invasion became a significant threat –
from Hitler during the Second World War, from Napoleon at the
beginning of the nineteenth century, and from Philip II of Spain at
the end of the sixteenth. On each of these occasions Britain had to
face the might of a great empire. In 1940 the German Empire, the
Third Reich, had seized control of Europe and North Africa too.
In 1805 Napoleon, recently crowned Emperor of France, was the
master of the European continent. In 1588 the power of domination
belonged to Spain.

By the 1580s Spain had gained control of Portugal, the Kingdom
of Naples and Sicily, and much of the Low Countries. It also owned
extensive colonial possessions in South America where gold and
silver mines contributed enormously to its financial strength. The
King, Philip II, was a Hapsburg, the most powerful royal family in
Europe whose other territories included Austria and Hungary.
Rudolf II, the Holy Roman Emperor, was Philip's nephew. Philip II
had also been King of England in the 1550s: before inheriting
the throne of Spain he had been married to Mary Tudor, Mary I of
England. On her death in 1558 he had proposed to her half-sister,
Elizabeth who had succeeded her as Queen, but Elizabeth declined.
For Philip marriage was always a political business, a matter of

strengthening his Hapsburg base through alliances with other great ruling families. His real interest was in religion. He was a devout Catholic and had reintroduced the Inquisition on becoming King of Spain. He was horrified at the spread of Protestantism in Europe – not only in his own possessions in the Netherlands but in Germany and England too. England, he knew, was prey to the curse of the Reformation, something that his religious orthodoxy could not endure.

England also presented him with another problem. The Queen who had demurred at his offer of marriage was turning out to be rather a law unto herself. She had refused to recognise the monopoly over trade to the New World that the Pope had given Spain. For Philip, as for all Catholics of that time, the Pope's decree in such things was infallible and beyond contention. England's buccaneers robbed Spanish treasure ships and investigated opportunities for their own trading interests, expressly disobeying the Pope's commands. Everywhere he looked, Philip saw England in his way, backing rebels against his rule in the Low Countries, supporting rival claimants to the Portuguese throne and interfering with his plans for international expansion. Measured, dutiful and severe, he began to contemplate an invasion of the country where once he had lived as its King.

Discussions for the building of an invasion fleet began in Spain in 1585. In 1586 Philip gave orders for an armada to be assembled in Lisbon, a squadron to be put together in Santander and ships and troops to be gathered in Cadiz and other ports on the southern coast of Spain. Tension was mounting. The crisis came in 1587.

Nearly twenty years before, in 1568, Mary Queen of Scots had fled her country after her Protestant nobility had rebelled against her. She had been deposed once and put in prison in Scotland. She had then escaped and been defeated in battle. With nowhere to turn she had run south to England where her cousin Elizabeth was Queen. Her arrival presented Elizabeth with enormous problems. For many Catholics, Mary, who was the great-granddaughter of Henry VII, was the legitimate heir to the English throne. They regarded Elizabeth, the daughter of Henry VIII and Anne Boleyn, as illegitimate. Elizabeth reacted by keeping Mary in prison, latterly at Fotheringay Castle in Northamptonshire where for nineteen years she remained the centre of intrigue and conspiracy. In 1586 another plot – the Babington Plot – came to light and this time there could be little doubt that Mary was implicated. Elizabeth's advisors, William Cecil and Francis Walsingham, urged her to get rid of Mary once and for all. Elizabeth vacillated, but ultimately agreed: executing rival queens was not something she did lightly. Mary Queen of Scots was executed in 1587 in the hope that her death would prevent England sliding into civil war. In helping to stop one conflict it precipitated another.

The news of Mary's death struck the Spanish like a hammer blow. The Duke of Parma, Philip II's commander in the Netherlands, wrote to the King urging him to invade England at the first opportunity. 'This cruel act must be the last of many which she of England has performed,' he said – and Philip was inclined to concur. He still had not made a final decision when, two months after Mary's death, Francis Drake arrived unannounced at Cadiz harbour with a small fleet, sank about thirty-five Spanish ships, caused panic ashore and sailed home again to announce that he 'had singe'd the King of Spain's beard'. His exploits were greeted in England with great jubilation, although Elizabeth herself remained uneasy. She had tried to cancel Drake's excursion, believing that Philip was still open to peace talks; but Drake had departed before her orders could be carried out. Peace was no longer possible. Philip had written to the Pope to ask for his support. The Pope had given it, promising him a million ducats if a Spanish army set foot on English soil. He also sent him a golden sword – symbol of the great religious crusade upon which the Spanish king was about to embark. In May 1588 the Armada set sail.

The Armada was led by the Duke of Medina Sidonia. He was a Spanish grandee, a powerful feudal lord, and one of the richest men in the country. He had been put in charge of preparations for the invasion following the death of another nobleman, the

Marques de Santa Cruz. Philip thought him the best administrator in the land: now he had the chance to prove himself its greatest admiral as well. Under his command he had about 130 ships, 7,000 sailors and 19,000 soldiers. The intention was that these would be reinforced by a further 27,000 troops from the Netherlands where the Duke of Parma was waiting to join the invasion fleet. The Spanish plan was to fight a land war. The great Armada would disgorge its army; Catholic rebels in England would join it and the crown would be taken back into Catholic control.

The English were to meet this majestic army of the high seas with a rather lighter force. They had only thirty-four royal galleons in their navy, but as preparations to tackle the Armada got under way these were supplemented by a large number of private vessels. They were mainly small ships, but their speed and manoeuvrability would prove to be an advantage against the clumsiness of the Spanish fleet. The English ships were also better armed with artillery that had a longer range. In command was Lord Howard of Effingham with Sir Francis Drake as his number two. Effingham was in the *Ark Royal* which had been built for Sir Walter Raleigh in 1587. Drake was captain of the *Revenge*. This was a battle that would depend entirely on English seamanship. If the Spanish landed all might be lost: they had to be driven away before they could get ashore. Their fleet ready, the English waited and watched.

We do not know if Francis Drake was told of the sighting of the Armada while he was playing bowls on Plymouth Hoe. The story of his remarking that he had time to finish the game and beat the Spaniards too must remain apocryphal, although judging by some of the other things he got up to, it does not sound too unlike the man. We do know that Elizabeth went to Tilbury to address her troops and made one of the most famous speeches ever made by an English monarch. She was, she told them, 'resolved in the midst and heat of battle to live or die amongst you. To lay down for God and for my kingdom and for my people my honour and my blood even in the dust. I know I have the body of a weak and feeble woman but I have the heart and stomach of a king and of a king of

England too.' There are no better words to evoke our image of Elizabethan England than those that were spoken by its queen on the eve of one of the most crucial battles in the country's history. They epitomise the nascent sense of nationhood to which England aspired at the end of the sixteenth century.

The Armada made slow progress. On the afternoon of 19th July a patrol of ships, disguised as merchantmen, caught sight of it near the Scilly Isles. On the 20th a watchman on the Lizard saw the Armada off the coast. One by one beacons were lit along the south coast of England, a long line of flame that announced the enemy had arrived. The Spanish saw it too, and knew that battle was imminent. During the night the English positioned themselves upwind of the Spaniards, and the following morning the Armada advanced on Plymouth. They bore down in a crescent formation, the tactics they had used in the Battle of Lepanto seventeen years before. That had been a famous Spanish victory and had saved all Europe from invasion by the Ottoman Empire. This time things did not go as well. A powder store on one of the Spanish ships exploded, killing 120 men; another was captured by the English. The Spanish changed tactics, putting their smaller ships to the fore to protect the larger galleons of the fleet and the following morning a fierce battle took place. The Spanish were trying to get close to the English so they could board and fight, but were unable to create the opportunity to do so. They desperately needed to get to Calais where they hoped the Duke of Parma's reinforcements were waiting, but the English clung on, following them every inch of the way. The running battles continued. The Spanish decided to try and make for the English coast and capture a port to use as a base. One English captain, Martin Frobisher, an experienced explorer with three voyages to the New World to his credit, used his skill to try and lure the Armada onto

'I know I have the body of a weak and feeble woman but I have the heart and stomach of a king and of a king of England too.'

rocks. The Spanish fleet was forced to withdraw further out to sea. It anchored off the coast of Calais and waited for the arrival of Parma and his troops.

This was to be an important moment in the battle. For five days the English had harried the Spanish invaders and so far they had prevented them from reaching the shore. Supplies were running low. They could not keep up the defence indefinitely: they needed to find a breakthrough. On the night of 28th July the English sent a fleet of fireships into the midst of the anchored Spanish galleons. There was panic and the Armada was split into two separate sections. At last the English could attack and on 29th July, Drake was given the order to do just that.

For nine hours the British and Spanish fought off the little port of Gravelines on the French coast. Drake led his ships straight towards the Spanish flagship the *San Martin* and the four galleons that accompanied her, getting within 150 yards before opening fire. Speed proved a better weapon than size, and the English fired on their Spanish enemy ceaselessly, manoeuvring their ships to come within range and then moving away before they could be caught. Three Spanish ships were sunk or abandoned and as the battle became more desperate the weather intervened to play its part. Heavy rain brought a respite, and when the skies cleared the depleted Armada could fight no more. It had received no reinforcements: Dutch rebels had created a blockade that prevented Parma from getting troops and ships to the Spanish fleet. Worse was to follow. A big storm and heavy winds drove the Armada northwards. It would be forced to return to Spain by sailing through the North Sea and the Scottish coast with further losses to come. England had been saved.

The winds that drove the Spanish into confusion were a sure sign for many that God was supporting the Protestant cause. More rational heads no doubt took the view that the mischievous nature of the English climate is often a blessing as much as a curse. The failure of the Armada protected England from foreign invasion and demonstrated that this little country off Europe's northern shore would always fight for its independence. But the failed invasion did not protect England from its internal quarrels. Fifteen years later Queen Elizabeth died. She had balanced England's internal divisions with great skill and her victory over the Armada had helped bind the nation together. It was a colossal achievement, but it had not resolved the nation's differences forever: far from it.

CHAPTER 4

The Battle of Naseby
1645

In 1645 the army of King Charles I was decisively beaten at Naseby in Northamptonshire by the New Model Army commanded by Oliver Cromwell and Sir Thomas Fairfax. The battle led to the ultimate defeat and execution of the King.

In March 1641, Thomas Wentworth, Earl of Strafford, stood before the House of Commons accused of treason. He had started his political career as an MP in opposition to King Charles I, but over time had parted company with his parliamentary colleagues to become one of Charles's most loyal and able supporters. 'Black Tom' as he was known did not suffer fools gladly. He could be fierce and cruel and he had a rather ominous name for the policies he pursued – 'thorough'. His days of power were coming to an end. Charles, having ruled without Parliament for eleven years, had been forced to recall it to see if he could raise taxes to pay for an ill-judged war against Scotland. He had tried to impose Anglican bishops on the mainly Presbyterian Scottish Church. The Scots had fought him off, Charles had been defeated and was now humiliated and in debt. The Parliament he had summoned was, not surprisingly, truculent. The King would not get money without sacrifices: 'Black Tom' was one of those.

Like many people caught up in the turbulent events of mid-seventeenth-century England, the Earl of Strafford was in many ways his own worst enemy. His determination to get things done meant that he rode roughshod over those who stood in his way. For the past seven years he had governed Ireland ruthlessly on behalf of the King, improving revenues through financial reforms, extending trade and industry, encouraging new settlers, driving the native Irish from their homes and subverting everything to the needs and requirements of the Crown. The beleaguered King had summoned him to London to assist with the mounting crisis. Despite Strafford's intervention Charles had dismissed Parliament and devised a plan to use the army from Ireland to help subdue the Scots. It had failed: the King had been defeated and had turned to Parliament once more. No wonder it was in rebellious mood: no wonder it had added 'Black Tom' to the list of sacrifices it required.

Undoubtedly Strafford had been somewhat overzealous in his support for his King. As with many others on both sides of the terrible conflict that was about to engulf the country, he demonstrated a remarkable inability to listen. But he was never a traitor. 'As to this charge of treason,' he told his accusers, 'I must and do acknowledge that if I had the least suspicion of my own guilt I would save your lordships the pains. I would cast the first stone. I would pass the first sentence of condemnation against myself.' His eloquence fell on deaf ears. Parliament secured a Bill of Attainder – a right to condemn someone without proof of guilt – and his fate was sealed. The King wrung his hands, but let his servant go and on 12th May 1641 Strafford was executed on Tower Hill. Eight months later, on 10th January 1642, Charles left London to prepare for war.

The causes of the English Civil War were both simple and profound. On the surface many of the issues, particularly at a distance of more than 350 years, seem fairly straightforward. There were obvious religious differences. John Pym, the passionate parliamentary leader who led the attack on the King in 1640, believed that the nation was in danger of being subverted to Catholicism. The Catholics, he had once said, would seek toleration, then equality, then superiority, and then 'they will seek the suppression of that religion which is contrary to theirs'. There were political differences as well. The King's belief in his divine right to rule, and his attempts to raise taxes without Parliament's authority, had called into question the whole nature of the constitution. During the reigns of Elizabeth and James I, Parliament had emerged with a greater influence over the affairs of the country than ever before. It wanted to see those extended, not cut back by an autocratic King. Added to all this was Charles's own indecisiveness. Unlike his father, who had negotiated the pitfalls of governing England with considerable care, Charles never seemed sure what to do next and, as doubt engulfed him, relied entirely on royal prerogative.

These clear-cut differences were not in themselves enough to drive England into civil war. The last act of the Long Parliament – the Parliament that called for the execution of Strafford and remained in session after Charles had quit London – had been to issue its 'Grand Remonstrance', a recital of the grievances that it had against the King. Organised by John Pym, it called, among other things, for Church reform and demanded that the appointment of the King's ministers should be approved by Parliament. These were all issues that had been at the forefront of the nation's arguments, but its contents were debated fiercely and it was only passed by a majority of eleven votes. England's divisions were deep, but they ran across the social structure of the country and through Parliament itself. The line that divided the country was jagged, not straight.

As the nation slid towards war, the man who would succeed Charles as ruler of England was still little known. Oliver Cromwell came to prominence as a soldier, not a politician. It was his victories against the Royalist armies that provided him with his power base and propelled him to political leadership. Rather like George Washington in another revolutionary war more than a hundred and thirty years later, he would first win on the battlefield what he would try later to consolidate in government. Like George Washington he was a dissatisfied country gentleman who learned the art of war. The man who, as MP for Cambridge, had been just one of a crowd of parliamentarians calling for the King to redress their grievances became in the space of a few years one of the most successful generals Britain has ever known.

The Civil War was fought in every corner of Britain. King Charles set up his headquarters in Oxford and armies representing both sides were raised throughout the country. The parliamentarians also formed an alliance with the Scots, the Solemn League and Covenant, which brought a powerful Scottish army to their side, but their greatest strength lay in the machine that they built themselves for the purpose of defeating the King. This was the New Model Army, a trained and disciplined force motivated not, as were most mercenary armies of the time, by drink, whores and the glory of a dashing cavalry charge, but by good pay, good leadership and an undying belief in its duty before God.

Cromwell was aware of the need to recruit and train a professional army from the moment he took part in the indecisive Battle of Edgehill, the first major engagement of the Civil War in 1642. His own military abilities became evident very quickly. As soon as the war started he raised a troop of horsemen and carried off plate and treasure belonging to Cambridge University to prevent it from falling into Royalist hands. By 1644 he had achieved the rank of Lieutenant-General of Horse and played a crucial part in Parliament's defeat of the King's army at Marston Moor in Yorkshire in the same year. The following year, 1645, was the year in which Parliament decided to unite its existing armies into one force – the New Model Army – under the command of Sir Thomas Fairfax. Members of Parliament were prevented from holding commands in this new army under the terms of the Self-Denying Ordinance that had been introduced in an attempt to weed out aristocratic officers from the House of Lords. Some parliamentarians believed that their lordships' pursuit of the Royalists was less than wholehearted. A few exceptions were allowed. One of these was Oliver Cromwell who was made second-in-command.

On the night of 13th June 1645, Charles I received news that a patrol of his had made contact with the enemy at Naseby. He decided to fight. His decision to do so was against the advice of his

The Civil War was fought in every corner of Britain.

Captain-General, Prince Rupert, and could be said to be the mistake that lost him the first stage of the war. Both sides got into position the following morning. Cromwell typically was sure that God was on his side. 'I could not ... but smile out to God in praises,' he wrote later, 'in assurance of victory.' The Royalists, too, were sure that God was on their side: after all, they were defending his appointed King. Whichever of the two sides God was on, the fact remained that they were unequally matched. The Royalist army was far outnumbered by the enemy and even though its cavalry charged with considerable success against the parliamentary army it did not have the strength to turn events in its favour. Cromwell's horsemen were far superior to their opponent's cavalry and routed it easily. As in earlier actions their commander then kept them tightly together as they rode in support of Fairfax in his battle against the King's infantry. This was Cromwell's great strength as a soldier. Having completed one action he would re-group his well-disciplined force and return to the battle to provide support wherever he was most needed. The King was totally defeated: 1,000 of his men died in battle and another 4–6,000 taken prisoner. The New Model Army suffered losses of less than 150. With total victory came astonishing cruelty. A group of Welsh women in the Royalist camp were brutally mutilated by the parliamentarian infantry, their faces cut and their noses slit, while others were killed outright. Many of the prisoners were paraded through the streets of London and then sent to disease-infested hulks on the River Thames where some of them would subsequently die. Charles I could not recover from this defeat. The following year he surrendered his stronghold in Oxford to Fairfax and Cromwell and ran to the Scots for shelter.

The end of the Civil War still lay several years ahead, years that would demonstrate Cromwell's invincibility as a general. Charles I tried to recover his throne by promising the Scots that if returned to power he would introduce Presbyterianism to England. The Scottish army raised to advance this cause was totally defeated by Cromwell at Preston in 1648. Cromwell then took his army to

Ireland to crush opposition from Irish Catholics and Royalists there, displaying merciless cruelty at the siege of Drogheda where his men massacred over 3,500 defenders of the town after they had already surrendered. His actions poisoned relationships between England and Ireland for hundreds of years afterwards. After Charles I was executed in 1649, Cromwell extinguished any immediate chance of the King's son gaining the throne by defeating his supporters at Dunbar in 1650 and Worcester in 1651. It is one of the most remarkable, if less than spotless, records in British military history. All his battles were fought in his own country against his own people, but Oliver Cromwell would not have found that amiss. For him the only battle was the one fought in the name of God for the true religion and the propagation of his work on earth. Nothing else mattered, not his own life, nor the lives of others, in the great cause to which he was devoted. God never had a better soldier, or a more successful one.

CHAPTER 5

The Battle of Blenheim
1704

In 1704 the French and Bavarians were decisively beaten
at Blenheim on the Danube in Southern Germany by
an allied army led by the Duke of Marlborough. The
victory halted the territorial expansion of France under
Louis XIV and opened the way for Britain to become
a major European power in the eighteenth century.

Britain's relationship with France has been deeper and more
complex than with any other country in Europe. In the Middle
Ages, as a result of the Norman Conquest, the Kings of England
owned and fought for territory throughout France and sometimes
aspired to become its monarchs. Once these ambitions had subsided France became Britain's principal rival and grew steadily in
power and influence as the Spanish Empire fell into decline. By the
late seventeenth century it was the strongest country in Europe. Its
King, Louis XIV, had inherited the throne at the age of four and a
half, but had taken full control of all aspects of government when
he was twenty-three. He was the absolute ruler of his country, the
Sun King whose remark – 'L'état c'est moi' – summarised perfectly
his philosophy of power. He presided over a centralised government where ministers and nobility were subservient to his wishes
and where everything revolved around his magnificent court at
Versailles.

One of Louis's greatest admirers was Charles II, son of the
English King executed in 1649, who spent much of his nine years of
exile in France during Cromwell's tenure of power. Charles II was
restored to the throne in 1660. Acutely aware of the fate that had
befallen his father, and of a rather more cynical temperament, he

was well equipped to negotiate the intricacies of the Britain he had inherited. The country was glad to have its King back and gave him more licence as a result. This was just as well: Charles was actually a Catholic sympathiser – he converted to Catholicism on his deathbed – and in 1670 signed the secret Treaty of Dover with Louis XIV. Under its terms Charles received payments from the French King in return for promises to help Louis fight against the Dutch and to return the Catholic religion to England. The Dutch proved tougher to defeat than Louis had anticipated and the French supply of cash ran out. Parliament agreed to continue funding the war, but Charles was forced to withdraw his 'Declaration of Indulgence', designed to promote Catholic toleration. Two years later, in 1674, it called a halt to the war as well. Like his father and grandfather, Charles II was tied to his Parliament whether he liked it or not and even a rich French King could not provide him with the means to wriggle free.

When Charles died in 1685 his brother James determined to prosecute publicly what Charles had tried to do by the back door and reopen England to Catholicism. Within three years he had been driven from the throne. William of Orange and his wife, Mary, James's daughter, became King and Queen. The relationship with France was finally over. William brought England into the alliance of Holland's United Provinces, Spain, the Holy Roman Empire and Prussia against France and in 1697 nine years of hostilities ceased with a treaty that rearranged France's European and colonial conquests. Crucially, Louis recognised William as the legitimate King of England and agreed, for the moment at any rate, to stop supporting the exiled James.

Louis XIV was not a man to give up easily. He actually reigned for seventy-two years, longer than any other European monarch in history. Although by no means always successful in his territorial ambitions, he never relinquished them, and his long period of power allowed him to pursue them with relentless determination. When the King of Spain died in 1700 he left his throne to Louis's grandson, Philip of Anjou, believing that an alliance with France would provide the best protection for Spain's crumbling empire. Louis responded to this new responsibility with typical bluntness. He marched French troops to the fortresses of the Spanish Netherlands on the Dutch border and, just to rub salt in the wound, removed the Spanish *asiento* that gave the English trading rights to provide slaves for the Spanish colonies. When, in 1701, the exiled James II died, Louis recognised his son as the true King of England. Four years after the last one had finished, Europe was once more at war with Louis XIV.

In 1701 the leading light in the British army was John Churchill, Earl of Marlborough, who had enjoyed a somewhat chequered career as a courtier and soldier. A supporter of James II, he had played an important role in suppressing the revolt against the King led by the illegitimate son of Charles II, the Duke of Monmouth. Monmouth's defeat at Sedgemoor in 1685 was the last battle to be fought on English soil. Churchill switched sides before James's deposition and supported the accession of William and Mary to the throne. He fought with distinction in the war against France, but his connections with James's exiled court aroused suspicions. He was accused of collusion, stripped of his military and civic duties, and imprisoned in the Tower of London. When war with France approached once more, William – by then ruling entirely in his own right following the death of his wife Mary – turned to him again. If this was a stroke of good fortune for Churchill, it was nothing compared to what happened next.

In 1702 William was killed in a fall from a horse and was succeeded by his sister-in-law, Anne. Anne's greatest friend and closest confidante was Sarah Churchill, John's wife. Sarah had known Anne since childhood and joined her service in 1683. The two had been placed under house arrest by Anne's father, James II, when he knew there was a plot to throw him out of power, but they had escaped together. Sarah and Anne were inseparable – even though Sarah often crossed the line with the Queen and was not afraid of arguing with her in public. Marlborough was now restored to full military command and joined England's Dutch allies fighting against France in the Netherlands. Being away from court did not worry him: his wife knew everything that was going on and kept him fully informed. The Anglo-Dutch alliance meant that Marlborough was forced to contain his operations to the area that understandably most worried the Dutch – their own country – but by 1704 it was clear that the centre of the war had moved further south. Louis XIV had decided to attack Vienna, capital of the Holy Roman Empire. If he succeeded France would become the master of Europe.

More often than not, great victories require great planning. In May 1704, the fall of Vienna was undoubtedly a possibility. A large Franco-Bavarian army – Bavaria was an ally of France – had gathered to the city's west. Another army was stationed in northern Italy ready to attack Vienna from that direction. Marlborough decided to carry the battle from where he was, in the far north of Europe, to where the enemy was gathering in southern Germany. He would have to get there by deception. If the enemy got wind of his plans, it would mobilise to cut him off. With superb skill he organised to march an army from Bedburg near the Dutch-German border to the Danube 250 miles to the south. He augmented his army as he went, bringing in troops from England's Prussian, Dutch and Hanoverian allies. The French knew he was on the march, but they could not decide where he was heading – and Marlborough drew them out of the Netherlands after him as they shadowed his movements. The French thought that he must be heading for Alsace and had a large force ready to meet him there. At the last moment they realised their mistake as the English and their allies swung southeast towards the Danube. Marlborough and his army had been on the march for five weeks – five weeks in which its commander had managed to keep his final destination secret until the very last moment. It was an extraordinary feat, brilliantly executed.

Marlborough now had to engage the Franco-Bavarian troops

If Louis XIV succeeded, France would become the master of Europe.

before the French reinforcements from Alsace arrived. His army was in good shape. The meticulous planning of the journey south had meant that the men had been well fed and watered on the way. But the enemy would not come and fight, preferring to wait for reinforcements even though Marlborough began to burn buildings and crops in an effort to force it on to the battlefield. He also hoped that by setting fire to the Elector's homeland he might persuade the Bavarian leader to switch sides and fight against the French. Finally, on 13th August 1704, the two huge armies met not far from the village of Blenheim, or Blindheim to give its proper German name. In fighting, as in marching, Marlborough displayed the strategic perception that made him one of Britain's greatest generals. He skilfully deployed his cavalry and maintained unrelenting artillery fire to keep the enemy forces at bay. Over 3,000 of its cavalry were driven into the Danube and drowned. The French commander, Tallard, was captured – he would spend seven years in prison in Nottingham – along with 13,000 of his men. A further 40,000 French and Bavarians had been killed or wounded. It was a convincing, bloody victory. Vienna was safe, and the might of Louis XIV had once more been held in check.

With fire and sword the country round
Was wasted far and wide,
And many a childing mother then
And newborn baby died:
But things like that, you know, must be
At every famous victory.

They say it was a shocking sight
After the field was won,
For many thousand bodies here
Lay rotting in the sun;
But things like that, you know, must be
After a famous victory.

Wars between Britain and France 1688–1815

1689–1697 The War of the Grand Alliance, or Nine Years' War

Under William of Orange, Britain joined Holland, Austria, Savoy and Spain in an attempt to limit the expansionist policies of the French 'Sun King' Louis XIV. In the 1697 Treaty of Ryswick a peace was negotiated, but it did not last long.

1701–1713 The War of the Spanish Succession

Britain again joined a coalition of European powers, and fought to curtail French ambitions towards Spain and her territories following the death of the Hapsburg King Charles II. John Churchill won a series of spectacular victories and was made Duke of Marlborough.

1740–1748 The War of the Austrian Succession

A war that involved almost all of Europe and broke out when the succession of the Archduchess Maria Theresa to the Austrian throne was disputed. Britain backed Maria Theresa and the French her enemies. When the fighting was over, Maria Theresa remained Empress of the Holy Roman Empire, but lost Silesia.

1756–1763 The Seven Years' War

A world war sparked by colonial tensions between Britain and France, as well as Austrian ambitions to retake territory lost in the War of the Austrian Succession. France lost colonies in America, the West Indies and India, while Britain's Empire was strengthened.

Robert Southey's famous ballad, 'After Blenheim', written more than ninety years after the event, describes how an old man from the area around Blenheim still digs up skulls when tending to his land. It is one of Britain's first anti-war poems. The old man tells the children the story of the battle, but he cannot remember why it was fought or what it achieved. (The ballad appears in full on p. 130.)

Blenheim remains one of the most famous victories ever won by a British commander. Marlborough went on to others. Elevated to a dukedom by a grateful Queen he defeated the French at Ramillies in 1706, at Oudenarde in 1708, and at Malplaquet the following year.

1775–1783 The War of American Independence

The war in which Britain lost its valuable American colonies forever.
The French formally joined this war on the side of the revolutionaries
in 1778. Their presence on land and at sea helped the Americans win a
decisive victory at Yorktown in 1781.

1792–1802 The French Revolutionary Wars

Begun at the time of the French Revolution, when foreign powers
tried to restore the Bourbon monarchy, the French Revolutionary
Wars soon became an opportunity for expansion as much as a defence
of France. This was the conflict that saw Napoleon and Nelson
establish reputations as brilliant commanders. A peace treaty was
signed at Amiens in 1802 but the following year hostilities resumed.

1803–1815 Napoleonic Wars

Britain joined forces with Spain, Portugal, Russia and the German
states to fight against the forces of the formidable Napoleon as he
sought to conquer Europe. He won control of much of the continent,
but by 1814 Paris had fallen and Napoleon was exiled to Elba. He soon
escaped, but the Battle of Waterloo in 1815 finally ended Napoleon's
dreams of empire. He was exiled to the island of St Helena, where he
died six years later.

By this time the English were tiring of the war and anxious to find
a way out. The casualty figures at Malplaquet were overwhelming –
the allies lost more than 20,000 men – and Marlborough's own
influence at court was waning. His wife had been supplanted in the
Queen's affections by Abigail Masham, and the Marlboroughs
ended Anne's reign out of favour, their splendid palace north of
Oxford only half-built, forced to depend on the gratitude of foreign
courts while their countrymen pursued trumped up charges of
embezzlement against the Duke. Only when Anne died did they
return to favour. George I, a Hanoverian whose army had marched

with Marlborough's, welcomed him back to power and the command of the army once more.

Louis XIV died in 1715. The war that had seen his army defeated at Blenheim ended in the Treaty of Utrecht of 1713 where he had to accept that the Spanish and French thrones would never be united. Britain had greatly strengthened her position in Europe as a result of the long war, although the cost of it in financial terms had been colossal. The stage was now set for the great imperial contest of the eighteenth century – a contest that would lead to further wars and battles fought well beyond the confines of Europe – as Britain and France sought to establish their influence around the world.

CHAPTER 6

The Battle of Trafalgar
1805

In 1805 the Royal Navy under the command of
Admiral Lord Nelson destroyed the combined French
fleet off the Spanish coast at Cape Trafalgar. It was
Britain's greatest naval victory and established its
maritime supremacy for the rest of the nineteenth
century.

When the news of Nelson's death at Trafalgar reached Britain, the
nation wept. He was, and is, a national hero. In the whole history of
Britain hardly any other man has been revered so deeply, both in
his lifetime and after his death. Wellington and Marlborough were
probably both his equals as commanders in the battlefield, and
Wellington's influence on Britain – he served as Prime Minister
as well as winning Waterloo – was far greater, but neither enjoyed
the love, respect and sheer adulation that Nelson did. Since his
death only Winston Churchill has managed to earn a similar place
in the country's affections, perhaps because both men communi-
cated instinctively with the people they had been chosen to lead.
Churchill did it through his speeches and writings, Nelson through
his character and actions. 'He was easy of access,' said one of his
contemporaries, 'and his manner was particularly agreeable and
kind. No man was ever afraid of displeasing him, but everybody was
afraid of not pleasing him.' Nelson did not always behave well –
few great men do – but in his leadership, his sense of duty and his
bravery he has few equals.

The life of a sea captain in the Royal Navy in the early part of
the nineteenth century was hard and unforgiving. The tours of
duty could be remorseless and maintaining morale among the crew

difficult. The Admiralty was an erratic paymaster and weary sailors frequently grew resentful at the treatment they received. Mutinies did happen but remarkably sailors seemed to retain their loyalty and sense of patriotism even when asked to serve in appalling conditions. Nelson, like other captains of the time, believed in building a loyal complement of men aboard each ship, creating a bond that could hold the crew together in many different situations. The Admiralty often wanted to move men about, providing resources where they were most needed at the time. Nelson, like his friend and contemporary, Cuthbert Collingwood – another of Britain's great naval leaders – knew the value of a team. It has been said that Nelson never flogged a man or had one flogged. That is doubtful; but whether true or not it is certainly the case that he and Collingwood represented a breed of seamen who understood the importance of humanity in command. They were modern-thinking men in a modernising age. Not all their contemporaries were like that. The lofty patrician manners of the eighteenth century could still be found aboard many a Royal Navy ship.

Nelson distinguished himself early in his naval career. In 1794 he played an important part in the capture of Corsica which the British needed as a Mediterranean base after they could no longer hold on to the French port of Toulon. This was supposed to be a combined army and navy assault, but in fact the Royal Navy played the most prominent part and Nelson was involved in the sieges of both the island's most important towns – Bastia and Calvi. It was at Calvi that he lost the sight of his right eye. A shell burst onto a wall of sandbags near where he was standing and a shower of stones and sand exploded in his face. He was lucky not to have been killed. His commander, Admiral Lord Hood, wrote of his 'unremitting zeal and exertion', but Nelson was disappointed that his role in the victory was not afforded more prominence. He always fought hard to make sure his name was at the front of his superiors' minds. Both his soldiering and his naval skills were strongly in evidence in the Battle of Cape St Vincent against the Spanish fleet three years later. Displaying the ability to think quickly and act decisively that were his outstanding qualities in war, he broke his ship from its position in the line, attacked the Spanish and succeeded in capturing two ships by leading boarding parties on to them himself. He made sure that this time people knew what he had done and was duly knighted for his actions. It was just as well: had his plan failed he would have been court-martialled.

A year after the Battle of Cape St Vincent found Nelson in command of his own fleet on the tail of Napoleon. By this time he had also lost his right arm in an unsuccessful assault on the Spanish port of Santa Cruz in the Canary Islands. The British had got wind that Napoleon was heading to the eastern Mediterranean but they could not work out what his intentions were. The French general had in fact devised a plan to invade Egypt although his reasons for such an escapade were at the time, and have remained ever since, something of a mystery. The most plausible theory is that Napoleon simply wanted glory and the Directory that governed post-revolutionary France wanted rid of the popular military leader in their midst. So the adventure suited both sides perfectly well. The rest of Europe, convinced that there must be some clever strategic purpose behind all this, assumed that Napoleon was going to attack the Ottoman Empire and then maybe head for India and the British possessions there. Nelson, chasing around the Mediterranean looking for Napoleon and his ships full of soldiers assumed, against prevailing wisdom, that Egypt must be the Frenchman's destination and set off in hot pursuit. He actually got there ahead of the French and thought at first that he had guessed wrongly, but a month later heard the news that the enemy had anchored in Aboukir Bay near Alexandria. Nelson fell upon them with fury. His attack came as a total surprise: the French thought that they were safe because they lay close to the shore and they could fend off any hostile forces with broadsides. Some British ships managed to slip into the shallow waters between the French and the shore. The French fleet was utterly destroyed and Napoleon's Egyptian adventure would ultimately end in withdrawal and defeat.

Nelson did not see full naval action again until 1801. He had become Baron Nelson of the Nile as a result of his astonishing success at Alexandria – the First Lord of the Admiralty fainted at the news of his victory – but had then caused people to doubt him. It was not just that he had begun a passionate affair with Emma Hamilton, wife of the British ambassador to Naples, that raised eyebrows. Rather more seriously he had chosen to meddle in the politics of the region and had fallen foul of the dangerous schemes of Queen Maria Carolina, wife of the Neopolitan ruler, Ferdinand, but in fact the person who pulled the strings. Nelson supported her ambitions to take revenge on France – she was a sister of the late Queen Marie Antoinette – and seize Rome. The plan failed, the army of Naples was defeated by the French and Carolina and Ferdinand had to flee to their second capital in Palermo. Nelson then participated in the recovery of Naples where the French had installed a puppet republic. A vicious civil war followed and terrible atrocities were committed against the republicans. Nelson, in trying to help the royal couple recover their throne, was implicated in these. The man who could cut through a line of enemy ships like a thunderbolt did not display the same sureness of touch in the love and politics of the Neapolitan court.

But, in 1801, he more than redeemed himself at the Battle of Copenhagen. The navy could not trust him with a full command after his Italian escapade – but they thought well enough of him to make him second-in-command to Sir Hyde Parker. Parker was despatched to Copenhagen to try to persuade the Danes to with-draw from their alliance with the Russians which they had entered into to resist the British searching their ships going in and out of French ports. The British considered the alliance supported French interests and was therefore a hostile act. If Parker could not per-suade the Danes to desist he was to use force, but he was elderly – aged sixty-one – and very slow. When the moment came to fight the Danes, Parker ordered Nelson to withdraw just at the moment Nelson knew he had to press forward for victory. He ignored his superior's orders by reading the flag signal with his blind eye. 'I have a right to be blind sometimes,' he told his flag captain. 'I really do not see the signal.' The British were victorious and Nelson went ashore to successfully negotiate the Danes' withdrawal from the Russian alliance.

By late 1805 Britain had waited and wondered for nearly two years as Napoleon prepared another plan for its invasion. The French Emperor had planned to unite the French Mediterranean fleet and the Spanish fleet at Martinique in the West Indies and then bring them both back to the French port of Brest where a third French fleet was bottled up by a British blockade. The combined French and Spanish ships would be sufficient to break the blockade and bring the Brest fleet out to sea to protect his invasion forces. This plan failed. The French Mediterranean fleet under Admiral Villeneuve escaped the clutches of the British and met up with its Spanish allies as planned in the West Indies. On its return it was attacked by a British squadron off Cape Finisterre and lost two ships. Villeneuve therefore decided to head, not for Brest, but to the port of Ferrol in northwest Spain. From there he was supposed to make his way back to Brest but, worried that he was being watched by the British, decided in August 1805 to link up with the rest of the Spanish fleet further south in Cadiz.

By the end of August 1805, Napoleon, exasperated by the failure of his fleet to come to his army's protection, abandoned his intentions to invade England and turned instead to Austria, which had mobilised to attack him. As he marched the Grande Armee towards the Rhine to one of its greatest victories at Austerlitz he left behind a Mediterranean fleet that would suffer one of its most devastating defeats. In September Nelson received news that Villeneuve, whom he had pursued to the West Indies earlier in the year, had joined the Spanish. Back in England after a spell of duty that had lasted for more than two years he spent only twenty-five days ashore. On 15th September he left for Cadiz aboard HMS Victory.

So it was that at 6 o'clock on the morning just over a month later, on 21st October 1805, Admiral Viscount Nelson aboard his flagship off the coast of Spain in the southern Mediterranean prepared to attack the combined forces of France and Spain. At home in England, in a little house in Merton near Wimbledon, Emma Hamilton waited for him. He had already begun a letter to her: 'My dearest beloved Emma, the dear friend of my bosom. The signal has been made that the enemy's combined fleet are coming out of port. May the God of Battles crown my endeavours with success ...'. Nelson decided to attack the enemy in two single columns, one led by him, the other by his good friend and second-in-command, Cuthbert Collingwood. This was a dangerous strategy. The English ships, bearing down in vertical lines against the horizontal barricade of the French and Spanish would be at the mercy of the enemy's broadsides as they approached. Unable to fire their cannons in return they would have to wait until they smashed through the enemy line before being able to inflict serious damage. Once they had broken through, however, they would be in a far better position to destroy their scattered target.

'England expects that every man will do his duty.'

Speed was important, but in late October 1805 the winds were light.

At 11.40 in the morning, as the two British lines slowly made their way towards the French and Spanish, Nelson sent his signal to his fleet: 'England expects that every man will do his duty.' Collingwood was the first to break through. Nelson's line suddenly began to veer towards the group of ships at the head of the enemy line, but this change of direction was a feint devised to prevent the enemy ships from turning and coming to reinforce the rest of their fleet. No sooner had he turned than Nelson turned again and headed straight for the French flagship the *Bucentaure*. It was stationed tightly against another French ship, the *Redoubtable*, which the captain of the *Victory*, Thomas Hardy, decided to ram. A sniper aboard the French ship seeing Nelson on deck in his uniform took aim and fired. Nelson fell to the floor as the musket ball drilled through his right shoulder and lodged in his spine. It was 1.15 p.m.

The battle had still got a long way to go, but Nelson had planned it well and his captains knew what to do. One of the most remarkable things about the Battle of Trafalgar is that it was won as the admiral who planned it lay dying. But it was his strategy, his trust in his officers, and his ability to explain to them and to empower them that gave the British fleet the upper hand in the fight. A midshipman who fought with Nelson remembered that 'the presence of such a man could not but inspire every individual with additional confidence. Everyone felt himself more than a match for any enemy.' That was the 'Nelson touch'.

The death of Nelson is an immortal moment in British history. At 4.30 p.m. Hardy brought him the news of victory. 'Thank God I have done my duty,' said the admiral as he died. His body was brought home to a state funeral. Today he towers over London, a sandstone statue on top of a granite column, 170 feet tall from plinth to tricorn hat, a monumental memorial to a remarkable man. The woman he left behind, his greatest love and the mother of his only child, a daughter Horatia, died in poverty in Calais in 1815 exactly five months before the battle of Waterloo.

CHAPTER 7

The Battle of Waterloo
1815

In 1815 an allied army under the command of the
Duke of Wellington defeated Napoleon at Waterloo.
The battle was the most famous in all of British history
and destroyed the dream of a Napoleonic empire
forever.

On 20th November 1852, the Duke of Wellington was buried in one
of the most spectacular public events of nineteenth-century
Britain. 'This event,' wrote the *Illustrated London News* 'may be said
to have surpassed in significant grandeur any similar tribute to
greatness ever offered in the world.' The windows of St Paul's
Cathedral, where the duke was to be buried alongside Lord Nelson,
were draped with heavy black cloth to exclude the sunlight; 6,000
new gaslights lit the Dome and the Whispering Gallery. A choir
of eighty men and forty boys supported by a further forty singers
and musicians played music specially composed for the occasion.
There were 10,000 marchers in the funeral procession. One and a
half million people filled the streets of London to watch it. Just
about every major figure in British public life was there including
Queen Victoria. He was, she wrote, 'The GREATEST man this
country ever produced.'

Wellington was eighty-three when he died. He had played a
prominent part in British public life ever since he had gone to
India as a colonel in his late twenties. He had served as Prime
Minister twice and in his first administration had overseen the
introduction of Catholic emancipation into Britain. He had been at
the forefront of the debate about parliamentary reform and had
resisted the Reform Bill of 1832 that greatly extended the right to

vote among the British people. He had served in the Tory cabinets of Sir Robert Peel and after retiring from political life had remained as Commander-in-Chief of the British army until his death. But as his vast catafalque moved through the streets of London the event that overshadowed all others in his life had taken place before many of its onlookers, including Queen Victoria herself, had been born. It was the event for which they revered him most. It had, they knew, helped make their comfortable, mid-Victorian world possible, and helped make their country the most powerful nation on earth. That event was the Battle of Waterloo.

Wellington was already a hard-bitten soldier by the time he faced Napoleon in 1815. When he returned from India in 1805 some dismissed him as a mere 'sepoy general' – a snobbish reference to his military successes in command of Indian native troops. Nepotism was another accusation levelled at him: his brother had been Governor-General of India throughout Wellington's time there. In fact Wellington had demonstrated his skills as both a politician and a soldier quite independently of his brother and if any doubts lingered, they were later dispelled by his long tours of duty fighting against the French in Spain and Portugal.

From 1808 until Napoleon's exile to Elba in 1814 Wellington spent most of his time fighting Napoleon's armies in the Iberian Peninsula. Here, against an enemy that always outnumbered him, in difficult and dangerous terrain and often facing enormous problems of supply he displayed the tactical and political skill that made him such an outstanding soldier. Against the finest that the French could throw at him – Marshals Junot, Masséna and Soult – he fought doggedly, sometimes going on the defensive but never afraid to push home the advantage when it presented itself. For the early period of the war he had to suffer under dithering commanders, but after 1809 was finally given the leadership of the whole British army in Spain and Portugal. His early experience of beating Soult at Talavera – before he was given full army command – convinced him, when he did finally become the military leader, to build the massive defences at Torres Vedras that prevented

Masséna reaching Lisbon. The 'Lines' were a series of remarkable fortifications 29-miles long which, built into the local mountainous landscape, created an impregnable fortress – a masterly example of ad hoc military architecture. Following the defence of Lisbon, Wellington managed, bit by bit, to drive his army northwards, resting when he had to, fighting when he must. He besieged the towns of Ciudad Rodrigo and then Badajoz where he is said to have wept when he saw the death and the destruction the battle had caused. In 1812 he fought and won at Salamanca and the following year carried the war into France itself, defeating the enemy at Vitoria and then crossing the Pyrenees. By 1814 he had spent five years of his life continuously in Spain, Portugal and France and was laying siege to Toulouse as the Napoleonic Empire collapsed – for the moment.

Wellington's painstaking slog through Spain was in marked contrast to the whirlwind that swept through Europe in the spring of 1815. Napoleon had gone – banished to the island of Elba off the coast of Tuscany under the terms of the Treaty of Fontainebleau. The French Emperor had tried to kill himself after signing it, but the poison he used had lost its strength and he survived to begin a new life running his tiny little kingdom. He kept himself busy organising its affairs and welcoming the British visitors who came to see him. The continent of Europe had been virtually closed to them while Napoleon was its master: new freedom of movement gave them an opportunity to go and look at the man who had kept them from the delights of the Grand Tour for so long. In England itself the press sniggered and talked of Napoleon's 'lack of Elba room'. Tabloid puns, it seems, are at least two hundred years old. Napoleon enjoyed his conversations with visiting English dignitaries. They allowed him to learn how he was being regarded in the world outside and to pick up useful intelligence about what was happening in European affairs. He had been promised a good pension as well as full sovereignty of the little island and he enjoyed the services of a large staff. He even had a ship and a small force of men. On 16th February 1815, the English Commissioner –

in effect, Napoleon's principal guard – left for a visit to Italy. When he got back twelve days later Napoleon had disappeared.

He had sailed to France. On 1st March he landed near Cannes in what is now the French Riviera and then made his way through Grasse and Digne to Grenoble. This was – and still is – the 'Route Napoleon', the pathway back to power of an exiled emperor who had landed with a tiny band of followers to reclaim the country he had ruled for twenty years. He had no firepower to speak of and hardly any other resources at all. All he had was himself and his hold over the minds of the French people. The strength of that hold faced its greatest test outside Grenoble on 7th March 1815 where, in one of the most famous scenes in the whole history of France, his party was met by a group of infantry from the 5th Line of the French Army sent to arrest him. Napoleon, wearing the heavy grey coat and three-cornered hat in which he was often portrayed in pictures, advanced towards them alone. Telling his own men to rest their arms he stood before them. '*Soldats du 5eme*,' he said, '*je suis votre empereur. Reconnaissez-moi.*' ('Soldiers of the 5th, I am your emperor. Recognise me.') Then he half opened his grey coat. '*Si'il est parmi vous un soldat qui veuille tuer son empereur, me voila.*' ('If there is a soldier among you who would shoot his emperor, here I am.') The soldiers of the 5th dropped their weapons and rushed forwards to greet him. 'Before Grenoble,' said Napoleon afterwards, 'I was an adventurer; at Grenoble I was a reigning prince.' By 20th March he had reached Paris. 'Before him,' wondered the novelist Balzac later, 'did ever a man gain an empire simply by showing his hat?'

Recapturing Paris from the restored Bourbon king, Louis XVIII, had been easy. Keeping it, Napoleon knew, would be much more difficult. His main hope lay in winning one of his famous victories – a quick and glorious battle that would restore him completely in the eyes of France and prevent the European powers from form-ing an effective coalition against him. He needed to attack as quickly as possible, first destroying the British and Prussians under Wellington and Blucher before turning to the Austro-Russian army on his eastern front. His plan was to prevent Wellington and

Blucher joining up. Setting out from Paris on 12th June, he seized Charleroi south of Brussels before the allies realised where he was. He then defeated Blucher at the Battle of Ligny, but Marshal Ney failed to beat Wellington at Quatre Bras. Wellington retreated and took up a position south of Waterloo. Napoleon advanced against him. This was the Emperor's last chance, the moment when he was either restored to new glories and new conquests, or finally destroyed forever. Blucher, he thought, was being held down after his defeat by Marshal Grouchy whom Napoleon had sent after him. All he had to do was to overcome the British army under the command of the Duke of Wellington. On 18th June 1815 he attacked.

'It was,' said the Duke afterwards, 'the most desperate business I ever was in: I never took so much trouble about any battle, and never was so near being beat.' The Battle of Waterloo lasted from about 11.30 in the morning until nine at night. Everything depended on Blucher, the seventy-two-year-old veteran Prussian commander, getting to the battlefield in time to support the British, Dutch-Belgian and Hanoverian troops commanded by Wellington, whose army had been put together hastily in the wake of the news of Napoleon's escape from Elba. The French Emperor was relying on the veterans from his previous campaigns, many of whom had rejoined his army out of loyalty. By attacking Charleroi so quickly, Napoleon had succeeded in separating Blucher from Wellington, but Blucher had escaped from Marshal Grouchy and was in a position to bring his army to support his British ally. Napoleon attacked with full force: Wellington stood his ground. By late afternoon, the Prussians began to arrive and Napoleon had to divert forces to deal with them. At 6.30 p.m. Marshal Ney captured a farmhouse near the centre of the Allied line and began to blast it with cannon. He thought he might be able to break through and called on his Emperor for more reinforcements. But Napoleon had none to give

It was the final flourish of the Napoleonic Empire.

him. Finally, as dusk began to settle, the French Imperial Guard made one last, hopeless charge in defence of their Emperor. It was the final flourish of the Napoleonic Empire. The battle was lost.

Napoleon was exiled to St Helena where he died in 1821. He had first come to power in the aftermath of the French Revolution at the end of the eighteenth century. As both a soldier and a statesman he has few equals in the history of Europe, but his thirst for glory and his love of power at almost any price destroyed him, and nearly destroyed the country he loved as well. Louis XVIII, who had fled to Ghent when Napoleon escaped from Elba, was now returned to power. Talleyrand, the French statesman who was a prominent figure during the French Revolution, the reign of Napoleon and the restored Bourbon monarchy – an unusual and remarkable record – observed that the Bourbons 'had learned nothing and forgotten nothing'. Their restoration did not bring stability to France: its government would suffer a series of crises throughout the nine-teenth century. It ultimately became a republic, as it has been ever since, in 1870.

For Britain it was a very different story. The Battle of Waterloo ended more than twenty years of European war, and the country emerged as the leading power in the continent. A long period of peace lay ahead – a period in which, fuelled by the Industrial Revolution at home and supported by the wealth of its imperial possessions abroad, Britain would expand and grow into the great-est power on earth. The Battle of Waterloo signalled the moment when this huge expansion could begin. It had, as Wellington said, been 'a damn'd close run thing'. Britain had squeaked through – towards global supremacy.

Poems about British History

'An Horatian Ode' by Andrew Marvell

Subtitled 'Upon Cromwell's Return from Ireland', this poem displays
the wit and intelligence of a poet who was also a politician. Andrew
Marvell rose to prominence during the Cromwellian era and then
served as MP for Hull throughout most of the reign of Charles II,
from 1659 to 1678. His output was small, but he is considered to be
one of the finest English poets of the seventeenth century. This is
an extract:

> So restless Cromwell could not cease
> In the inglorious arts of peace,
> But through adventurous war
> Urgèd his active star:
>
> And like the three-fork'd lightning, first
> Breaking the clouds where it was nurst,
> Did thorough his own side
> His fiery way divide:
>
> For 'tis all one to courage high,
> The emulous, or enemy;
> And with such, to enclose
> Is more than to oppose.
>
> Then burning through the air he went
> And palaces and temples rent;
> And Cæsar's head at last
> Did through his laurels blast.
>
> 'Tis madness to resist or blame
> The face of angry Heaven's flame;
> And if we would speak true,
> Much to the man is due,
>
> Who, from his private gardens, where
> He lived reservèd and austere
> (As if his highest plot
> To plant the bergamot),

Could by industrious valour climb
To ruin the great work of time,
And cast the Kingdoms old
Into another mould;

Though Justice against Fate complain,
And plead the ancient rights in vain—
But those do hold or break
As men are strong or weak—

Nature, that hateth emptiness,
Allows of penetration less,
And therefore must make room
Where greater spirits come.

'Absalom and Acitophel' by John Dryden

'Absalom and Acitophel' is one of the greatest verse satires in the English language. Dryden was the dominant literary force in England throughout the second half of the seventeenth century, This poem uses the biblical events of the rebellion of Absalom against David as an allegory to poke fun at the political situation during and following the Duke of Monmouth's rebellion against James II in 1685. This is its famous opening; the whole poem is more than a thousand lines long.

In pious times, ere priestcraft did begin,
Before polygamy was made a sin;
When man on many multiplied his kind,
Ere one to one was cursedly confined;
When nature prompted, and no law denied
Promiscuous use of concubine and bride;
Then Israel's monarch after Heaven's own heart,
His vigorous warmth did variously impart
To wives and slaves; and wide as his command,
Scatter'd his Maker's image through the land.

'After Blenheim' by Robert Southey

'After Blenheim' is one of English literature's first anti-war poems. It first appeared in *The Morning Post* in 1798. Robert Southey was one of the so-called 'Lake Poets', who lived and worked in the Lake District at the beginning of the nineteenth century. Their most famous member was William Wordsworth who succeeded Southey as Poet Laureate.

> It was a summer's evening,
>   Old Kaspar's work was done,
> And he before his cottage door
>   Was sitting in the sun;
> And by him sported on the green
> His little grandchild Wilhelmine.
>
> She saw her brother Peterkin
>   Roll something large and round,
> Which he, beside the rivulet,
>   In playing there, had found.
> He came to ask what he had found,
> That was so large, and smooth, and round.
>
> Old Kaspar took it from the boy,
>   Who stood expectant by;
> And then the old man shook his head,
>   And, with a natural sigh,
> ''Tis some poor fellow's skull,' said he,
> 'Who fell in the great victory!
>
> 'I find them in the garden,
>   For there's many hereabout;
> And often when I go to plow,
>   The plowshare turns them out;
> For many thousand men,' said he,
> 'Were slain in that great victory!'
>
> 'Now tell us what 'twas all about,'
>   Young Peterkin he cries;
> And little Wilhelmine looks up
>   With wonder-waiting eyes;
> 'Now tell us all about the war,
> And what they fought each other for.'

'It was the English,' Kaspar cried,
  'Who put the French to rout;
But what they fought each other for
  I could not well make out.
But everybody said,' quoth he,
'That 'twas a famous victory!'

'My father lived at Blenheim then,
  Yon little stream hard by:
They burned his dwelling to the ground
  And he was forced to fly;
So with his wife and child he fled,
Nor had he where to rest his head.

'With fire and sword the country round
  Was wasted far and wide;
And many a childing mother then
  And new-born baby died.
But things like that, you know, must be
At every famous victory.

'They say it was a shocking sight
  After the field was won;
For many thousand bodies here
  Lay rotting in the sun.
But things like that, you know, must be
After a famous victory.

'Great praise the Duke of Marlborough won,
  And our good Prince Eugene.'
'Why, 'twas a very wicked thing!'
  Said little Wilhelmine.
'Nay, nay, my little girl,' quoth he,
'It was a famous victory!'

  'And everybody praised the Duke
    Who this great fight did win.'
  'But what good came of it at last?'
    Quoth little Peterkin.
  'Why, that I cannot tell,' said he,
  'But 'twas a famous victory.'

'The Burial of Sir John Moore after Corunna' by Charles Wolfe

This is the only poem written by the Irish poet, Charles Wolfe, which is still remembered today. It appeared in the *Newry Telegraph* in 1817. Sir John Moore was a British commander in the Peninsula War fought in Spain against the French. He was killed in 1809 while his army was defending the garrison port of Corunna before its evacuation. He was buried in the ramparts of the town.

> Not a drum was heard, not a funeral note,
>   As his corse to the rampart we hurried;
> Not a soldier discharged his farewell shot
>   O'er the grave where our hero we buried.
>
> We buried him darkly at dead of night,
>   The sods with our bayonets turning,
> By the struggling moonbeam's misty light
>   And the lanthorn dimly burning.
>
> No useless coffin enclosed his breast,
>   Not in sheet or in shroud we wound him;
> But he lay like a warrior taking his rest
>   With his martial cloak around him.
>
> Few and short were the prayers we said,
>   And we spoke not a word of sorrow;
> But we steadfastly gazed on the face that was dead,
>   And we bitterly thought of the morrow.
>
> We thought, as we hollow'd his narrow bed
>   And smooth'd down his lonely pillow,
> That the foe and the stranger would tread o'er his head,
>   And we far away on the billow!
>
> Lightly they'll talk of the spirit that's gone,
>   And o'er his cold ashes upbraid him –
> But little he'll reck, if they let him sleep on
>   In the grave where a Briton has laid him.
>
> But half of our heavy task was done
>   When the clock struck the hour for retiring;
> And we heard the distant and random gun
>   That the foe was sullenly firing.

Slowly and sadly we laid him down,
From the field of his fame fresh and gory;
We carved not a line, and we raised not a stone,
But we left him alone with his glory.

'The Eve of Waterloo' by George Gordon, Lord Byron

Byron's description of the Battle of Waterloo comes from the third part of his long poem, 'Childe Harold's Pilgrimage'. It was published in 1816, the year after the battle itself. It opens with a description of the Duchess of Richmond's ball in Brussels at which the Duke of Wellington heard that Napoleon had crossed the French border into Belgium. 'Napoleon has humbugged me, by God;' Wellington is reported to have said. 'He has gained twenty-four hours' march on me.' The following day the Allied and French armies fought an inconclusive engagement at Quatre Bras, and two days after that met at Waterloo.

There was a sound of revelry by night,
And Belgium's capital had gathered then
Her beauty and her chivalry, and bright
The lamps shone o'er fair women and brave men.
A thousand hearts beat happily; and when
Music arose with its voluptuous swell,
Soft eyes looked love to eyes which spake again,
And all went merry as a marriage bell;
But hush! hark! a deep sound strikes like a rising knell!

Did ye not hear it? – No; 'twas but the wind,
Or the car rattling o'er the stony street;
On with the dance! let joy be unconfined;
No sleep till morn, when youth and pleasure meet
To chase the glowing hours with flying feet.
But hark! – that heavy sound breaks in once more,
As if the clouds its echo would repeat;
And nearer, clearer, deadlier than before;
Arm! arm! it is – it is – the cannon's opening roar!

Within a windowed niche of that high hall
Sate Brunswick's fated chieftain; he did hear
That sound the first amidst the festival,
And caught its tone with death's prophetic ear;
And when they smiled because he deemed it near,
His heart more truly knew that peal too well
Which stretched his father on a bloody bier,
And roused the vengeance blood alone could quell;
He rushed into the field, and, foremost fighting, fell.

Ah! then and there was hurrying to and fro,
And gathering tears, and tremblings of distress,
And cheeks all pale, which, but an hour ago,
Blushed at the praise of their own loveliness.
And there were sudden partings, such as press
The life from out young hearts, and choking sighs
Which ne'er might be repeated; who would guess
If ever more should meet those mutual eyes,
Since upon night so sweet such awful morn could rise!

And there was mounting in hot haste; the steed,
The mustering squadron, and the clattering car,
Went pouring forward with impetuous speed,
And swiftly forming in the ranks of war;
And the deep thunder, peal on peal afar;
And near, the beat of the alarming drum
Roused up the soldier ere the morning star;
While thronged the citizens with terror dumb,
Or whispering, with white lips – "The foe! they come! they come!"

'The Revenge: A Ballad of the Fleet' by Alfred, Lord Tennyson

The Revenge, commanded by Sir Richard Grenville, fought alone against a fleet of fifty Spanish ship off the Azores in 1591. Grenville refused to abandon his sick men who were ashore when the British admiral, Lord Howard, decided that the Spanish force was too big to fight. Tennyson, who succeeded William Wordsworth as Poet Laureate in 1850, wrote several poems about British History including 'The Charge of the Light Brigade'. This poem appeared in a collection that was published in 1880; these are two extracts from it:

At Flores in the Azores Sir Richard Grenville lay,
And a pinnace, like a flutter'd bird, came flying from far away.
'Spanish ships of war at sea! We have sighted fifty three!'
Then sware Lord Thomas Howard: "fore God I am no coward;
But I cannot meet them here, for my ships are out of gear,
And half my men are sick. I must fly, but follow quick.
We are six ships of the line; can we fight with fifty three?'

Then spake Sir Richard Grenville: 'I know you are no coward;
You fly them for a moment to fight with them again.
But I've ninety men and more that are lying sick ashore.
I should count myself the coward if I left them, my Lord Howard,
To those Inquisition dogs and the devildoms of Spain.

. . .

And the sun went down, and the stars came out far over the summer seas,
But never a moment ceased the fight of the one and the fifty three.
Ship after ship, the whole night long, their high-built galleons came,
Ship after ship, the whole night long, with her battle-thunder and flame;
Ship after ship, the whole night long, drew back with her dead and her shame.
For some were sunk and many were shatter'd, and so could fight us no more—
God of battles, was ever a battle like this in the world before?

'Drake's Drum' by Sir Henry Newbolt

Sir Henry Newbolt was the author of several patriotic poems whose style went out of fashion after the First World War. 'Drake's Drum' is his most famous. Published in 1897 it evokes the swashbuckling activities of the great Elizabethan sailor with tremendous vigour.

Drake he's in his hammock an' a thousand mile away,
(Capten, art tha sleepin' there below?)
Slung atween the round shot in Nombre Dios Bay,
An' dreamin' arl the time o' Plymouth Hoe.
Yarnder lumes the island, yarnder lie the ships,
Wi' sailor lads a-dancin' heel-an'-toe,
An' the shore-lights flashin', an' the night-tide dashin'
He sees et arl so plainly as he saw et long ago.

Drake he was a Devon man, an' ruled the Devon seas,
  (Capten, art tha sleepin' there below?),
Rovin' tho' his death fell, he went wi' heart at ease,
  An' dreamin' arl the time o' Plymouth Hoe,
'Take my drum to England, hang et by the shore,
  Strike et when your powder's runnin' low;
If the Dons sight Devon, I'll quit the port o' Heaven,
  An' drum them up the Channel as we drummed them long ago.'

Drake he's in his hammock till the great Armadas come,
  (Capten, art tha sleepin' there below?),
Slung atween the round shot, listenin' for the drum,
  An' dreamin' arl the time o' Plymouth Hoe.
Call him on the deep sea, call him up the Sound,
  Call him when ye sail to meet the foe;
Where the old trade's plyin' an' the old flag flyin',
  They shall find him, ware an' wakin', as they found him long ago.

'Recessional' by Rudyard Kipling

Rudyard Kipling wrote this poem to celebrate Queen Victoria's
Jubilee in 1897 and its refrain 'Lest we forget' is often used in services
remembering those who have died in war. Kipling was a strong
believer in the values of the British Empire. In 1907 he became the
first British writer to be awarded the Nobel Prize for Literature.

God of our fathers, known of old—
  Lord of our far-flung battle-line—
Beneath whose awful Hand we hold
  Dominion over palm and pine—
Lord God of Hosts, be with us yet,
Lest we forget – lest we forget!

The tumult and the shouting dies—
  The captains and the kings depart—
Still stands Thine ancient sacrifice,
  An humble and a contrite heart.
Lord God of Hosts, be with us yet,
Lest we forget – lest we forget!

> Far-call'd our navies melt away—
>   On dune and headland sinks the fire—
> Lo, all our pomp of yesterday
>   Is one with Nineveh and Tyre!
> Judge of the Nations, spare us yet,
> Lest we forget – lest we forget!
>
> If, drunk with sight of power, we loose
>   Wild tongues that have not Thee in awe—
> Such boasting as the Gentiles use
>   Or lesser breeds without the Law—
> Lord God of Hosts, be with us yet,
> Lest we forget – lest we forget!
>
> For heathen heart that puts her trust
>   In reeking tube and iron shard—
> All valiant dust that builds on dust,
>   And guarding calls not Thee to guard—
> For frantic boast and foolish word,
> Thy Mercy on Thy People, Lord!

'Anthem for Doomed Youth' by Wilfred Owen

Wilfred Owen was the most famous of the so-called 'War Poets' whose poems revealed the truth about the terrible misery of the First World War battlefields. Owen joined the army in 1915 and wrote this poem in 1917 while he was recovering from shell shock in an Edinburgh hospital. He returned to the Western Front the following year and was killed in action a week before the war ended. He was twenty-five.

> What passing-bells for these who die as cattle?
> Only the monstrous anger of the guns.
> Only the stuttering rifles' rapid rattle
> Can patter out their hasty orisons.
> No mockeries now for them; no prayers nor bells;
> Nor any voice of mourning save the choirs,
> The shrill, demented choirs of wailing shells;
> And bugles calling for them from sad shires.

> What candles may be held to speed them all?
> Not in the hands of boys but in their eyes
> Shall shine the holy glimmers of good-byes.
> The pallor of girls' brows shall be their pall;
> Their flowers the tenderness of patient minds,
> And each slow dusk a drawing-down of blinds.

'War Poet' by Sidney Keyes

Sidney Keyes was a poet and soldier who was killed in action during the Second World War during the Tunisian campaign of 1943. He was twenty-one. His poetry demonstrated a great, unfulfilled talent.

> I am the man who looked for peace and found
> My own eyes barbed.
> I am the man who groped for words and found
> An arrow in my hand.
> I am the builder whose firm walls surround
> A slipping land.
> When I grow sick or mad
> Mock me not nor chain me;
> When I reach for the wind
> Cast me not down
> Though my face is a burnt book
> And a wasted town.

CHAPTER 8

The Battle of the Somme
1916

The Battle of the Somme was fought for five months
from 1st July to 18th November 1916. There were more
than a million casualties on all sides; 125,000 soldiers
from Britain and the Empire were killed.

The history of the First World War fills us with revulsion and
despair. Europe's fading empires, swollen with misplaced pride
and mutual mistrust, crashed into each other with disastrous
results. The war destroyed much but resolved little. The German
invasion of France in the summer of 1914 followed the lines of the
Schlieffen Plan. Schlieffen himself died in 1913, so he never lived to
see the carnage that his military tactics created, but his plan had
been the central strategy of the German General Staff for nearly a
decade before the First World War began. The Germans believed
that they could defeat France easily as they had in the Franco-
Prussian War more than forty years before when the German
Empire had first come into existence. They intended to sweep
westwards in a great northern arc while maintaining a defensive
position further south on the Franco-German border. With typical
Prussian precision, they envisaged the fall of Paris within thirty-
nine days. This time things did not go according to plan. In the
Franco-Prussian War of 1870–71, the Prussians invaded France on
4th August and had beaten and captured the French Emperor,
Napoleon III, within a month. They then laid siege to Paris before
the final victory was theirs.

The military architect of this rapacious onslaught had been
General von Moltke, whose nephew was Germany's Chief of the
General Staff in 1914. The nephew was not as decisive as his uncle

had been. Always worried about an attack from Russia to the east he did not move with the unstoppable speed the plan required and the German advance was halted in the Battle of the Marne. Both sides dug in. They each built a line of trenches, stretching eventually from the Belgian coast through France to its border with Switzerland. This was the Western Front, Europe's killing fields for the next four brutal, murderous years. The hopeless, inconclusive battles would result in men dying in thousands for each hour they fought. The Somme was one of these.

'The lamps are going out all over Europe,' said the British Foreign Secretary, Sir Edward Grey, to a friend one evening as he watched street lamps being lighted just before the start of the First World War. 'We shall not see them lit again in our lifetime.' It was a prophetic remark. As Foreign Secretary it had been his job to impress upon the German government that if it invaded Belgium, which was the route into France that the Schlieffen Plan required, Britain would have no choice but to come into the war against Germany. Belgian neutrality was protected under the Treaty of London of 1839, and both Prussia and Britain were signatories to it. The German Chancellor, Theobald von Bethmann Hollweg, was contemptuous: he could not believe that the two countries would go to war over a 'scrap of paper'. They did exactly that: they were the last piece of the diplomatic jigsaw that ostensibly bound the nations of Europe together in a way that, once broken, drove them to war.

The superficial reasons for the struggle that was about to engulf the world were straightforward. Austria had declared war on Serbia after the Austrian Archduke, Franz Ferdinand, was assassinated by Serbian revolutionaries in Sarajevo. Russia then mobilised in Serbia's defence; Germany, allied to Austria declared war on Russia; France, bound by treaty to Russia, found itself at war with Austria and Germany; and Britain declared war on Germany to protect Belgian neutrality when the Germans entered Belgium to invade France. These diplomatic obligations were really just dance steps to the sinister tune of rivalry, fear and aggression that had been driving the European powers towards confrontation with one another for most of the twentieth century. At the heart of it lay the ambitions of the new German Empire which had strengthened its political base through its alliance first with Austria in 1879 and then with Italy in 1882 and wanted to compete with Britain and France for overseas territory as well. The small German states that had existed independently before the creation of the Empire in 1871 had never been able to colonise like Britain, France and Holland. As one united nation they could now look for their 'place in the sun' and had already begun to lay claim to parts of Africa. Theirs was an empire founded on military success and born out of war and they continued to build up their armaments as the rest of Europe watched them suspiciously. The country most alarmed by their activities was France which had lost all of Alsace and part of Lorraine to Germany after its defeat in the Franco-Prussian War. It turned to Britain for support and the two countries formed an 'entente cordiale' in which they agreed to settle their differences over colonial expansion and to work together in peaceful co-operation. In 1908 they celebrated their new-found friendship with an exhibition in London. They built a field of white pavilions in Shepherds Bush, better known today as White City, the west London home of the BBC.

Such pleasant diversions were long forgotten eight years later in the catastrophic mud bath of the Western Front. The Allied High Command, meeting at Chantilly, decided that the time had come to make a great push forward. The Germans had attacked further south at Verdun and the French were fighting desperately to prevent their advance; threatening to 'bleed France white' with the strength of their attack the Germans had, by late June, nearly broken through. The Allies planned a huge assault of 120,000 troops along a 20-mile front. Their advance would be preceded by a five-day-long bombardment – in the event extended for a further two days – in which the German defences would be utterly destroyed. By the time it had finished the British troops would be able to stroll towards the German lines. Or so they thought. Like a lot of the military planning of the First World War it was horribly and utterly wrong.

On the morning of 1st July 1916, the pounding of the Allied guns began. They could be heard by Londoners standing on Hampstead Heath in north London. People living in East Anglia claimed to have felt the ground tremble beneath their feet. In the first hour of the bombardment almost a quarter of a million shells were launched; powerful underground mines were detonated as the British and French set about trying to destroy the German defences.

Once the artillery had finished their work, the British commander, Sir Douglas Haig, sent in the troops. Many of them were filled with a sense of optimism about their coming advance into enemy lines. Captain Bill Nevill brought two footballs along with him and kicked them into no-man's-land to encourage his men forward. What he and the rest of the British forces did not realise was that the huge bombardment had achieved virtually nothing. The German defences had proved too strong and many of the Allied shells were badly made and failed to go off. The Germans, instead of being pulverised into submission, were waiting with their machine guns ready as the Allied soldiers went over the top. Line after line of advancing soldiers were killed or wounded, including Captain Nevill and his footballing comrades: there were 57,000 British casualties on the first day of battle alone. Haig determined to fight on. His attack against the German lines had succeeded in drawing the enemy away from Verdun so he could argue – in the curious logic with which so much slaughter was then justified – that his strategy had been a partial success. The French encouraged Haig in his plans. They had nearly lost everything at Verdun but had been greatly relieved as the Germans turned to attend to Haig's assault further north and so all through the rest of the summer and into the autumn the British continued to try to break through the German lines. By the middle of November, snow, rain and mud brought their efforts to a standstill. They had gained 7 miles of ground. They had suffered 420,000 casualties.

The forward march of the British Empire ground to a halt in the trenches of the Somme. A nation that had entered into war in a blaze of patriotic superiority learned the news of death and watched with speechless dismay as horrifically wounded and disfigured men made their way home from the front. Many of them had enlisted together with their friends or workmates, little groups from the same town or village to which they would return as the crippled messengers of sadness and despair. King and Country no longer had quite the same resounding ring. People looked up less and began to turn to each other more. Three weeks after the end of the Battle of the Somme, in December 1916, Britain got a new Prime Minister, David Lloyd George, a man who believed passionately in social reform and had opposed the build-up of British armaments in the years before 1914. Lloyd George's approach chimed much better with the new mood of the British people than that of his predecessor, Herbert Asquith. He understood the aspirations of a nation where trade union membership had increased by 50 per cent during the war years. He introduced the idea of a war cabinet, pulling together representatives of all the main parties to direct operations. Although he never achieved total control over its direction, the national war effort became better coordinated. In 1917, following Germany's decision to resume unrestricted submarine attacks on Atlantic shipping, America entered the war on the side of the Allies. In 1918, Germany surrendered. Nearly fifty years previously it had humiliated France, not only by defeating it in the Franco-Prussian War, but also using the historic palace of Versailles to proclaim the formation of the German Empire. At the Treaty of Versailles of 1919 that empire was dismantled and destroyed. Britain settled down to the task of, in Lloyd George's words, 'building a land fit for heroes to live in'.

Twenty years later Britain would need its heroes again. Germany was forced to accept very harsh terms at the Treaty of Versailles: France was determined to revenge the years of humiliation it had suffered at the hands of its militaristic neighbour. Germany lost all its colonial possessions and many of its European ones too; it lost half its iron and steel industry and 16 per cent of its coalfields; it had to accept military restrictions so that it could not rebuild its armed forces; it had to accept total responsibility for causing the war; and it had to pay huge reparations for the damage it had caused. These provisions would prove disastrous, as the British economist John Maynard Keynes, foresaw. In his book, *The Economic Consequences of the Peace*, published in 1919, he remarked that: 'Great privation and great risks to society have become unavoidable.' He urged renegotiation to 'promote the re-establishment of prosperity and order, instead of leading us deeper into misfortune'. His words fell on deaf ears. Within fourteen years, Adolf Hitler was elected Chancellor of Germany. The dead and wounded of the Somme fought, they were told, to end all wars. Their sacrifice was in vain.

CHAPTER 9

The Battle of Britain

1940

In the summer of 1940 Hitler announced that Germany intended to invade and conquer Britain and the German air force, the Luftwaffe, was ordered to destroy all Britain's air defences. The Royal Air Force responded by fighting the Luftwaffe in the air. This was the Battle of Britain when Britain stood alone against the aggressive might of Nazi Germany.

In October 1941, the British Prime Minister, Winston Churchill, went back to his old school, Harrow, to give a speech. 'This is the lesson,' he said. 'Never give in, never give in, never, never, never, never – in nothing, great or small, large or petty – never give in except to convictions of honour and good sense.' In those words he summed up the spirit of the nation. His resilience and determination had become its embodiment.

'You ask,' he had said to the House of Commons in his first speech as Prime Minister eighteen months before, 'what is our aim? I can answer in one word. It is victory. Victory at all costs. Victory in spite of all terror. Victory however long and hard the road may be. For without victory there is no survival.' With growling clarity he identified for the British people what their purpose had to be. He had always warned that trying to appease Hitler and his government was a mistake. In 1938, when his predecessor Neville Chamberlain returned from Munich with an agreement with Hitler that, he claimed, would ensure peace, Churchill described it as a 'total and unmitigated defeat'. Not many had listened then. The country had no appetite for war and Churchill seemed too much of a maverick to attract widespread support. No one had any doubt that he had brilliant gifts but he was thought untrustworthy: after all, he had changed sides twice in his political career. He was also regarded as being out of touch because he was a strong opponent of Indian independence and a critic of the leaders of the independence movement, Gandhi and Nehru. But Churchill's warnings about Hitler had proved right. Britain declared war on Germany in September 1939. Neville Chamberlain was still Prime Minister, but clearly not equal to the task. In April 1940 he was still maintaining that Hitler had 'missed the bus' as far as an invasion of Western Europe was concerned even though Germany had already captured Poland and invaded Norway. On the morning of 10th May, the day Churchill became Prime Minister, German troops occupied Belgium, the Netherlands and Luxembourg. He had been chosen to lead the nation because he was the only person who it was felt could command the support of all the main parties in Parliament. That support depended entirely on Britain's ability to win the war.

To win a war you have to want to win it. Churchill knew that he had to prepare the British people for what they were about to face. Just over a month after he took office, France fell to the Germans. Britain was now entirely alone, barely 20 miles away from an army intent on its capture as its last, ultimate European prize.

> *To win a war you have to want to win it.*

Hitler expected Britain to come to some form of peace agreement once France had fallen but he underestimated the country's resolve. In July 1940 the Luftwaffe attack began with the bombing of British shipping. Hitler issued a directive: 'As England, despite the hopelessness of her military situation, has so far shown herself unwilling to come to any compromise, I have ... decided to begin preparations for, and if necessary to carry out an invasion of England ... If necessary, the island will be completely occupied.' This chilling announcement led to the planning of Operation Sea Lion, the gathering of a fleet of landing craft ready to ferry the German army across the Channel to the shores of Britain. In advance of this, and to pave the way for the arrival of the victorious forces of the Third

Reich, the Luftwaffe extended its fight to Britain's air defences.

An RAF recruiting film of the late 1930s described the organisation as 'the great freemasonry of the air'. In this, historically the youngest division of the British armed forces, there was an instinctive sense of camaraderie. On the whole young men joined because they loved the idea of flying: it was something, new, exciting and different. Once it came to confronting the enemy, the sense of adventure that had prompted men to join in the first place became transformed into a sense of mission – a determination to prevent the Luftwaffe from destroying Britain from the air. The RAF had been founded in 1918 when the Royal Flying Corps and the Royal Naval Air Service were amalgamated. By the time the Second World War began it had three fighting divisions – Bomber Command, responsible for carrying out bombing attacks on German installations; Coastal Command, responsible for protecting British shipping from the air; and Fighter Command, responsible for engaging with and trying to destroy enemy aircraft in the air. Led by Sir Hugh Dowding – known as 'Stuffy' because of his prickly temperament – Fighter Command shouldered the main responsibility for beating off the Luftwaffe in 1940 and was divided into four sections each looking after a different area of the country. Dowding was an RAF veteran who had served with the Royal Flying Corps in the First World War. His experience had taught him that to win air battles you needed good intelligence and fast, reliable fighter aircraft. His plan for the Battle of Britain was therefore to develop effective monitoring of enemy movements through radar and then to attack the oncoming enemy squadrons with planes specifically built for the purpose. Not long before the outbreak of the war the RAF was still dependent on biplanes, but late into the 1930s it unveiled two new additions to its fleet – the Hawker Hurricane and the Supermarine Spitfire. These two single-seater fighter planes were prepared for combat in the nick of time. Without them Britain would never have defeated the Luftwaffe. The Spitfire was the pride of the RAF – light, fast and, just as importantly, less likely to catch fire than the Hurricane. But it also took twice as long to manufacture so the RAF relied equally heavily on its more tradi-tional companion. The Hurricane was the plane responsible for most German losses in the battle itself.

Fighting in the air at the new high speeds that both the British and German planes could achieve was something neither side had experienced before. Bullets could penetrate a cockpit easily if fired within 200 yards and the Germans also used explosive shells in the sky. It was fire that the pilots most feared. If a plane's fuel tank caught fire a pilot could be burned to death in a few seconds: those that survived suffered terrible injuries. If a plane was disabled and was going to crash there was no choice but to bail out – most pilots who survived several weeks of combat had to bail out of their planes at some point. There were ghastly risks associated with this as well: a parachute might not open, particularly if the mechanism had been hit by a bullet. It could also get trapped on a part of the plane preventing final escape. Hugh Dundas joined the RAF as a pupil pilot in 1939. In his book, *Flying Start*, he described his experiences in the Battle of Britain, including his first dogfight on 28th May 1940:

With sudden, sickening, stupid fear I realised that I was being fired on and I pulled my Spitfire round hard, so that the blood was forced down from my head. The thick curtain of blackout blinded me for a moment and I felt the aircraft juddering on the brink of a stall ... I was close to panic in the bewilderment and fear of that first dogfight ... the consideration which was uppermost in my mind was the desire to stay alive.

Britain was saved by men like that, men who fought their fears in order that they might fight the enemy: 2,917 airmen took part in airborne operation during the Battle of Britain; 544 of them lost their lives. All these were, in Winston Churchill's words, 'the few' to whom so many in Britain owed so much; men who, given the newness of the whole experience, given the astonishing risks and the sheer, terrifying danger of it all, displayed the courage and discipline their country required in its summer of greatest need.

Up until August 1940, the battle was mainly contained to

German attacks on British airbases and fights in the air, but in September all that changed as Hitler set out to destroy British morale by bombing the big cities in the Blitz. This shift in tactics failed to work. Morale could not be bombed into oblivion, and the RAF, with German attention elsewhere, was able to rebuild its airfields and damaged infrastructure. The Luftwaffe launched a huge aerial bombardment on 15th September, but suffered a reversal, losing fifty-six aircraft in one day. Two days later, on the 17th, Hitler postponed Operation Sea Lion and the invasion of Britain indefinitely. The Battle of Britain was over.

The war itself, of course, had only just begun. The Blitz continued and away from the shores of the British Isles its scope widened as Japan entered the conflict with the attack on America's Pearl Harbor in December 1941. Eventually in the summer of 1944, due mainly to the involvement and support of America, an allied force left the shores of Britain to carry out its invasion of the continent of Western Europe and to take it back from Nazi Germany's control. In Eastern Europe, the forces of the Soviet Union rolled forward to reach Berlin. Finally, in the last great eruption of the war, the Japanese were forced to surrender when atomic bombs were dropped on Hiroshima and Nagasaki. On 14th August 1945 the Second World War finally ended.

Victory, Churchill's ultimate, relentless aim, had been achieved, but the price Britain paid in every way was very high. It had large debts to repay to the United States that had helped it meet the cost of the war effort. Its empire had disintegrated; 330,000 of its people had lost their lives. The man who had led it so forcefully and helped give it the inspiration it needed to survive and win was not the person it turned to in its hour of victory. Churchill was defeated in the general election of 1945: this more than anything symbolises the change that had come over Britain as the war ended. Churchill had been successful as a war leader because he represented the aims and values of the old nation, a nation of Empire and world pre-eminence. The struggle of the war changed the social structure of the country; class divisions had broken down as rich and poor had fought side by side against a common enemy; and women had emerged with a far more influential role than before. Britain was no longer a great world power and had to defer to the new global masters, America and the Soviet Union. These great new influences meant that life in Britain could never be the same again.

In 1962, the former Secretary of State in the post-war American administration of President Truman, Dean Acheson, made a famous speech about America and Britain. 'Great Britain,' he said, 'has lost an empire and not yet found a role.' His remark captured the essence of Britain's position in the post-war world. The Labour Party that defeated Churchill's Conservatives in the 1945 election set about the business of reforming Britain, modernising a nation where many people felt they deserved a greater share of wealth and opportunities. Britain's new health service became the envy of the world. At the same time the problems associated with the management of a declining international role created mixed feelings. There were many who felt that Britain was just a forgotten global power with lingering imperial pretensions as the country, weakened by war, struggled to enrich its people at home and discharge its responsibilities abroad. The years following the Second World War were some of the most difficult that Britain ever faced as the few who fought so bravely in the Battle of Britain and the many who fought after them in all the battles that followed, tried to rebuild their nation from the disappointments of victory.

The Blitz 1940

After Hitler failed to invade Britain he decided to try to bomb it into submission. Between 7th September 1940 and 11th May 1941, the German Luftwaffe attacked several of the country's most important cities in an endless series of air attacks.

The first bombing raid, carried out over London, killed 430 people and injured 1,600. London was bombed for the following fifty-seven consecutive days, driving people to find shelter in underground stations or in hastily constructed Anderson shelters erected in their gardens. The bombing raids were mainly carried out at night, the more to frighten people and deprive them of sleep. London was the city which was hardest hit, but other towns and ports were also attacked – particularly Swansea, Cardiff, Bristol, Southampton, Birmingham, Coventry and Liverpool. In November 1940 the biggest air raid of the whole war struck Coventry killing 554 people and destroying more than 4,000 homes.

The Blitz killed about 40,000 civilians and seriously injured a further 87,000. Two million homes were destroyed. It tested the British nation to its uttermost, which rose to the occasion with extraordinary courage and solidarity.

CHAPTER 10

The Battle of Goose Green
1982

In April 1982, Argentina invaded the British-owned
Falkland Islands in the South Atlantic. The British
government decided to fight a difficult and
controversial war.

South America has not been much blessed by good governance.
Simon Bolivar, the great liberator of Venezuela, Colombia, Bolivia
and Peru, had dreams of a United States of South America but
by the time he died in 1830 such ideas had virtually no support. As
countries became free from Spain, their former colonial master,
they set about building their independence in their own way. In the
case of Argentina this was mainly through a series of dictatorships.
Although the country encouraged immigration from Europe – it
has always been one the most 'European' of the South American
states – its wealth remained concentrated in the hands of a few.
By the early 1980s the responsibility for mismanaging the country
had passed to a military dictatorship led by General Galtieri.
His regime was not only unpleasant – he and his predecessors had
disposed of hundreds of political opponents by kidnapping and
murdering them – it was also incompetent. The country was bank-
rupt. Galtieri decided to improve domestic support by taking the
Falkland Islands – *Las Malvinas* as they are called in Spanish – away
from Britain. A modest foreign conquest would, he assumed,
improve his popularity. He was right. Many people in Argentina
greeted the invasion of the Falklands in 1982 with big popular
demonstrations. Eight thousand miles from Britain, with a population then of about 1,300 people, the Falklands are made up of two
large islands, East and West Falkland and about 778 smaller ones.

In the 1980s the main, virtually the only, source of wealth was sheep farming. Galtieri felt sure that all this could be repossessed by Argentina without too much difficulty.

The general and his colleagues in the Junta could be forgiven for assuming that Britain would be unlikely to fight for possession of these islands in the South Atlantic. Argentina had claimed the Falklands as its own since 1820, following its independence from Spain, but Britain had always denied this. It traced its ownership back to the time when a British expedition landed there in 1690 and named the sound between the islands after Viscount Falkland, a politician and later First Lord of the Admiralty. Britain then seized the islands from Argentina in 1833 and set up a new settlement. It was this that the Argentinians joyously captured 150 years later.

The islands themselves had always been of little or no strategic importance. In the eighteenth century Samuel Johnson made the following rather cool observations about them: 'What, but a bleak and gloomy solitude, an island thrown aside from human use, stormy in winter and barren in summer; an island which not even southern savages have dignified with inhabitation ... of which the expense will be perpetual, and the use only occasional.'

Remote they might be, strategically unimportant they certainly were – but what the generals in the Argentinian Junta had not realised was that the British Prime Minister was, like them, also looking for an opportunity to improve her popularity. Margaret Thatcher had become Britain's first (and as yet only) woman Prime Minister in 1979. Unemployment was high; racial tensions had led to riots in London and Liverpool and Manchester, and in Northern Ireland the historic sectarian conflict between Catholics and Protestants seemed to be deepening. Viewed from the Argentinian capital, Buenos Aires, these difficulties seemed more than enough to keep the new British Prime Minister occupied – but the Junta underestimated her temper and mettle. Margaret Thatcher had become Prime Minister because she was not afraid of confronting the problems her country faced, however difficult they might be to resolve. She knew instinctively that to walk away from the Falkland Islands would lose her the ability to deal effectively with pressing domestic issues. She was about to engage in a significant battle with the power of the trade union movement in Britain. Her chances of winning it would be severely undermined if she were seen to be sent packing by a group of Argentinian generals.

She was also possessed of the sort of patriotism that the British people understood. When she said that Falkland islanders were 'of British tradition and stock' and wanted to stay part of the country that had governed them for a century and a half, she appealed to the prevailing mood of the nation. The territory of the Falkland Islands did not matter much to anyone in Britain, but the people who lived there did. General Galtieri waited for British submission but none came. Instead, a task force of warships, aircraft carriers and amphibious assault ships, as well as a fleet of requisitioned civilian ships, including the passenger liner, the QE2 was assembled; harrier jets, helicopters and other aircraft planes were also prepared; and 28,000 troops – many of them from elite units such as the SAS, the Royal Marine Commandos and the parachute regiments – made ready. The day after the invasion the United Nations Security Council demanded the immediate withdrawal of the Argentinian troops and urged both sides to come to a diplomatic solution. There would be no withdrawal – and no diplomacy either.

Margaret Thatcher was about to engage in a significant battle with the power of the trade union movement in Britain.

The Argentinian capture of the Falkland Islands had seemed to take the British government by surprise, even though a curious incident a few weeks earlier warned it that something was afoot. When a British survey ship called at the island of South Georgia in the middle of March 1982, it discovered that a group of Argentinian workers who had landed there with a contract to remove scrap metal were flying the Argentinian flag. South Georgia is a remote, uninhabited island that operates administratively as part of the

Falkland Islands and the illegal flying of the Argentinian flag was interpreted as a hostile act. The British ship alerted the Governor of the Falkland Islands to the situation and the scrap metal merchants were told to lower their flag. This they did, but from that moment on tensions between the two countries started to intensify. A group of British marines was landed on South Georgia to keep an eye on the workers who turned out to have Argentinian troops among them. Throughout the last two weeks of March the situation became more critical. In Argentina the idea of repossessing the Malvinas grew in popularity. Even the leaders of the country's trade unions, who opposed the Junta on most domestic issues, supported its stance on ownership of the islands. 'This is a question of national sovereignty,' said one of them, 'and other things are subject to it in importance.' The Malvinas were, said another, more important than 'internal domestic problems'. In Britain the events leading up to the war did not command the same attention. Although some diplomats and MPs warned that Argentina was preparing to invade, the British people remained remarkably unconcerned about the events that were about to unfold 8,000 miles away. By the end of March it was clear that something was about to happen. The United States President, Ronald Reagan, closely allied to Margaret Thatcher in his approach to economic policies, telephoned General Galtieri on 1st April and asked him not invade. It was too late. The Falklands War had begun.

It took until the end of May – nearly two months after the invasion – for British forces to put themselves in a position where they could land on the islands and repossess them. The recapture of South Georgia came quite easily, on 25th April – Mrs Thatcher when questioned about it at a press conference responded by telling the British people to 'rejoice' – but the main battles would prove much harder. A week after the fall of South Georgia, the Royal Navy sank the Argentinian cruiser, the *General Belgrano*, with the loss of 368 lives. Argentina replied with an attack on the British destroyer HMS *Sheffield*. The ship was sunk and twenty of her crew killed.

The Miners' Strike 1984–1985

The miners' strike of 1984–1985 was the biggest confrontation
between a British government and the trade union movement in the
second half of the twentieth century. The Conservative Prime
Minister, Margaret Thatcher, was determined to reduce the power of
the trade unions, which she believed stood in the way of essential
economic reforms. In Britain, the miners had always been seen as a
symbol of the integrity and courage of the ordinary working man.
Their strike was not just about the mining industry. It represented a
battle for the whole future direction of Britain.

In 1984 the National Coal Board announced that it was going to
close twenty mines. For mining communities in the North of England
and South Wales the implication of these closures was disastrous.
They were entirely dependent on the mines for their livelihoods.
Many of the men who worked there had never known anything else.
On 12th March, the leader of the National Union of Mineworkers,
Arthur Scargill, announced a national strike. For it to be effective, the
miners had to reduce the country's coal supplies to a point where the
government would be forced to negotiate with them. But the
government was prepared. It had stockpiled coal in preparation for
such an eventuality, and the miners turned to other methods to try to
win their battle.

The first land battle of the war was at Goose Green – an isthmus
about 5 miles long and a mile wide – and the second largest settlement on the Falklands. It was a battle won almost entirely thanks
to the determination and skill of the British soldiers, and in particular the 2nd Parachute Regiment whose commander, Colonel
Jones, was killed in action. The British had fewer troops – about 500
against an enemy's estimated strength of about 1,500. The assault
was announced on the BBC World Service before it had begun and
appalling weather conditions meant that to begin with air attacks
on enemy positions were not possible. The Argentinian forces were
well armed – but many of them had been told frightening stories

In May 1984, the Union of Mineworkers organised a mass picket of a British Steel plant at Orgreave, South Yorkshire. Their intention was to close the plant by preventing coal from reaching it. The authorities responded by drafting in 20,000 extra police. As the pickets tried to stop the coal lorries carrying out their deliveries, the police intervened and a day-long riot began: 41 policemen and 28 strikers were injured and 81 people arrested. 'The Battle of Orgreave' was the violent centrepiece of the whole strike: a tense and decisive test of government power.

The strike lasted for around nine months after Orgreave, but the miners, unable to force the government to change its position, had to abandon their protest on 3rd March 1985. By that time many of them, who were only receiving small amounts of strike pay, were facing serious financial hardship. The end of the strike cleared the way for the economic and industrial reforms of the Thatcher administration, including the de-regulation and privatisation of Britain's national industries. It was the brutal moment when the country parted company with the fading legacy of its industrial past.

about how British troops, particularly the Gurkhas, behaved. The advancing paratroopers found some of them cowering in their sleeping bags at the bottom of their trenches: they believed the British took no prisoners, or forced their captives to walk across minefields. These myths aside, the battle was hard and long. The British assault lasted for fourteen hours, but it ended in total victory. From this point on, the British were in a position to organise the recapture of Port Stanley, the capital of the Falkland Islands. It fell to their forces on 14th June, but not before fifty soldiers were killed by enemy aircraft as they waited to disembark from their landing ships at Bluff Cove, to the south of the town, in preparation for the final assault. Argentina surrendered. Within days General Galtieri had fallen from power: he would later serve five years in prison.

For the victorious politician in Britain, the outcome of the war was rather more beneficial. It strengthened Margaret Thatcher's hand and gave her the political base she needed to carry through important economic reforms. Her landslide victory in the 1983 election was in large part due to her determination and resolution during the conflict. 'The lesson of the Falklands,' she said, 'is that Britain has not changed and that this nation still has those sterling qualities which shine through our history.' This appeal to the country's pride was irresistible. It had seen its power wane steadily since the end of the Second World War: the Falklands War reminded it of its fighting ability. On the other hand, all this was achieved in a completely different atmosphere from that which prevailed in the hour of Britain's victory over Nazi Germany in 1945. The BBC, which in 1945 had been the mouthpiece of the nation's patriotism, remained determinedly neutral in its attitude, never using phrases such as 'our troops'. Some newspapers took a similar line. The *Daily Mirror* remained against the war throughout. Britain may have been renewed by the Falklands War, but the patriotic upsurge it generated was not enough to extinguish the scepticism that post-war decline had bred.

3 The Sea

Britain at Home and Abroad

Introduction

An elderly Indian gentleman was flying to London for the first time. During the journey he turned to the person sitting next to him, and asked quietly and courteously: 'Excuse me, sir, but would you mind telling me where Britain is exactly?' A little taken aback but anxious to help, his fellow passenger retrieved the airline magazine from the seat pocket and turned to the map of airline routes on the back pages. He pointed to Britain. 'It's just here,' he said.

The Indian looked at it gravely for quite a long time and then observed: 'It's very small.'

'Yes it is,' replied his fellow passenger, 'a small country with quite a lot of people in it.'

The Indian man was silent again. Then he said, 'How did such a small country become so powerful and rule so much of the world?'

In asking that question he put his finger on one of the most important points about Britain and its history. How did a small island off the northern coastline of the European continent, over-run in turn by Romans, Vikings and Normans and forced to fight for survival against stronger neighbours, develop into one of the largest empires the world has ever known? Where did that empire come from? What happened to it? And once it had disappeared, how did Britain manage to retain such a large measure of world influence through its language, culture and political structures? Britain is a small nation, but it once managed to dominate most of the world. It is impossible to appreciate who the British are without

ALASKA

DOMINION
OF CANADA

NEWFOUNDLAND

Heligoland
1814–90

GREAT
BRITAIN

GERMAN

UNITED
STATES
OF AMERICA

FRANCE

Hawaiian Is.
1898

SPAIN

MEXICO

Bahamas

Bermuda

Gibraltar

MALTA

BRITISH
HONDURAS

JAMAICA

Turks and Caicos Is.

Pacific Ocean

Atlantic Ocean

Galapagos Is.

Barbados

Trinidad

BRITISH
GUIANA

FRENCH
WEST AFRICA

GAMBIA

NIGERIA
1884–1900

Marquesas

Cook Is.

PERU

SIERRA LEONE
1896

GOLD COAST
1874–96

Pitcairn I.

BRAZIL

(British 1888, to
New Zealand 1901)

Ascension I.

St. Helena

CHILE

ARGENTINA

Tristan da Cunha

Gough I.

Falkland Is.

South Georgia

Pacific Ocean

JAPAN

Weihaiwei 1898

MONGOLIA

C H I N A

TIBET

Hong Kong

SIAM

BURMA
1886

INDIA

Andaman
Is.

Nicobar
Is.

MALAYA
1875-95 Singapore

CEYLON

Laccadive
Is.

Maldives

Cocos Is.

RUSSIAN EMPIRE

OTTOMAN
EMPIRE

PERSIA

CYPRUS
(leased, 1878)

KUWAIT

OMAN

EGYPT

ANGLO-
EGYPTIAN
SUDAN
1898
(under
British
control)

Aden

HADHRAMAUT

Socotra
1876

BRITISH
SOMALILAND
1884

Chagos Archipelago

BRITISH EAST
AFRICA 1886

Seychelles

UGANDA

Indian Ocean

Mauritius

NYASALAND 1891

NORTHERN RHODESIA 1891

SOUTHERN RHODESIA 1890

Bay

BECHU-
ANALAND
1885

SWAZILAND 1895

BASUTOLAND 1871

UNION OF
SOUTH AFRICA

BRITISH NEW
GUINEA

NORTH
BORNEO
1881

BRUNEI

SARAWAK
1888

AUSTRALIA
(Commonwealth, 1901)

NEW ZEALAND

TASMANIA

Gilbert Is.
1892

Ellice Is.
1886

Solomon Is.
1893

Samoa
1888–99

Fiji
1874

Tonga
1900

New Hebrides
1906

Norfolk I.

THE BRITISH EMPIRE AT 1900

British Empire

major British investment
outside of Europe

1893   date of British control

major sea routes

sphere of effective control

Major raw materials exported to Europe

∅	grain	▬	jute	◇	diamonds
O	meat	◄	silk	▬	gold
T	tea	o	rubber	S	silver
▥	cane sugar	⊖	veg oil	T	tin
🐄	dairy produce	◓	copra	I	copper
▸	cotton	▲	wool		

trying to understand the achievements and mistakes of their imperial history.

The history of Britain from the beginning of the eighteenth century to the outbreak of the Second World War is dominated by the story of its Empire, something that in the late twentieth century it became fashionable to disparage. In our anxiety to embrace multi-culturalism we became critical, even ashamed, of this aspect of our history. Today the Empire still remains a source of controversy.

The story of the British Empire actually begins in the sixteenth century when the British joined the European enthusiasm for global exploration triggered by Christopher Columbus's discovery of America in 1492. The British followed their Spanish and Portuguese rivals, but Sir Francis Drake's circumnavigation of the globe between 1577 and 1580 brought them to the forefront of the action.

In the seventeenth century Britain began to develop colonies abroad, driven almost entirely by commercial interests. Some of the first settlers were religious dissidents such as the Pilgrim Fathers who in 1620 took advantage of the new trading climate to try to develop their own self-governing communities overseas.

The passion for trade led to a passion for speculation with sometimes disastrous results. The South Sea Bubble, with its bogus promises of quick wealth from overseas investment, expanded and burst between 1711 and 1720. It ruined thousands of people and reminded everyone of the pitfalls of commercial expansion abroad.

By the middle of the eighteenth century, Britain's colonial interests could be found all over the world but principally in India, America and the West Indies. At the Battle of Plassey in 1757 the British East India Company demonstrated that it was far more than just a trading organisation by defeating local Indian princes and establishing itself as the effective ruler of a large part of the Indian sub-continent.

In America, Britain fared much worse. Its failure to respond to the demands of the colonists resulted in the War of Independence and the British defeat at Yorktown in 1781. In the West Indies, moral concern over the way slaves were used to fuel the colonial economy led to a long campaign at home led by Christian evangelists. They succeeded in abolishing the slave trade in 1807 and slavery itself in 1833.

In the nineteenth century the British Empire was the most powerful in the world, although its underlying weaknesses sometimes proved shocking. The Afghanistan Massacre of 1842 reminded people at home of the perils of managing vast lands abroad.

Meanwhile new territories were opened up. David Livingstone's huge journeys, and in particular his discovery of the Victoria Falls in 1855, revealed Africa to Britain and gave it a new colonial destination.

In the twentieth century, as Britain careered from one terrible global conflict to another, its hold over its colonial possessions began to decline. With the end of the Second World War the process of withdrawing completely from imperial control began with the partition of India in 1947. A year later, in 1948, the arrival of several hundred West Indians aboard the SS *Empire Windrush* at Tilbury Docks brought the British people face to face for the first time with significant numbers of the people its empire had once ruled. The pendulum had begun to swing the other way: the Empire was starting to come home.

CHAPTER 1

Sir Francis Drake and the Circumnavigation of the Globe 1577–1580

Sir Francis Drake was the first sea captain to sail round a world that had started to open up to European explorers. Britain's imperial ambitions began when it followed the Spanish and Portuguese to the wealth of the New World.

Sir Francis Drake was not simply a sailor. Think of him instead as Elizabethan England afloat. His exploits captured the essence of the age in which he lived – courage, curiosity and creativity. He was by no means the first European to set out on an arduous voyage to the New World, but he was the first commander to complete the whole journey round the globe. The Spanish explorer, Ferdinand Magellan, had managed to reach the Philippines over fifty years before Drake, but he had been killed in a fight with natives, so never got any further. Between 1577 and 1580 Drake sailed from Plymouth to South America, travelling through the Straits of Magellan and up the coastline of Chile and on north as far as San Francisco. From there he set out west across the Pacific, through the Philippines to the East Indies – and then on across the Indian Ocean to the Cape of Good Hope and back to England. It was an astonishing voyage. Drake not only discovered places that no European had been to before but he also brought back a vast amount of treasure.

Europeans had known about the wonders of America ever since Columbus had reached it at the end of the fifteenth century in 1492.

The Kings of Spain and Portugal, rather more adventurous perhaps than their Tudor counterparts in England, had licensed and paid for the explorers who had gone on to open up Central and South America and they were now enjoying the benefits of their foresight with imported silver and bullion. To be fair to Henry VII and Henry VIII – the great Tudor kings who preceded Elizabeth – they had had fairly sizeable domestic problems to contend with. Henry VII had established the Tudors as a powerful dynasty thanks to his shrewd management of the kingdom following his victory in the Wars of the Roses. He had supported an expedition by John Cabot who went off in search of the North West Passage across America to the Pacific. Cabot touched the shores of the vast lands of Canada, believing he had discovered Asia, but on a later adventure in 1498 he disappeared altogether never to be heard of again. Henry VIII, having broken with the Catholic Church over his divorce from Catherine of Aragon, had to think about the defence of his country against Europe's Catholic powers. In doing this he had done much to improve the English navy – he was extremely interested in guns and ships – but it was for war rather than commerce that he had invested in shipbuilding, earning him the sobriquet 'Father of the English Navy'. By the time Elizabeth I came to the throne things had changed: ships were no longer just useful for war, they had become the engines of commercial expansion.

'I'll have them fly to India for gold,/ Ransack the ocean for orient pearl,' so exclaims Dr Faustus in Christopher Marlowe's play. The world had become a big place, ripe for exploration and adventure, and its wonders were being brought before English playgoers in the magnificent language of Marlowe, Shakespeare and their contemporaries. Drake was part of this world. It is hard for us to imagine what it must have been like to realise the earth on which you lived seemed to have no boundaries and the shores of the island of Britain were not an end but a beginning of something extraordinary and new. That was the world which the Elizabethans inhabited. It was the moment when the British spread their wings and began their journey towards the Empire.

On 13th December 1577, five ships carrying 164 men – mariners, artisans and gentlemen – set out from the Barbican at Plymouth. The reasons for the voyage were never written down before it began and many of those on board believed they were about to embark on a peaceful trading mission. Their commander had rather more ambitious goals in mind but he had to keep his intentions secret. There were spies and informers everywhere and Drake, who had received support from Queen Elizabeth herself, could not be seen to be planning attacks on Spanish shipping. He would claim later that the Queen told him: 'I would gladly be revenged on the King of Spain for divers injuries I have received.'

Francis Drake was the son of a Protestant farmer and preacher. He had taken to the seas at the age of thirteen, and quickly distinguished himself. He made his first trip to the Americas when he was just twenty-three and had been attacked by the Spanish while on a slaving expedition. His 1577 expedition was one of the most dangerous and audacious the world had ever seen. His ships were tiny by modern standards. The largest, at 120 feet long, was Drake's own, the *Pelican*, later renamed the *Golden Hind*. Next came the *Elizabeth*, the *Swan*, the *Marigold* – and finally the little *Benedict*, weighing not much more than 12 tons. By modern standards these ships were small; but they were fast and on the sort of expedition Drake had in mind that would come in extremely useful.

The voyage started badly. The December departure was in fact Drake's second attempt to get out to sea. His first had been brought to a halt a month earlier, only one day in, by terrible storms. Life on board the small boats was tough: the men lived in cramped conditions and the close quarters caused arguments. The sailors' diet was poor and the men fell ill with scurvy. The morale of many of them doubtless dipped further when they realised that they had signed up, not as they had been told for a simple trading trip to the North African coast, but for a frightening journey into the unknown. However, Drake seems to have been a fair commander who inspired loyalty among his men. He did not see himself as being above menial tasks and could man the ropes with the best of them. He had a fearsome reputation among his Spanish adversaries, who called him 'El Draque', the dragon.

He headed first for the Cape Verde Islands in the mid-Atlantic, where he captured the Portuguese merchant ship, the *Santa Maria*, whose skilled captain, Nuno da Silva, gave him helpful information about navigating in South American seas. From there his fleet made its way to South America, arriving at the coast of Brazil on 5th April. It then headed southwards towards Port St Julian in Patagonia where Magellan had dropped anchor fifty-eight years earlier.

Fifty-eight years is a long time. Today the exploits of the seventeenth-century seamen seem to roll into one. We think about them as a single group, but their adventures unfolded over a century or more. The rest of the world did not yield its secrets easily. It turned out that Drake was following in Magellan's footsteps in more ways than one. In the harbour at Port St Julian he was greeted by the sight of a gibbet where the Portuguese explorer had probably hanged a mutinous member of his crew. Francis Drake now faced the same problem.

He suspected that one of his officers – a friend called Thomas Doughty – had committed treachery by trying to incite mutiny. Doughty was put on trial, found guilty and executed. On 17th August, now with only three ships in his fleet – the *Pelican*, *Elizabeth* and *Marigold* – Drake set sail again. The trial and execution of Doughty had unsettled his men and he had had to steady the nerves of an increasingly restless force. 'Let us show ourselves all to be of a company, and let us not give occasion to the enemy to rejoice at our decay and overthrow,' he told them in an emotional speech. It did the trick. The expedition was back on course. In late August of 1578 it reached the crucial waterway discovered by Magellan that links the Atlantic with the Pacific between the foot of Chile and Tierra del Fuego – the Magellan Straits. It took Drake and his fleet nearly three weeks to navigate these dangerous waters and when they finally reached the Pacific they discovered their charts were wrong. They were lost. The weather was atrocious. The *Marigold* sank with all hands. The *Elizabeth* became separated from Drake's own ship,

DRAKE'S VOYAGE

Drake, 1577–80

English trading company

now sailing under its new name of the *Golden Hind* and, after three weeks' fruitless attempts to become reunited, turned round and headed home. Meanwhile the storms drove Drake south leading him towards Tierra del Fuego, which he called the Elizabeth Islands in honour of his Queen. He was the first person to discover that this remote corner of the globe was not, as his contemporaries believed, one land mass that stretched unbroken to the South Pole.

When after two months the storms abated Drake found himself alone. Of the five ships that had left Plymouth a year earlier only his was left. He sailed north along the Chilean coastline where he raided Valparaiso and carried off its gold. The Spanish had no idea that an English ship was in their waters and Drake was able to turn up where he wanted, taking what he could. According to one contemporary report, the *Golden Hind* was in the process of being welcomed by the crew of a Spanish ship at Valparaiso which only realised its mistake when an energetic seaman called Tom Moone threw one of the Spaniards aside with a cry of: 'Go down, dog!' Drake sailed on to Peru and raided Lima's harbour, Callao, where he picked up news of a Spanish treasure ship heading north for Panama and subsequently set off in pursuit.

The *Nuestra Senora de la Concepcion* ('Our Lady of Conception') was a stately Spanish galleon of 120 tons that plied the Peru-Panama route. Its sailors called it the *Cacafuego*, or '*fireshitter*'. Drake tracked it down off the coast of Ecuador and drew alongside disguised as a merchantman. The engagement was swift and decisive, the *Cacafuego* surrendered and Drake loaded its treasure into his hold. It was a huge catch. We cannot be sure how much because contemporary accounts vary. Besides, the final tally had to be kept secret because of the Queen's own involvement.

Drake next went north to Mexico and then to northern California, an area that he called Nova Albion and where he became revered as a god by the local Miwok people. He and his crew were almost certainly the first Europeans to land in this part of America which may explain why his relationships with the natives were so friendly. Elsewhere the local people had been more suspicious and aggressive – perhaps because of their experiences in dealing with the Spanish – and some of Drake's men had been killed in fights. Drake had thought that in travelling north he might come across signs of a north-west passage, a sea route through the continent of North America and back to Britain, but none came to light. He decided that his only way home was across the Pacific Ocean and on 23rd July 1579, nineteen months after leaving England, he set sail due west. He and his crew saw no land for more than two months. When they did it was part of the Caroline Islands, an archipelago that sits to the north of New Guinea and east of the Philippines. Drake and his crew were now on Asia's doorstep. Yet another world, yet more prizes awaited them.

Drake and his men tried to trade with the locals for supplies, but the natives of the Caroline Islands preferred to steal from the ship. About twenty islanders were killed in the fight that followed. The Englishmen moved quickly on, through the Philippines themselves where Magellan had met his death over fifty years before, and then into the East Indies and the Molucca Islands. The Moluccas were the centre of the spice trade. They were ruled by Islamic sultans, the most powerful of whom was Babu, the sultan of the small island of Ternate. He welcomed the crew of the *Golden Hind*. He was looking for allies against the Portuguese who had become the dominant European force in the region and were beginning to monopolise his valuable trade in cloves. Babu offered Drake his part of the spice trade in exchange for English help against the Portuguese. Drake agreed and, with his ship loaded with spices, sugar cane, fruit and fresh meat, set sail once more. Off the coast of Celebes, just west of Ternate, the *Golden Hind* ran aground and Drake nearly lost her. They were 18 miles from land: he and his men would probably have drowned if the wind had not changed and blown the ship back into the water. They carried on, along the southern shore of Java (which Drake was able to prove was definitely an island), across the Indian Ocean to the Cape of Good Hope at the tip of southern Africa and then up the western side of the African continent.

On 26th September 1580, after a voyage lasting three years, the *Golden Hind* sailed up the English Channel and into Plymouth Sound. Drake and his crew had travelled 36,000 miles. They had been to places no European had been to before. They had brought back an immense amount of treasure, as well as spices and other valuable commodities. But despite these huge achievements, Drake was nervous. How would he be received? How would his Queen feel about his rumbustious activities? Had he damaged or helped his country's relationship with the Spanish Empire, then the greatest power on earth? He stayed on board his ship anxiously waiting to hear.

He need not have worried. Elizabeth I was keen to meet her intrepid explorer and to hear the stories of his astonishing journey. Anyway, she had made a profit on her original investment in the voyage of around £160,000. England rejoiced while the Spanish seethed.

The empires of history have been created as much by mankind's thirst for adventure and the natural aspirations of human exploration as they have by greed and the desire for conquest.

Drake could fairly be described as a pirate – he robbed and plundered Spanish ships. England and Spain were officially at war but they were deadly enemies and eight years after Drake completed his voyage, the Spanish king, Philip II, would send a great Armada to try to seize the English throne from Elizabeth I. For England the struggle against Spain was simply a matter of survival. For Spain it was a matter of preserving its valuable territories in the New World, and maintaining the power of the Catholic Church against the Protestant heretics. Drake the pirate would also become Drake the hero of the Armada. They are one and the same man.

The story of Francis Drake is an essential part of England, and an important piece of British history symbolising the moment when the country began to take its place in the world. The empires of history have been created as much by mankind's thirst for adventure and the natural aspirations of human exploration as they have by greed and the desire for conquest. The one is inextricably bound up with the other. The historian, J. A. Froude, said something about Drake and his fellow seamen that seems as true today as it did when he delivered it in a lecture at Oxford 120 years ago: 'The instinct of their countrymen gave them a place among the fighting heroes of England from which I do not think they will be deposed by the eventual verdict of history.'

CHAPTER 2

The Voyage of the Pilgrim Fathers
1620

The Age of Exploration led to an age of colonisation and settlement. In 1620 a group of Puritans, persecuted for their beliefs at home in Britain, set sail for America where they established an important and successful colony.

There is a famous painting by John Everett Millais called 'The Boyhood of Raleigh', which depicts the young Walter Raleigh and his half brother, Humphrey Gilbert, listening enraptured to the tales of the sea being told them by an exotic-looking sailor. Both Gilbert and Raleigh would later sail to America but they never created permanent settlements there. That came in 1607 when the adventurer Captain John Smith established Britain's first colony in Virginia. Smith is famous, among other things, for claiming that an Indian princess, Pocahontas, had saved his life. Like Millais's sailor he was a great storyteller so we cannot be sure whether this was true, but his eloquence and passion played a big part in promoting the opportunities of the New World to his countrymen back home.

Among those who heard and began to dream about a new life far away from religious torment in Europe were the 'Pilgrim Fathers'. To discover a new place and to bring back its treasures to enjoy at home is one thing. To decide that the new place is where you want to be, permanently, is quite another. That is what the Pilgrim Fathers did in 1620. They decided that the country of their birth was no longer tolerable and that in order to worship and live their lives in the way they wanted they would need to start life afresh, in an 'undiscovered world'. The fierceness of their convictions, their belief that they could create something far better than that which existed around them in Europe, drove them across the Atlantic to the eastern seaboard of what is now the United States. Devout, determined and defiant, they were a central part of the foundation of the nation that has become the most powerful the world has ever seen.

Europeans had been travelling westwards to the Americas, and settling there, for more than a century before the Pilgrim Fathers set sail. The Spanish Conquistadors – Cortes in Mexico and Pizarro in Peru – ruled their lands decisively and violently. In a sense their approach was similar to that taken by the Normans when they conquered Britain in the middle of the eleventh century: take control of everything and make it yours. Now, 3,700 miles to the north of the lands the Conquistadors had taken, a new group of conquerors had arrived. They would use guns, but they preferred bibles. They would order things their way, but they would try

In order to worship and live their lives in the way they wanted they would need to start life afresh, in an 'undiscovered world'.

to be inclusive. They were unafraid of war, but they sought peace. They were, as one American historian has said, 'the spiritual ancestors of all Americans'.

The Pilgrim Fathers were Puritans who wanted to live as a separate community. By 1607 a hundred and fifty men, women and children had fled their homes near Doncaster in Yorkshire to start a new life, first in Leiden, Amsterdam, and then in Holland. They had been given official permission by the Dutch authorities to settle there, but while the religious climate was more to their liking everyday existence was not. They had to do tough manual work in the local textile industry in order to earn the money to survive and the longer they stayed the more their children became drawn into Dutch society. In order to manage their community in their own way they would have to find their own place, their own land.

As often happens to desperate people, the Puritans fell prey to commercial speculators. The London Virginia Company had been set up in 1606 with a charter from James I to allow it to establish colonies on the eastern seaboard of the American continent. It had not found many takers – and the Leiden Puritans, lured by promises of religious freedom, seemed like an ideal catch. The Puritans built two boats financed by merchants anxious to make a profit out of the New World, and set sail in August 1620. They shared their journey with a group of ordinary settlers – people leaving their home country simply to try to create a new life abroad. Only a third of the passengers who left for America were in fact pilgrims.

The voyage was unspeakably awful. At the first attempt one of the ships, the *Speedwell*, sprang a leak and the little fleet which had originally left from Southampton was forced to return to Plymouth. A month later they set out again, this time in just one ship, the *Mayflower*. Two passengers died; all suffered from scurvy. The conditions were cramped and the ship's stores of firewood ran out. After more than two months they finally arrived on the shores of Cape Cod, ill, exhausted and afraid. The Cape today is an affluent place – an American playground where attractive little seaside places litter its shores – a far cry from how it was in 1620.

The pilgrims had anchored in what is today Provincetown on the southern side of the furthest seaward point of the Cape. They set out to explore and eventually decided to build a colony at a place they called Plymouth, to remind them of the port they had left behind three months earlier. In Cape Cod pleasant summers give way to fierce winters. Four months later, by the spring of 1621, half the colonists were dead, including their first governor, John Carver. The others struggled on. They were made of stern stuff. When they had arrived at 'Plymouth', forty-one men had signed an agreement, known as the Mayflower Compact, in which they promised to work with each other for the good of the colony. Helped by the local Indians they managed to grow food and, after their first harvest in 1621, gave thanks to the Lord in a celebration that became the Thanksgiving holiday, which remains a central celebration in

The Mayflower Compact

In ye name of God, Amen. We whose names are underwriten, the loyall subjects of our dread soveraigne Lord King James, by ye grace of God, of great Britaine, franc, & Ireland king, defender of ye faith, &c.

Haveing undertaken, for ye glorie of God, and advancemente of ye Christian faith, and honour of our king & countrie, a voyage to plant ye first colonie in ye Northerne parts of Virginia, doe by these presents solemnly & mutualy in ye presence of God, and one of another, covenant & combine our selves togeather into a civill body politick; for our better ordering & preservation & furtherance of ye ends aforesaid; and by vertue hearof to enacte, constitute, and frame such just & equall Lawes, ordinances, Acts, constitutions, & offices, from time to time, as shall be thought most meete & convenient for ye generall good of ye colonie: unto which we promise all due submission and obedience. In witnes wherof we have hereunder subscribed our names at Cap-Codd y^e. 11. of November, in ye year of ye raigne of our soveraigne Lord King James of England, France, & Ireland ye eighteenth, and of Scotland ye fiftie fourth. An^o: dom. 1620.

American society to this day. They had also elected a new leader, William Bradford, whose statue still stands in the town that he and his fellow pilgrims founded nearly 400 years ago. He was re-elected thirty times and died in the late 1650s, by which time Plymouth had been established as a successful enterprise. Bradford kept a journal in which he told the story of the Pilgrim Fathers and their struggle for survival:

Being thus passed ye vast ocean, and a sea of troubles before in their preparation... they had now no friends to welcome them, no inne to entertaine or refresh their weatherbeaten bodys, no houses or much less townes to repaire too, to seek for succoure ... May not and ought not the children of these fathers rightly say: 'Our fathers were Englishmen which came over this great ocean, and were ready to perish in this wilderness; but they cried unto ye Lord, and he heard their voice, and looked on their adversitie.'

The first few years of the colony proved hard. New arrivals came from England in 1621, but it was not until 1625 that Bradford could record they had begun to taste 'the sweetness of the country'. Their population began to grow – reaching nearly 300 by 1630, and just about double that number seven years after that. They began to develop a thriving fur and timber business, shipping goods back to England, and new towns were set up nearby, many with names familiar to English ears such as Taunton, Yarmouth and Sandwich. By 1648, as their homeland slid into the crisis created by parliamentary opposition to the King, the English Civil War, the colonists succeeded in paying off the last of the debts incurred by their courageous journey to the New World.

The British had arrived in America, lock, stock and Christianity.

CHAPTER 3

The South Sea Bubble
1711–1720

> Trade from the colonies was making men rich – and
> everyone wanted a share of the wealth. Between 1711 and
> 1720 investors speculated furiously in the South Sea
> Company which owned trading rights to South
> America. The company became overvalued and when
> the bubble burst, it nearly destroyed the British
> financial system.

By the end of the seventeenth century many English men and
women were enjoying a standard of living rather higher than their
predecessors. The fruits of imperial expansion were being felt at
home as tea, coffee and their inevitable accompaniment, sugar,
began to make their way into English homes. Throughout the
seventeenth century, the European powers had built on their
earlier exploratory journeys to discover new lands. The Dutch, English and French had overtaken the Spanish and Portuguese as
the main colonial powers. The Iberian countries, transfixed by the
treasure mines of Central and South America, had not been as
quick to take advantage of the many commodities to be found elsewhere and their rivals had fanned out across the globe in steadily
increasing numbers. The British had settled in North America, the
West Indies and India. The Dutch had established themselves in
Indonesia and South Africa. The French were colonising in the
Caribbean, West Africa and India. The Western powers were on
the brink of capturing the rest of the world for their own.

The principal way in which they had achieved this was through
the formation of trading companies. In the seventeenth century,
the greatest of these was the Dutch East India Company. Founded

in 1602, the VOC (Veereenigde Oostindishce Compagnie) had been granted a monopoly over the trade routes to the East Indies, where the new Dutch Republic was now in competition with the Portuguese for control of the spice trade. Seventy years on, the VOC had become a huge and lucrative enterprise operating 150 merchant ships as well as forty warships. It employed more than 50,000 people around the world and had its own military force of 10,000 men.

The British version, later known as the Honourable East India Company, had been founded in 1600, but was not as successful as its Dutch rival during those first seventy years of the seventeenth century. The Dutch dominated the spice trade in the East Indies – so the British turned their attention to the Indian sub-continent where they began to establish a number of successful commercial operations. These would later provide the basis of what became the British Raj – but for that their owners would have to wait a great deal longer. In 1670 British merchants also set up the Hudson Bay Company to try to profit from the Canadian fur trade.

In 1688 the interests of the Dutch and English nations were united when King James II was forced off the throne and the Dutch William of Orange and his English wife, Mary, were invited to take his place. Dutch financial management was rather better than the British. The sober merchants of Amsterdam knew a thing or two when it came to commerce, and their ideas and institutions began to be adopted in Britain. In particular they understood the value of credit. In 1694 the Bank of England was created to help fund government borrowing. This combined with an altogether more sophisticated approach to trading fuelled the British expansion abroad. Bit by bit its tentacles reached into new and different corners of the world.

Then, in 1711, the South Sea Company was created.

War is an expensive business and by the end of the first decade of the eighteenth century the British government was millions of pounds in debt thanks to the cost of the war against France – the War of the Spanish Succession. By this time Queen Anne had succeeded William and Mary. One of her principal ministers, Robert Harley, Earl of Oxford, spotted an opportunity. He suggested the formation of a company to take on the government's debt in return for a monopoly over the lucrative slaving routes to the Spanish territories in South America. The investors in the company would, in effect, fund government debt in return for trading profits. Harley was one of the cleverest politicians of his age – it was he who formed the political group that many regard as the precursor to the Tory Party in British politics. He knew that one of his jobs while he was in power was to bring to an end the European war that had been dragging on since the century began. The Duke of Marlborough's great victories in the war – particularly at the Battle of Blenheim in 1704 – had given the British the upper hand, and the approaching peace would, Harley knew, give his country the opportunity to strike a few beneficial deals. He was proved right. Britain won the *asiento* – the rights to the South American slave trade – and the South Sea Company began operations.

This was a time when men everywhere in England were looking to get rich quick. Peace, the growth of trade and comparative political stability, brought with them a new sense of affluence. Landowners were enclosing the countryside so they could develop and improve it for profit; great houses were being expanded and modernised; and men in the city spent lavishly. This wealth, or belief in the importance of wealth, had developed out of a financial system that had become more dependent on credit and loans. The South Sea Company, although it purported to be a trading concern supported by its monopolies, very quickly turned into a financial corporation intent on being a rival to the Bank of England. The enterprise depended on the close relationship between politicians and the City of London. Together they set out to make each other rich. Together they wrought financial disaster.

By 1719, the directors of the South Sea Company decided to exploit the public appetite for overseas speculation by launching a scheme to convert a huge slice of government debt into a loan on which the government would pay interest at less than the rate at which it had contracted it in the first place. Stock in the company would be offered in return for the surrender of government securities – £1 of stock for every £1 of debt. The stock would then be sold to speculators at a far higher price, based on the inflated expectations of the company's South Sea trading prospects. The ambitious Chancellor of the Exchequer, John Aislabie, himself a partner in the plan, presented the scheme to the House of Commons. The Bank of England tried to outbid the South Sea Company, but the government, mesmerised by a proposition that seemed to offer a painless solution to its indebtedness, backed its Chancellor.

What then happened was very similar to the 'dotcom' boom that grew and then crashed in the financial markets of the West in the late 1990s. The directors of the company, desperate to drive up the market price of their shares in order to cover their obligations, devised a series of operations to inflate it. Excitement over the prospects for the stock meant that it was at first over-subscribed, and the price shot up accordingly. To provide an incentive for further buying, the company then offered loans against the stock: £100 stock entitled depositors to a loan of £250 at 5 per cent as long as they bought more. Through this and other manipulative measures the price of a £1 share had risen to £1,000 by the end of June 1720. Other companies were invented purporting to offer fantastic opportunities. There was one for making soup, another for importing walnut trees from Virginia. There was a company for creating a wheel of perpetual motion and even one for 'carrying out an undertaking of great advantage', although it failed to mention what this might be. These madcap schemes were called 'bubbles'.

The directors of the South Sea Company had launched their plan with the backing of Parliament in February 1720. By August of that year they could no longer maintain the fiction that their stock

What happened was very similar to the 'dotcom' boom that grew and then crashed in the financial markets of the West in the late 1990s.

was worth the prices at which they were selling it and the 'South Sea Bubble' burst.

The crash when it came was fast, deep and disastrous. Men who had covenanted to buy stock when prices were high faced ruin if they were forced to honour their agreements. Others who had bought stock on the instalment plan provided by the company's loan scheme were left with nothing. By the autumn of 1720 people everywhere were calling for revenge. They were angry with ministers of the Crown, as well as the King and his court, all of whom were deeply implicated in the venture. The scale of the collapse was huge. It nearly destroyed the British banking system. The King – George I was now on the throne – broke off his stay in Hanover and returned to London where in December Parliament reassembled. There was no doubt that the company had been selling bogus stock. It would take the skill and patience of the new Lord Treasurer, Robert Walpole, to steady a nation in anguish. He had been an opponent of the South Sea scheme from the start – although his opposition was based as much on his association with the company's rivals in the Bank of England as anything else. Walpole devised a scheme for reapportioning South Sea stock into both the Bank of England and the East India Company. Some debtors were relieved of part of their obligations on condition they repaid 10 per cent of their contracted debt.

One distinguished victim of the crash was the mathematician and astronomer Sir Isaac Newton – one of the cleverest men Britain has ever produced. He remarked ruefully that he could 'calculate the movements of stars but not the madness of men'. But it was left to the sharpest commentator of the age, the poet Alexander Pope, to sum up the whole dreadful episode:

> *At length Corruption, like a gen'ral flood,*
> *(So long by watchful Ministers withstood)*
> *Shall deluge all; and Av'rice creeping on,*
> *Spread like a low-born mist, and blot the Sun;*

Statesman and Patriot ply alike the stocks,
Peeress and Butler share alike the Box,
And judges job, and Bishops bite the town,
And mighty Dukes pack cards for half a crown.
See Britain sunk in lucre's sordid charms ...

Lucre's sordid charms were to a large extent what the British Empire was all about. From the moment that Drake returned from his momentous voyage, to the sad spectacle of the South Sea Bubble 130 years later, Britain had been trying to ascertain how best to get its hands on the profits that it knew existed in the development of the world's discoveries. As a small country with powerful rivals it had made sure it had a share of the action. The events leading up to the South Sea crash in 1720 demonstrated just how fragile these commercial activities could be. From then on Britain had to make sure its commitments were properly protected. Trade and profit would go on being the reasons for expanding abroad: men at arms would be the means by which they were secured.

CHAPTER 4

The Battle of Plassey
1757

British trading interests began to require military protection. In 1757 Clive of India won a victory over Indian forces at Plassey, and Britain made its first steps towards establishing imperial rule.

Great men tend not to kill themselves. Presumably suicide does not fit with their vision of destiny. However, on 22nd November 1774, at his home in Berkeley Square in London, Major General Robert Clive, the first Baron Clive, better known as 'Clive of India', stabbed himself to death with a penknife.

Clive's story is inseparable from the story of the British Empire. Because of what he achieved, and in particular because of his victory at the Battle of Plassey, he established India as the corner-stone of Britain's imperial strength for two hundred years after his death. His contemporaries were often uneasy about his activities and when he died few would have foreseen the role that India was to play in Britain's fortunes. Clive's career marks the point at which trade alone no longer stood as the single ambition of British expansion overseas. Power and control began to play their part.

The world was already getting smaller by the time the eigh-teenth century was underway. At the beginning of the second decade of the eighteenth century, following the end of the War of Spanish Succession, Britain emerged as a major new power in Europe. As a result of the Act of Union of 1707 it was now known as the United Kingdom. Thanks to its success in the way it had helped to curb the ambitions of the French under Louis XIV it was regarded as the principal bulwark against French supremacy. This made it a formidable power-broker. Furthermore, the success of its navy had made it Europe's strongest maritime power. All this helped support its trading ambitions in the territories that it had started to colonise all over the world. In the Caribbean, in North America and in India, Britain began to extend its influence. People at home revelled in the goods that these new possessions provided – sugar, calico, spices and tobacco. The slave trade was now in full swing and the plantations of the West Indies were crowded full of captured Africans forced to work for their European masters.

Wealth also meant power: merchants and politicians were the natural allies of the comfortable oligarchy that had taken control of the national interest. But although Britain had emerged as a great European power, its old rivals – particularly France – were not inclined to sit back and watch it grab the wealth of the world for itself alone. France remained active in the Caribbean and in North America, where in the War of Independence, its support for the revolutionaries would prove decisive in Britain's defeat.

The growth of the British Empire in India began with the gradual dissolution of another. The Mogul emperors had commanded most of the Indian sub-continent since the beginning of the sixteenth century. One of the longest lived, Aurangzeb, died in 1707 and the Mogul Empire, which until this point had been highly centralised, began to fragment under pressure from its enemies. In 1739, a Persian army swooped through the Khyber Pass, plundered Delhi and took control of the continent's western territories. Meanwhile, the Hindu confederacy of the Marathas in northern India had grown into a powerful threat to Mogul power. The Empire survived, at least in principle, but much of its authority began to be devolved to regional nawabs and these were the men with whom the European traders had to deal. Some of them were fairly unscrupulous – but in that they probably did not differ much from the colonial adventurers who were establishing ports along their coastline. They were also dazzlingly rich, although their personal finery was in stark contrast to the poverty of the people they ruled. For Britain, India would prove to be a poor substitute for the loss of the American colonies, at least in terms of the wealth it would return to its imperial masters.

It was the French who got the hang of ruling India first. Louis XIV's minister of finance, Jean-Baptiste Colbert, had founded the French East India Company (La Compagnie français pour le commerce des Indes orientales) in 1664. Though its arrival on the scene was more than sixty years behind its British and Dutch rivals, by the middle of the eighteenth century it was beginning to operate highly effectively in its chosen territory. In 1742 Joseph Francois Dupleix became Governor of Pondicherry in south-east India and rose to be the effective ruler of the whole of the southern part of the continent. He lived magnificently. His army was more than a match for the local native forces and the British found it difficult to develop their trading operations in the region. Their salvation came in the form of the Treaty of Aix-la-Chapelle in 1748 which ended another European war between the French and the British with the swapping of foreign possessions. The British got Madras and the French Louisburg in Canada. Dupleix was no longer master of all he surveyed: there was now another power in the land. The two rivals decided to entrench their authority by backing different princes as the local rulers, each hoping to have control over his candidate once victory was achieved. A nasty little war began which the British won, thanks largely to the seizure and defence, in 1751, of the town of Arcot – headquarters of the prince that the French supported. The hero of this engagement was Robert Clive.

It was an astonishing feat of arms and typical of the man. Clive had come to India as an East India Company 'writer' – a sort of merchant's clerk – but in a fit of depression had twice tried to blow his brains out. The pistol failed to go off both times. Life in the warehouses of the Indian seaports in the early eighteenth century was a wretched existence: drink, fights and whores were the main attractions for young Englishmen who found themselves stuck there. Clive complained that he had not 'enjoyed one happy day since I left my native country' and, desperate for a change of scene, enlisted in the East India Company's soldiery. He was a far better soldier than he was a clerk. Back home in Market Drayton in Shropshire he had once formed a gang and tried to run an extortion racket against local shopkeepers. His bravado was breathtaking. He did not seem to hold his own life in much regard and that, combined with his natural cunning, made him a formidable enemy.

Captain Clive, as he had become since enlisting, captured Arcot with a small force of 200 British troops and 300 natives recruited as regular soldiers – or sepoys. Having scattered the small garrison, he pursued them to their camp in the night and killed a large number. He then set about protecting his prize – a run-down little fort with few defences. For fifty-three days, from 23rd September to 14th November, he held out as the enemy reinforced and grew larger. This is what he had planned: he knew that the enemy ranks were being swelled from forces in other parts of the region and that once depleted the other British troops in the area would find them easier to defeat. In the last round of the fighting he was down to 120 soldiers and 200 sepoys. The enemy had a force of about 10,000 including armed soldiers mounted on elephants. Razah Sahib, the commander of the attacking forces, told Clive that if he did not surrender he would kill every man in the garrison. Clive declined his offer. Razah Sahib then sent his elephant cavalry into battle. The animals had iron plates fastened to their foreheads so they could push down the gates of the fort, but when Clive's men fired their muskets at them, they stampeded and crushed their own men. After several attempts to break through, the Indian forces finally withdrew and Clive won the day. He had turned round the fortunes of the British and put them in a position where they could win their war.

Clive's bravado was breathtaking. He did not seem to hold his own life in much regard and that, combined with his natural cunning, made him a formidable enemy.

Dupleix was recalled to France where he died in disgrace. Clive came back to England as a celebrated soldier, but in 1755 he was back in India, this time as a lieutenant-colonel and the deputy governor of Fort St David, a hundred miles south of Madras. It was here he would hear the news of the so-called 'Black Hole of Calcutta'.

The Black Hole of Calcutta is the stuff of legends. In June 1756, the new Nawab of Bengal, Siraj-ud-Daula, had launched an attack on Fort William in Calcutta. The small British and European contingent, many of whom were civilians, surrendered. According to an unsubstantiated account by one of the survivors, John Holwell, the Nawab locked 146 of them, including one woman, in a cell 14 by 18 feet wide. They were so tightly packed together that it was impossible to move. Some quickly became delirious and some were trampled on. Others – 123 in all – died from heat stroke or suffocation. The story that Holwell told caused outrage in England. Clive was despatched to retake Calcutta, which he did, and then settled down to the business of getting the Nawab to make reparations for the plunder he had taken.

On 23rd June 1757, Clive and his army of 2,800 men – 800 Europeans and 2,000 sepoys – faced the might of Siraj-ud-Daula's force of 50,000 men at a small village called Plassey, which stood in a mango grove on the east bank of the Bhagirathi in West Bengal. Clive positioned his small force behind some mud banks and waited for the Nawab to attack. He began with a huge bombard-ment, but the East India Company troops were well protected and the artillery fire had little more effect than to use up most of the enemy's ammunition. In fact, the outcome of the battle was virtually decided before it even began. Clive had done a deal with the Nawab's principal general and rival for his throne, Mir Jafir, who had agreed to desert his leader. For the first part of the battle Mir Jafir did nothing, but eventually he led his troops away, leaving Siraj-ud-Daula to fight alone and Clive to win the day easily. It was a very small encounter but its results were immense. Bengal, a country three times larger than the United Kingdom, had fallen into British hands and Clive, thanks to his secret deal, was rewarded by Mir Jafir, who had got the throne he wanted, to the tune of more than £200,000 – a colossal sum in those days.

It is easy at this distance to be less than complimentary about Clive. Nobody could claim he was an easy man, and he seems to have had violent mood swings, possibly because of an opium habit. But no one can deny that he was brave. Yes, he had reason to believe that Siraj-ud-Daula would be deserted by his troops – but he cannot have been sure. He stood his ground, as he had done previously, before an army that outnumbered his by tens of thousands and won a victory that would eventually make his countrymen the masters of India. Historians are divided about him. Simon Schama has called him 'the hooligan of Market Drayton'. Lord Macaulay, who lived in an age when such exploits were more easily forgiven, felt that: 'Clive committed great faults ... But his faults, when weighed against his merits, and viewed in connection with his temptations, do not appear to us to deprive him of his right to an honourable place in the estimation of posterity.'

Clive believed that Bengal should be governed by the Crown and tried to persuade the Secretary of State, William Pitt the Elder, to achieve this. But Pitt would have none of it. Taking the country away from the East India Company, which in effect now owned it, was, he felt, the wrong thing to do. Clive himself, on his third tour of duty in India, did much to try and bring good governance to the territories that he had delivered to his country. He established local nawabs in their positions and made sure they were supported by Company troops; he stopped private trading among the Company's officials; he improved the pay and conditions of officers, and he set up a fund to help retired servants of the Company. In many ways he was like Cecil Rhodes in southern Africa 120 years later. He was an entrepreneur as well as a soldier, a man with his own agenda and the force of will to drive it through. His vision of an India that would provide endless profit to Britain if only the British got hold of it and governed it properly was one that came to be shared by many of his countrymen in the century that followed. But at the time many of them did not like it. They were jealous of his conspicuous wealth: they thought him just another nawab like the rest of them. Nevertheless the British government realised something had to be done. In 1773 Parliament passed the Regulating Act, which reorganised the Court of Directors of the East India Company and provided for the appointment of a royal governor-general to supervise Madras and Bombay. The foundations of the Raj had been laid.

Two years after Plassey, on the other side of the world, another brave Englishman, General James Wolfe, captured Quebec from the French, giving Britain the mastery of Canada as well. Britannia not only ruled the waves: she ruled an awful lot of land as well. But not all the people who lived in these newly conquered territories were happy. In 1773 some of the citizens of Boston, determined to maintain a boycott against imported British tea, threw a cargo of it into the harbour. Lord North, the British Prime Minister, decided that Clive was just the man to send to America to sort out these rebellious colonials, as he had the disobedient Indians. But Clive was dead. Lowered by criticism of his activities, subject always to depression and, possibly, a certain self-loathing, he had finally succeeded in doing what he had first attempted when living out in India, and committed suicide. His countrymen would have to find another hero to carry out their colonial ambitions in America. They would not find one.

Ten Men of Empire

Sir Francis Drake (1540?–1596)

The Elizabethan explorer and sailor is best known for his circumnavigation of the globe and leadership in the fight against the Spanish Armada. He was also a pirate – something that troubled his Victorian admirers; here is a defence from one of the best of them, James Anthony Froude:

We English have been contented to allow Drake a certain qualified praise. We admit that he was a bold, dexterous sailor, that he did his country good service at the Invasion. We allow that he was a famous navigator, and sailed round the world, which no one else had done before him. But – there is always a but – of course he was a robber and a corsair, and the only excuse for him is that he was no worse than most of his contemporaries.

(James Anthony Froude, *English Seamen in the Sixteenth Century, Lectures Delivered at Oxford Easter Terms 1893–1894*)

Sir Walter Raleigh (1554?–1618)

Explorer, writer, poet and favourite of Elizabeth I, Raleigh was involved in early attempts at English settlement in America, including the first failed British colony on Roanoke Island. He also travelled twice to South America in search of 'El Dorado'. He was executed by James I on the charge of treason.

He hath been a star at which the world has gazed; but stars may fall …

(Attorney General Sir Edward Coke at Raleigh's execution)

William Bradford (1590–1657)

One of the group of separatist Puritan pilgrims who travelled to America on the *Mayflower*, Bradford became the official leader of the Plymouth Colony during its first, difficult years. His writings ensured that later generations would never forget the story of the Pilgrim Fathers.

Here was Mr Bradford, in the Year 1621 unanimously chosen the Governour of the Plantation: The Difficulties whereof were such, that if he had not been a

Person of more than Ordinary Piety, Wisdom and Courage, he must have sunk under them.

(Cotton Mather, in his 1702 *Magnalia Christi Americana*, a book on the ecclesiastical history of New England)

Robert Clive (1725–1774)

An East India Companyman and military commander whose actions helped establish the British Raj in India. A cunning and ruthless tactician, as well as a highly talented leader of men, he led the British to victory at the Battle of Plassey in 1757. He committed suicide after being investigated for suspected corruption.

Clive, like most men who are born with strong passions and tried by strong temptations, committed great faults. But every person who takes a fair and enlightened view of his whole career must admit that our island, so fertile in heroes and statesmen, has scarcely produced a man more truly great either in arms or in council.

(Thomas Babington Macaulay, essay, the *Edinburgh Review*, 1840)

Major-General James Wolfe (1727–1759)

A British general who successfully secured Canada for the British. He defeated the French at Louisburg in 1758, and the following year took Quebec in a brilliantly planned assault. He was killed in the battle.

In days of yore, from Britain's shore,
Wolfe, the dauntless hero came,
And planted firm Britannia's flag,
On Canada's fair domain.
Here may it wave, our boast, our pride,
And joined in love together,
The thistle, shamrock, rose entwine
The Maple Leaf forever!

(Canadian song 'The Maple Leaf Forever', 1867, Alexander Muir)

Captain James Cook (1728–1779)

An explorer, navigator and cartographer who led three historic expeditions across the Pacific. In his first, on HMS *Endeavour*, he became the first European to sail the length of Australia's eastern coast. He claimed New South Wales for Britain, but was frustrated in his attempts to find the elusive north-west passage. On his last voyage, aboard HMS *Resolution*, he was killed by Hawaiian islanders, during a disagreement over the theft of a boat.

His great Qualities I admired beyond anything I can express – I gloried in him – and my Heart bleeds to this Day whenever I think of his Fate.

> (David Samwell, surgeon on HMS *Discovery*, which sailed with Cook on his last voyage)

Charles Cornwallis, 1st Marquess Cornwallis (1738–1805)

Commander of British troops in the American War of Independence whose surrender to a combined army of French and American soldiers at Yorktown in 1781 ended the war. He subsequently became Governor-General of India, but it is mainly for his role in the American Revolution that he is remembered.

… [his career was] devoted to cleaning up the messes made by the British Empire.

> (Simon Schama, *A History of Britain*, 2002)

David Livingstone (1813–1873)

Scottish missionary and explorer, whose travels did much to increase European knowledge of Africa. He was also fervently opposed to slavery and hoped that by discovering trade routes through Africa he might help eradicate it. He was the first European to travel from one coast of Africa to the other.

… the quintessential hero of the age, sprung from humble origins, blazing a trail for British civilization in what was manifestly the least hospitable of all the world's continents … Livingstone had become a one-man NGO – the nineteenth century's first médecin sans frontières.

> (Niall Ferguson, *Empire*, 2003)

Edward John Eyre (1815–1901)

Vicar's son who emigrated to Australia, where he became a farmer and explorer. In an epic journey which took over a year, from 1840 to 1841, he became the first man to travel across the desert from Adelaide to West Australia. After rising to the position of magistrate and protector of the Aborigines on the Murray River, he joined the British colonial service, serving in New Zealand and the Caribbean. Eyre was recalled to Britain after he brutally suppressed a rebellion and had a black political opponent hanged while he was Governor of Jamaica. Several distinguished people called for his trial on a charge of murder, but he retired to Devon where he died at the age of eighty-six.

I believe ... that Mr. Eyre has either been guilty of, or has tolerated under his authority, crimes of violence and cruelty which no man of even ordinarily tender conscience or good heart could be capable of.

(John Stuart Mill in a letter to a constituent, 1868)

Cecil Rhodes (1853–1902)

Politician, businessman and founder of the De Beers diamond company, which dominated South African diamond production, Cecil Rhodes was an avowed supporter of a British African empire. He set up the British South Africa Company in 1889 in the hope that it could become a commercial colonising force like the East India Company. The land he colonised, Rhodesia, was named after him: he was a brutally successful one-man band. The following description of him by Mark Twain sums him up very well:

He has done everything he could think of to pull himself down to the ground; he has done more than enough to pull sixteen common-run great men down; yet there he stands, to this day, upon his dizzy summit under the dome of the sky, an apparent permanency, the marvel of the time, the mystery of the age, an Archangel with wings to half the world, Satan with a tail to the other half.

(Mark Twain, *Following the Equator*, 1897)

CHAPTER 5

The Surrender of the British Army at Yorktown, Virginia 1781

On 19th October 1781 the British army under Lord Cornwallis surrendered to the combined American and French forces commanded by George Washington. Britain had lost its American colonies forever.

'We hold,' states the Declaration of Independence, 'these truths to be self-evident, that all men are created equal, that they are endowed by their Creator with certain inalienable Rights, that among these are Life, Liberty and the pursuit of Happiness.' When people in eighteenth-century Britain read those words they should surely have realised they were facing resistance on a scale they had not witnessed before. 'Self-evident' equality – in other words beyond proof, requiring no further explanation; 'inalienable Rights' – in other words unbreakable, never to be removed. These words alone should have been enough to tell the British that their attempt to subvert the colonies to British parliamentary rule was bound to end in failure. For Britain at the time, its thirteen American colonies were simply a source of supply – a trading opportunity to support British interests wherever they might lie. For America, the colonies were emerging states, creating a new world independent of the attitudes and behaviour of the Europe its inhabitants had left behind more than a century ago. So when the British government tried to tax them they felt huge resentment. But nothing created opposition as much as the declaration which confirmed parliamentary authority over its American possessions. Here was the heart of the matter: this was a battle about who was in charge.

Parliament and the King, George III, had been warned. William Pitt the Elder, Earl of Chatham, had told Parliament in 1775: 'The spirit which now resists your taxation in America is the same spirit … which called all England on its legs and by the Bill of Rights vindicated the English constitution … This glorious spirit of Whiggism animates three millions in America who prefer poverty with liberty to gilded chains with sordid affluence; and who will die in defence of their rights as freemen.' In this great oratorical condemnation of the government's policy he echoed another famous Member of Parliament of the time, Edmund Burke, who had argued a year earlier that the government's attempt to tax the colonies would end in failure. 'Do not burden them with taxes,' he said; '… you will teach them by these means to call … sovereignty itself in question … If that sovereignty and their freedom cannot be reconciled, which will they take? They will cast your sovereignty in your face. Nobody will be argued into slavery.' William Pitt and Edmund Burke were the voices of opposition. Power in Britain at this point in time belonged to rather different men.

In 1760, Lord George Sackville was court-martialled for his behaviour at the Battle of Minden during the Seven Years' War – a war in which Britain and its allies fought against France for the control of Europe and European possessions overseas. Sackville had refused an order to conduct a cavalry charge and as a result the British victory over the French had been less than complete. The court found him guilty. In its verdict it stated that he was 'unfit to serve his Majesty in any military capacity whatsoever'. Fifteen years later, however, as Lord Germain, he became Secretary of State for the American Colonies and was put in charge of directing the strategy of one of the most important wars the British would ever fight. History has not been kind in its judgement of 'Lord George', but his actions and behaviour did little to earn its better opinion. With bad maps and bad ideas he tried to direct a war in a country he had never seen and did not know against a people he arrogantly despised and completely underestimated. He was a member of a British government that thought, as it has in our own time, that an overseas war against a less well-developed country could be prosecuted with ease. Such wars are not as easy as they might first seem. Unexpected difficulties led to isolation and defeat.

The American colonists and their British masters had not seen eye to eye for a long time before the American War of Independence began. In 1675 – exactly a century before – a man called Nathaniel Bacon had led a revolt against the Royal Governor of Virginia, Sir William Berkeley, but his rebellion was soon quashed by a powerful force of British soldiers. An army of redcoats was permanently stationed in the colonies acting, in effect, as a sort of police force to carry out the orders of the British government and its representatives. Inevitably this standing army came to be resented by many colonists whose ancestors had arrived in America to escape such coercion and control. This friction was exacerbated by the miserable failure of the attempt to conquer Canada between 1709 and 1711. Some New England colonists – though not the Quakers of Pennsylvania who always abhorred any form of warfare – thought that capturing Canada and removing the French privateers who interfered with their trade would be a good idea and sought the help of Britain in the enterprise. Eventually a British expeditionary force arrived in Boston but found when it got there that the Americans were by no means of one mind about the plan. Many had no interest in supporting the British in a military enterprise and the expedition was plagued by desertion and a refusal to furnish it with proper supplies. The invasion force finally set off, got lost in the St Lawrence seaway and was forced to cancel the entire operation. The British blamed the colonists. One colonel, writing to the Secretary of State in London, criticised the 'ill nature and sowerness of these people', whom, he believed, 'will grow every day more stiff and disobedient'.

His prediction was accurate. By the end of the Seven Years' War in 1763, Britain's finances were thoroughly drained. The war had been fought on a global scale: it has been described as the first 'world war' in history. The British had emerged victorious, but the cost had been immense. One particular success had been in Canada where, thanks to General Wolfe's brilliant action at Quebec, the French had lost all their territory, thus securing the safety of Britain's colonies to the south. The British government, which felt that the colonists had not fully played their part in this success, demanded that they should now help pay for it, and decided to impose new taxes.

The sombre warnings of Pitt and Burke fell on deaf ears. The King, George III, the Prime Minister, Lord North, and the Secretary for the American Colonies, Lord Germain, refused to back down and the situation drifted into war. They had no generals of the temper of Robert Clive, whose audacity in India had won them such prizes, although in Charles Cornwallis they had a steady soldier who understood honour and service. He had been opposed to the plan to tax the American colonies, but when his country demanded that he go and fight for the British right to do so, he saw it as his duty to obey. He served under both Sir William Howe and Sir Henry Clinton, the two generals in charge of the British offensive, and was then given command of the southern campaign where the war was concentrated during its latter half.

By 1781, after six years of fighting, both sides in the war were tiring. There had been victories and defeats on both sides, but final success eluded both. The early part of the war had been concentrated in the north: Howe captured Philadelphia in 1777, but the British were forced to surrender at Saratoga in New England the same year. This British defeat encouraged the French to join in on the colonists' side: they had been looking for an excuse to take revenge on the British ever since their defeat in the Seven Years' War fourteen years earlier. The intervention of the French was crucial: not only could they provide much needed infantry support on land, they were also able to attack the British at sea. George Washington, who had become Commander-in-Chief of the American armed forces, in 1775, knew that the Royal Navy's superiority at sea put his enemy at a distinct advantage. Because they controlled American ports, the British could prevent supplies reaching the colonists and were also better able to reinforce their own armies. Washington's strategy had been to create a specially trained army – the 'Continental Army' – to do battle with the redcoats on their own terms; but even with this improved force he was unable to secure outright victory. In 1781, three years after France had entered the war, their intervention finally gave him what he wanted.

The British under Sir Henry Clinton had won one of the biggest victories of the war at Charleston, Virginia in 1780 and Cornwallis had followed this up by defeating the American forces at Camden in South Carolina. The British now believed that they could finally take control of the south, but their task proved far bigger than they realised. Cornwallis won another battle at Guilford Courthouse, in North Carolina, but his army was by this time depleted and his most able – and ruthless – officer, Banastre Tarleton, had suffered a defeat in the Battle of Cowpens. Cornwallis led his tired and reduced army into Virginia where he was under orders to protect British naval shipping. He dug in at Yorktown hoping to be reinforced by troops brought in by sea by the Royal Navy. Unfortunately for him, it was the French who turned up first.

The French admiral, the Comte de Grasse, in command of a fleet in the West Indies, made a daring attack on Chesapeake Bay off Yorktown in 1781. Although he was challenged by the Royal Navy, he still had control of the approach to the town when George Washington heard of his arrival. This was the crucial turning point in the whole war. Washington was camped outside New York at a place called Dobbs Ferry on the Hudson River, trying to work out how to attack Sir Henry Clinton and the British army which had control of the town. He had been joined by the French General, Jean-Baptiste Rochambeau. Suddenly Washington switched plans. Instead of staying and continuing to try to winkle Clinton out of New York he decided to take his armies south – to Virginia and Yorktown. He had to make sure that Clinton did not get wind of his plans in case he sent reinforcements to the beleaguered Cornwallis. On 19th August 1781 he and his French allies began the 600-mile march south. The route that the armies took has become one of the most famous in America, running from New York through New Jersey, Pennsylvania, Delaware and Maryland to Virginia.

Cornwallis in Yorktown was in a hopeless position. At his back lay the sea and the French fleet. In front of him was a large combined army that was, he knew, more than a match for his battered band of soldiers. Clinton sent no reinforcements. He remained convinced until it was far too late that Washington's plan was to attack him in New York. On 19th October, two months after the French and Americans had left their camp by the Hudson, Cornwallis realised that he had no option but to capitulate and the British army surrendered. On hearing the news, the British Prime Minister, Lord North, exclaimed: 'Oh my God! It's all over.' It was. America was lost.

The American War of Independence was always going to be a difficult one for Britain to win, as its opponents had pointed out even before it had begun. British military might was undoubtedly superior, but directing a war against a determined and sophisticated enemy 3,000 miles away proved an impossibly difficult task. Although Washington and his generals suffered defeats as well as winning victories, they triumphed in the war because they stayed in the field, always ready to face an enemy which eventually ran out of energy and resources.

Britain absorbed its defeat at the hands of the American colonists with resignation. Five years after Yorktown, a comedy called *The Heiress* opened in London to wild acclaim. Its plot involving legal chicanery, forged wills and incriminating documents was delightfully amusing, while the characters of two snobs, Mr and Mrs Blandish, were said to be expertly drawn. All London laughed – but not, as far as we know, with a trace of irony, despite the fact that the author of this entertaining piece was John Burgoyne who, in 1777, at the head of 7,000 British troops had been the general who had surrendered to the Americans at Saratoga. In the same year as Burgoyne was enjoying success as the darling of the London theatre, a new Governor-General arrived in Bengal. He too had served in America, and he too had tasted defeat – the bitterest taste of all, in fact, for the new Lord of India was none other than Charles Cornwallis who had made that final surrender to Washington at Yorktown.

Just as the disgraced Lord Germain had managed to rehabilitate himself sufficiently to become the political director of the war's strategy, so John Burgoyne was allowed to return to captivate London society with his witty drama. Cornwallis, too, had been forgiven. To be fair he had always been unconvinced by the war's objectives but had slogged it out as a faithful servant of his country. It was Britain's new Prime Minister, William Pitt, son of the great Earl of Chatham who had asked Lord Cornwallis to come to India and take charge of the country. Cornwallis had some misgivings: would this be another poisoned chalice? Ringing in his ears, perhaps, was the oratory of Edmund Burke who had told the House of Commons that: 'Were we to be driven out of India this day's end nothing would remain, to tell that it had been possessed, during the inglorious period of our dominion, by anything better than the ourang-ourang or the tiger.' In other words, India looked set to go the same way as America. Something had to be done. That something was to send out a soldier, someone who had experience of command, and someone who could rule. While the East India Company would remain at the heart of British interests in India for another fifty years or more, the emphasis was beginning to change. The final great phase of the British Empire was about to begin, heralded by military fanfares rather than profitable trading monopolies.

The British lost America because they lost touch with their own natural beliefs in liberty and toleration. In preserving what was left of their overseas dominions they would try to rediscover these, underpinned always by their strengths as a great military power. They had learned the lessons of Yorktown and everything that led up to it. They would try to be liberal but they would always shrink from showing weakness. No further territories would slip from their grasp: the British Empire would be British and would bring British values to the world.

CHAPTER 6

The Abolition of Slavery
1833

Although the slave trade in the British Empire had been formally abolished by the Act of 1807, existing slave ownership was allowed to continue. In 1833, Parliament passed an act that liberated all slaves throughout the Empire, finally destroying a practice that had been at the heart of its economic success for more than two hundred years.

Slavery is a disgusting business. To uproot human beings from their homelands and ship them to plantations thousands of miles away, forcing them to work long hours, depriving them of all basic liberties, and treating them repressively in order to instil obedience, might seem unfathomable to us today. Yet for more than two hundred years that is exactly what British and other European traders did. The majority of their countrymen, regarding it as perfectly acceptable, turned a blind eye. As early as the Elizabethan age the British sailor, Sir John Hawkins, had made big money shipping slave cargoes from West Africa to Spanish settlers in the Caribbean. He was regarded as something of a hero by his contemporaries – not least because he successfully created trading links with the Spanish colonies even though their masters in Madrid strongly disapproved of their relationship with an enemy. Discovery took sailors further afield. Sugar from the West Indies and tobacco from America became staple fare for Europeans. As the plantations grew so did the requirement for cheap labour to keep them going. British ships carried 3 million Africans as slaves between the end of the seventeenth century and the year of formal abolition in 1807. Slaves poured into the colonies bought with bartered goods – guns, cloth and booze – from tribal chiefs and native traders. Always violent, inevitably corrupt, the trade prospered while gentlemen in England puffed their pipes or added another teaspoon of sugar to their tea or coffee.

First had come trade, then control, then conscience. Britain's management of its empire went through each of these phases in turn. To begin with it simply wanted to trade – granting licences to companies to form enterprises abroad from which the mother country would profit. As competition for these international opportunities grew, the British government decided to protect its overseas operations with force. It failed in America, but continued to maintain its hold in India and most of its other territories. Finally, realising that it was master of a huge part of the world, Britain decided that the principles by which its foreign possessions would be governed would, as far as possible, be good British ones. Nothing demonstrates this better than the abolition of slavery: as the British Empire made its few last steps towards global supremacy, authority and conscience hugged each other in an awkward embrace.

As the British Empire made its few last steps towards global supremacy, authority and conscience hugged each other in an awkward embrace.

A British Prime Minister, talking about the activities of British forces in the West African country of Sierra Leone, said: 'From the day of their arrival ... [they] have helped to bring ... hope to a people who have suffered terribly ...'. The troops had demonstrated, he went on, that 'the rest of the world would not abandon [the people of Sierra Leone] to their fate', adding that the soldiers had acted as they had because of Britain's 'historic responsibilities'. These fine words came not from some nineteenth-century politician surveying Britain's colonial splendour, but from Tony Blair in the year 2000. He had ordered a British force to go into Sierra Leone to protect the people from violent rebels who were threatening to overthrow the democratically elected government. The operation was a success. The rebels were defeated and law and order were restored. Most people in Sierra Leone were grateful for the British intervention. Many would have liked them to stay. Some went as far as to call Tony Blair their 'saviour'. Britain's 'historic responsibilities' had been met. What Tony Blair did not say is that those responsibilities are directly related to slavery and the slave trade.

The capital of Sierra Leone, Freetown, was in fact established by an anti-slavery campaigner called Granville Sharp in 1787 as a place for housing emancipated slaves. He bought land from a local African chief and shipped 400 British and American freed slaves to West Africa to start a new life there. The little settlement struggled to survive, but eventually grew into a sizeable community. In 1794, Zachary Macaulay, father of the Victorian historian, became its governor: his experiences in Freetown provided him with the information and ideas to become one of the most effective campaigners for the abolition of slavery.

While eighteenth-century British merchants set about trying to enslave the population of Africa, their countrymen at home were intent on pursuing greater freedoms for themselves. The period of European history that saw the development of ideas about freedom and individual liberty – from the British Bill of Rights of 1689 to the ideas of the American Declaration of Independence and the French Revolution – coincided almost exactly with the growth of slavery. The force that exposed this contradiction was only partly based in intellectual ideas of liberty – after all, Thomas Jefferson, the principal author of the American Declaration of Independence, was also a slave owner. Much more important – and more effective – was Christianity.

In the early 1780s the MP for Hull, William Wilberforce, became an evangelical Christian. With his discovery of religion came a burning mission to improve human society. He became the parliamentary spokesman for a group known as the Clapham Sect – a collection of well-heeled, like-minded Christian radicals who were determined to see the world rid of the evil of slavery. Armed with Wilberforce's eloquence and Zachary Macaulay's grasp of detail they proved a formidable opposition to those who sought to preserve this lucrative trade. 'We are all guilty,' Wilberforce told the House of Commons in 1789; 'we ought all to plead guilty, and not to exculpate ourselves by throwing the blame on others.' And, he continued by explaining how his investigations into the slave trade had convinced him of its wickedness: 'A trade founded in iniquity ... must be abolished ... I from this time determined that I would not rest till I had effected its abolition.' Slowly but surely the rhetoric began to do its work. There were some who had doubted whether Wilberforce was up to the task, but now they changed their minds. James Boswell, the biographer of Samuel Johnson, remarked that he had seen a man whom he had thought a 'shrimp' become a 'whale'.

When they first came together at Holy Trinity Church on the north side of Clapham Common, the abolitionists decided to devise an emblem that would symbolise their mission. They designed the figure of a 'kneeling Negro', naked with his hands clasped, looking upwards in supplication. Above the image were written the words: 'Am I not a man and a brother?' Thanks to the fact that one of their supporters was the successful pottery manufacturer, Josiah Wedgwood, this figure was produced as a jasper ware cameo and became popular not only in Britain but also in America. The abolitionists knew the power of effective marketing. As Christians they wanted to spread the word of the Gospel. They founded the Church Missionary Society and the British and Foreign Bible Society, as well as societies for helping the poor and improving conditions in prison. When the charter of the East India Company came up for renewal in 1793, Wilberforce argued unsuccessfully for a clause to be inserted saying that part of its responsibility was to introduce 'Christian light into India'. The abolitionists believed fervently that slavery was inhumane and immoral but equally fervently they wanted to see African souls delivered into the brotherhood of their church, united in worship of the Lord. They enjoyed some unusual allies in the pursuit of this campaign – among them John Newton, a former slave ship owner who converted to Christianity, became a priest and wrote the words to the hymn 'Amazing Grace'. Another campaigner was a former black African slave called Olaudah Equiano who bought his freedom, became a successful writer and journalist in London and married an Englishwoman. Equiano was a devout Christian, relentless in his pursuit of pro-slavery supporters. 'Remember,' he warned one, 'the God who has said, vengeance is mine and I will repay ...'.

When vested interests are attacked they produce fierce arguments to defend themselves. So it proved with slavery. Many slave owners presented themselves as having the same principles and values as those who criticised them. They were, they claimed, industrious and loyal British citizens providing a commercial service to the nation. They were not despotic or cruel: rather, as one writer called them, they were 'humane and indulgent' masters. Furthermore, slavery was positively beneficial for those who were enslaved because they were protected by their benevolent owners. When these arguments failed to convince, the slave owners argued for evolution rather than radical reform – always a good tactic for those who believe that through delay you can prevent change. They appeared to believe in its abolition just as their opponents did: it was only in the method and timing by which this should happen that they differed. All this, of course, was nonsense. The slave owners had no intention of giving up their profitable business. The fight to destroy it would be long and hard.

Fine ideas of individual liberty were not in themselves enough to rid the world of the evils of slavery. Philosophy was not on its own tough enough. It needed the fire and brimstone of the radical evangelical and the moral passion that went with it, to drive the practice away. Today, in a more secular age, we may feel that some of the attitudes of those in the anti-slavery movement were rather condescending: they wanted to convert slaves and make them part of their own Christian civilisation. The young Thomas Macaulay, son of old Zachary – practising the eloquence that would one day make him a household name – said at an anti-slavery meeting: 'The peasant of the Antilles will no longer crawl in listless and trembling dejection round a plantation ... but when his cheerful and voluntary labour is performed he will return with the firm step and erect brow of a British citizen from the field which is his freehold to the cottage which is his castle.' Freedom would make slaves British citizens – and good Christian ones at that. Lordly rhetoric and religious zeal were the powerful and effective weapons of the day. And they achieved their purpose.

When the final bill for emancipation came before the House of Commons the Colonial Secretary, Edward Stanley, remarked that the slave owners had done nothing that could be called a step 'towards the ultimate extinction of the system'. The fight against slavery had indeed proved a long one. William Wilberforce had made his first parliamentary speech on the subject eighteen years before the slave trade was finally abolished. It would be another twenty-six years before all British owned slaves were set free. Wilberforce heard the news three days before he died in 1833. By then he had led the battle against slavery for nearly half a century.

There are memorials to William Wilberforce and both Macaulays in Westminster Abbey. The one to Wilberforce reads: 'His name will ever be specially identified with those exertions which, by the blessing of God, removed from England the guilt of the African slave trade and prepared the way for the abolition of slavery in every corner of the Empire.' Below the one to Zachary Macaulay is a medallion with the kneeling figure of a slave in supplication asking: 'Am I not a man and a brother?'

CHAPTER 7

The Afghanistan Massacre
1842

In 1842 a combined force of 4,500 British and Indian
troops, with 12,000 camp followers, were killed by local
tribesmen in the cold wastes of Afghanistan. The massacre
destroyed the idea of British imperial invincibility.

Landlocked in the mountainous heart of central Asia, Afghanistan
is inhospitable, lawless and strange. It is a European graveyard. In
recent times the might of the Soviet Union was defeated by the
difficulties of managing a war in the region. Russian forces invaded
on Christmas Day 1979, but were forced to withdraw eight years
later with nothing to show for their occupation other than deaths,
casualties and humiliation. It was a futile war, which contributed
to the collapse of the Soviet Union in 1991. Today, around 7,000
British troops are stationed in the country to help protect the
development of the democratically elected government. When they
went there in 2001, the British Secretary of State for Defence said
they would not be needed for more than a few years: seven years
later many people, including army commanders on the ground,
believe that a British presence might be needed for twenty-five or
even thirty more.

In 1842, as the British Raj took an increasingly stronger hold
over the whole of India, its imperial experience in Afghanistan
demonstrated that colonial supremacy could never last forever.

> *When you're wounded an' left on Afghanistan's plains,*
> *And the women come out to cut up your remains,*
> *Just roll to your rifle an' blow out your brains*
> *An' go to your Gawd like a soldier.*

So wrote Rudyard Kipling, balladeer of the Raj and a writer skilled in capturing both the excitement and complexity of the British experience in India. In his novel *Kim*, Kipling portrayed what he called the 'Great Game' – the power struggle between Britain and Russia for the control of the area on the North-West Frontier of the Indian sub-continent, where Asia begins its long climb into Eastern Europe. Kipling was writing at the end of the nineteenth century, but his evocation of the conflict between Russian and British interests was as relevant then as it would have been sixty years earlier when Britain began the First Afghan War.

In 1838 the Governor-General of India, Lord Auckland, issued a proclamation in which he declared that India had to have a friendly ally on its North-West Frontier. The country could not be safe, he argued, unless this border was secure. In order to implement his policy, he announced that Britain would support an army to return the deposed king, Shah Shujah, to his throne in the capital, Kabul. Once he had been installed safely the troops would leave. They were needed in the first place, said Auckland, to protect the new king's government from 'foreign interference and factious opposition'. The language may be somewhat arcane, and the enemy may be different, but the message is surprisingly similar to that which is used to justify the intervention of British troops in Afghanistan today. Shah Shujah had ruled Afghanistan nearly thirty years previously and had formed an alliance with Britain before he was overthrown. He proposed to reinstate this arrangement in return for getting his kingdom back. An imperial force of about 20,000 men was assembled, together with a further 38,000 servants and supporters. British officers did not travel light in those days: each was entitled to twelve servants. In addition to the army commander, a political officer called William Macnaghten was sent along too. The invasion went well. The army crossed into Afghanistan in March 1839, captured the town of Kandahar and by August had reached Kabul. Shah Shujah was reappointed as emir; William Macnaghten became the British envoy and the new arrivals began to make themselves at home.

Back in Britain, the Duke of Wellington had warned that the expedition would mean a 'perennial march' into Afghanistan, but his warnings seemed unnecessarily pessimistic as colonial life in Kabul got under way. There was horse racing, gambling, cricket and polo. Bit by bit the settlers moved out of the fortified city and established themselves in a cantonment on the lower slopes outside. Behind the scenes, however, tensions were beginning to emerge. Shah Shujah was corrupt and incompetent and complained that the British interfered with his ability to run his country properly. Macnaghten was under pressure from headquarters in Delhi to cut costs and sent several contingents of troops home. His relationship with the military was not good and deteriorated further when a new commander, William Elphinstone, arrived.

There can be few more disastrous appointments in British military history than that of William Elphinstone to the command of the army in Kabul in 1841. He was nearly sixty, ailing and indecisive. He had last seen action at the Battle of Waterloo, some twenty-six years earlier. He had not wanted to come to Afghanistan, but his friend, Lord Auckland, had persuaded him by telling him that Kabul's bracing air would suit his health better than the hot plains of India. Elphinstone arrived at a time when the garrison had been severely reduced and a large part of it stationed at Jalalabad, 85 miles away from the capital. It was also the point at which the tribesmen of Afghanistan, under Akbar Khan, had decided to remove the British and Shah Shujah from their midst.

In November one of the British political officers in Kabul was murdered. As the month wore on the British came under repeated attack from Afghan warriors. Elphinstone dithered and then despatched a small force of soldiers, getting them to form up in squares as they might have done on the field at Waterloo. To the horror of the British residents watching from their quarters, the party was cut to pieces. One of the most stirring accounts of the whole war comes from the journal kept by Florentia Sale, wife of the general commanding the British force in Jalalabad. She was known as 'the grenadier in petticoats' and she seems to have survived the disaster against all the odds. Wounded and then captured she was eventually saved by her husband. As the tribesmen closed in on Kabul she recorded that 'by keeping behind the chimneys, I escaped the bullets that continually whizzed past my ear'.

William Macnaghten lost patience with his military colleagues and a few days before Christmas decided to go and parley with Akbar Khan in person. Dressed in a frock coat and silk top hat, he marched out with his aides to meet the Afghan leader, and was promptly executed and mutilated, his dismembered body dragged round the streets of the city. Isolated and insecure, Elphinstone made an agreement with the Afghan leader. One major involved in the discussions complained he felt 'obligated to negotiate for a parcel of fools who were doing all they could to ensure their own destruction'.

On 6th January the entire garrison – civilian men, women and children as well as Elphinstone's full complement of troops – left the city in return for promises of safe conduct back to Jalalabad. They were required to surrender all their weapons – apart from three mountain guns and one horse artillery – and 130 personnel, mainly married officers and their families, who were to remain behind as hostages. It was the middle of winter. The snow was already thick on the ground. Elphinstone had been led into a terrible trap. From the moment the column left Kabul it was attacked. As its numbers were depleted, either killed by pursuing tribesmen or left wounded to die in the perishing cold, Akbar Khan demanded more hostages, including Elphinstone himself. Leaderless and abandoned, the British force staggered through the mountains to its destruction. The idea of crossing 'the stupendous pass, in the face of an armed tribe of bloodthirsty barbarians was frightful', wrote one soldier. Frightful and deadly. A week later, as they watched anxiously from their fortifications in Jalalabad, the British stationed there saw one man ride towards them. He and his horse were exhausted. It looked as if he might not make it the last few yards to the city walls. 'Where is the army?' they asked him.

'I am the army,' he replied. His name was William Brydon, an assistant surgeon, the only man apart from those few who had been taken prisoner out of a total company of 16,000 people to make it safely home.

The British took reprisals of course. An 'army of retribution' was despatched the same year and captured Kabul. Shah Shujah was assassinated by his Afghan enemies and Akbar Khan died, possibly poisoned by his father who succeeded him as emir. The political experiment was over. The British withdrew. It had demonstrated – catastrophically – that they could be defeated. Fifteen years after the Afghan disaster, the British army would face mutiny in its own ranks as the infantry and cavalry regiments of the Bengal Army rose against them. The Indian Mutiny of 1857 took place exactly a century after Robert Clive had won his famous victory at Plassey, an action which set Britain on the road to becoming masters of the Indian

'Where is the army?' they asked him. 'I am the army,' he replied.

sub-continent. At that time the principal governing force had been the East India Company – but the Afghan War and the Indian Mutiny demonstrated that the fiction of a country managed by a trading concern protected by British troops could not be maintained any longer. The Mutiny was suppressed. Parliament then abolished the East India Company and the British government itself took total control of the country.

A contemporary historian later remarked that Britain seemed 'as it were to have conquered and peopled half the world in a fit of absence of mind'. By that time, Queen Victoria had been proclaimed Empress of India and the British had begun expanding into Africa and the Far East. Absence of mind or not, British imperialism was proving remarkably successful. With the growth of this new imperialist outlook came a new view of Britain's role in the world, summed up in a phrase later used by Rudyard Kipling:

Take up the White Man's burden,
Send forth the best ye breed –
Go, bind your sons to exile
To serve your captives' need ...

The process by which Britain had become a great imperial power was beginning to coalesce into a sense of duty – a responsibility that a civilised country had to undertake in order to bring civilisation to other parts of the world. By challenging British power and reminding the British people that they were by no means all-powerful the Afghan tribesmen who massacred General Elphinstone's army helped set Britain on the road towards total imperial control. The 'Great Game' had several more rounds to go yet.

CHAPTER 8

The Discovery of the Victoria Falls by David Livingstone
1855

In 1855 the explorer David Livingstone became the first
European ever to see the Victoria Falls in Africa. This
and his other discoveries opened up central and eastern
Africa to colonisation in the second half of the
nineteenth century.

He had the energy of St Paul and the constitution of an ox. In an
age that produced many remarkable men he was, perhaps, one of
the most extraordinary. In the words of South Africa's most famous
soldier, Jan Smuts: 'He lifted the veil from Southern Africa, and
added more to the knowledge of her mysterious interior than
perhaps any other man has done.' David Livingstone – a man from
a poor, hard background in the cotton mills of Lanarkshire –
almost single-handedly brought Africa to Britain. His vision:
'civilisation, commerce and Christianity', epitomised the Victorian
view of imperial power, but he learned the hard way how these
linked together. While he started his life in Africa as a missionary,
he became an explorer when he realised that religion on its own
could not provide people with everything they needed.

Livingstone was born in Blantyre in Scotland. His father, a door-
to-door tea salesman, was a devout Christian and tried to persuade
his son to read nothing but theological works. The young
Livingstone earned his living at the local cotton mill, working ten
or twelve hours a day to help support his impoverished family.
He made enough money to be able to attend Anderson's College in
Glasgow, founded to bring education to the poor. Here he learned

science and technology and eventually received a qualification from the Royal Faculty of Physicians and Surgeons in Glasgow. He also became ordained as a minister. Self-taught, self-willed, uniquely convinced of his own driving energy, he applied to the London Missionary Society and was accepted subject to further training. 'My constitution,' he told them, is 'capable of enduring any ordinary share of hardship or fatigue.' His judgement of his own strengths would prove to be perfectly accurate.

In December 1840 he went to Africa – he had hoped for a posting in China but the outbreak of the first Opium War between the British and Chinese made such a journey unwise – and joined a mission station at Kuruman, the so-called 'oasis of the Kalahari desert'. He then travelled further north, first to a place called Mabotswa where he was mauled by a lion – he suffered from pain in his arm ever afterwards – and then to Kolobeng in what is now Botswana, where he established a mission station. Here he also became fluent in the local language, Tswana. The work was hard and the climate unforgiving. Persistent drought threatened the livelihoods of natives and missionaries alike. There was another, and in some ways for Livingstone, more troubling problem. The local people were reluctant to convert to Christianity. However much Livingstone tried to teach them simple subjects – his wife started an infants school at Kolobeng – however much he tried to persuade them of the 'glories of the Gospel', they were not willing to accept the new teachings of this well-meaning Scotsman in their midst. In coming to terms with this, Livingstone made one of his most important discoveries.

'In the early ages,' he said later in one of his speeches, 'the monasteries were the schools of Europe, and the monks were not ashamed to hold the plough.' He realised – unlike other Europeans toiling to convert non-Christians to the word of God – that religion on its own was not enough. He could see that in many respects Christianity represented a threat to tribal customs – particularly on issues such as polygamy. He knew Africa would only open its secrets if its people and their cultures were understood and their material needs met. Whenever he used his skills as a doctor he was met with warmth and openness: the Gospel on its own made poor provision for the improvement of African lives. 'My desire,' he said, 'is to open a path ... that civilisation, commerce and Christianity might find their way there.' He would not only convert Africa, he would 'civilise it', but to do that he had to find it first. He left the mission station at Kolobeng and struck off into the dark heart of the African continent.

Livingstone began exploring the Zambezi in 1851. At that point he still had his wife and children with him but, realising the dangers of disease, particularly malaria, he decided to send them home. By 1855, working on his own and travelling light – unlike other explorers of the time he did not try to bring the trappings of home life with him into the jungle – he had traced the upper course of the Zambezi to near its source, travelled back westwards across to the Congo basin, then through Angola until he reached the Atlantic coast of Africa. Completely exhausted and thoroughly emaciated he had recuperated for long enough to allow him to go back eastwards again. It was on this part of his journey, in the company of a group of natives from the Makolo tribe, who always acted as his helpers, that he made his most famous discovery.

The Victoria Falls are one of the natural wonders of the world. Their beauty and magnificence defy description. Only by standing in front of them yourself can you begin to realise what it must have been like to be the first European to see them. They come as something of a surprise. For a long way above them the Zambezi River flows across level, flat land. There are islands in its midst – but no mountains or deep gorges, nothing in fact to suggest what is going to happen to it next. Suddenly the whole wide river pours in a single drop into a chasm 400 feet wide and 360 feet deep. Where just a moment before hippopotamuses basked in the pleasant waters, observed by birds in the tall trees on the islands and the bank, a boiling torrent cascades over the edge. It is as if the river suddenly stops. The Falls are a natural weir – on a vast, astonishing scale.

In 1855 a group of natives offered to show Livingstone the 'smoke that thunders'. They led him down the wide Zambezi River in a canoe. He heard the 'thunder' and began to see the 'smoke' – columns of spray thrown up by falling water. Only 5 or 6 miles later did he see the falls themselves. 'No one,' he said, 'can imagine the beauty of the view from anything witnessed in England. It had never been seen before by European eyes; but scenes so lovely must have been gazed upon by angels in their flight.' Livingstone then got out of the canoe he was travelling in and climbed inside a smaller, lighter boat in which his native guides took him into the middle of where the water began its long fall into the depths below. It was November and the water was quite low. He was able to reach an island in the middle of the stream – something that would have been impossible at other times of the year when the height of the water would have swept him and his little craft over the edge. He recorded meticulously everything that he saw – his descriptions, measurements and soundings were always extremely accurate. It was, he said, 'the most wonderful sight I had witnessed in Africa ... Its whiteness gave the idea of snow, a sight I had not seen for many a day.'

The long arm of British imperialism had penetrated the heart of Africa.

He named the glorious torrent of water to which the natives led him the 'Victoria Falls', out of loyalty to his Queen. It was the only English name, he said, he had 'affixed to any part of the country'. He went back to England to an ecstatic public welcome. He had a private audience with Queen Victoria. His book – *Missionary Travels and Researches in South Africa* – was a bestseller. The long arm of British imperialism had penetrated the heart of Africa.

When Livingstone began his journeys of exploration, the interior of eastern and central Africa was quite unknown to Europeans. For the rest of his life he would attempt to change that, in particular fighting hard against what he regarded as the worst of its evils – the slave trade. 'By trading with Africa,' he had told his audiences at home, 'we should at length be independent of slave-labour, and thus discountenance practices so obnoxious to every Englishmen.' On his famous first expedition he had become the first man to travel across the continent from the Indian Ocean to the Atlantic. Following this success, the British government paid for him to return, but the organisation of an expedition on a large scale defeated him and his wife who, once again travelling with him, died of malaria. He had persuaded her to accompany him despite the concerns of friends and family. He was forced to return home. This second expedition had proved a disaster: public opinion turned against him. No trade, no converts, no civilisation: Livingstone's mission seemed an empty dream.

He refused to give up, and in 1866, a little over a year later, he was back. This perhaps was to be his most famous journey of all. The people of Britain heard nothing of him for six years. Then a newspaper decided to go and look for him. In November 1871, almost exactly sixteen years after Livingstone had made his breath-taking discovery of the 'smoke that thunders', the Welsh-born American journalist Henry Morton Stanley, on assignment from the *New York Herald*, tracked him down on the shores of Lake Tanganyika. He may have said: 'Dr Livingstone, I presume?' That's what he told his readers anyway. More importantly, he found a dying hero, a man who had given himself to Africa in the name of God and whom Africa would soon take back to itself. Livingstone told Stanley he would not give up his travelling. He was sick with malaria and dysentery and his mind was confused. Within two years, by May 1873, he was dead. His heart was buried under a tree where he died, and his body was carried a thousand miles by his faithful attendants and then returned to Britain for burial in Westminster Abbey – barely ten years after he had been so castigated by the press.

Stanley went on to become a highly successful explorer in his own right, but he used rather different methods. He was well equipped and well armed: he preferred guns to the Gospel. At the same time other Englishmen, excited by the prospect of the new continent that was opening up before them, finally joined the mission that he had so devotedly led. Their enthusiasm, too, came at a price. Stanley's exploits in the Congo were taken up by King Leopold of Belgium who paid him to try to conquer and annexe the territory for his country. The other great powers, Britain and also Germany – which had just emerged as a new empire with Bismarck as its Chancellor – became alarmed. A conference was convened in Berlin in 1884 – and here the powers of Europe solemnly divided Africa for themselves. They simply took the map and carved it up, deciding that each of them could exercise a 'sphere of influence' over its various sections. They signed a declaration prohibiting the slave trade and proclaimed that no country could just set up a colony where it felt like it. It had to have proper agreements from local chiefs. If all this sounds like some grisly board game with human beings and real territories as the counters, then that is not too far from the truth. This was the so-called 'scramble for Africa'. Throughout the rest of the nineteenth century, the powers of Europe would seek to conquer and control the land that David Livingstone had helped bring to their attention.

The colonisation of Africa is not a happy chapter in the history of Europe. David Livingstone was one of the first men to realise how difficult it would be to bring to the continent the ways of his native country. Though he never gave up hope that this could be achieved, he also sought to understand it and immersed himself in it in order to realise how this could be done. He failed, not least because he was a man alone. In his last days his wanderings in its unknown places were perhaps more for his own reasons than for a wider purpose, but he was, and remains to many, an inspiration. Statues and memorials to him in the parts of Africa he explored still stand proudly today – even though we live in an age when Africa does not look kindly on the activities of other white men who have involved themselves in its affairs. Christianity, commerce, civilisation: taken individually there does not seem to be a great deal wrong with any of those things. Taken together they brought the full force of European ambition to the continent that

Livingstone loved. His heart, buried under that tree near Lake Tanganyika, might feel a wrench of despair at how his mission was eventually pursued.

CHAPTER 9

The Partition of India
1947

In 1947 the British granted independence to the peoples
of the Indian sub-continent whom they had ruled in
one form or another for two centuries. Partition created
two new countries, India and Pakistan, and signalled
the end of the British Empire.

The British took over two hundred years to colonise and rule India.
They cut it up in just over two months. The idea of independence
for India was at the forefront of British politics for much of
the twentieth century. The idea of partition – dividing the sub-
continent between its Muslim and Hindu peoples – came at the last
minute, and was carried out with astonishing speed. The British
had created an empire in India that extended from Kashmir in the
north to Kanyakumari in the south; from Baluchistan in the west to
Assam in the east; from the wilds of the Hindu Kush to the great
cape where sunset and sunrise can be seen together; from the
wilderness of the Bolan Pass to the great Brahmaputra River. This
vast land, united under its colonial master and ruled by a small
corps of soldiers, civil servants and business or professional people
– in 1931 there was one British person to every 4,000 Indians –
could not be bequeathed to its successors in one piece. While the
British Raj reigned supreme, it dealt with India collectively. Once it
let in the idea of self-government, issues of difference – political,
racial and religious – became just as important as independence
itself and could no longer be contained when the moment of
separation from Britain arrived.

The idea that India would one day govern itself had occurred to
its British rulers almost as soon as their command of it began. In

INDIA UNDER BRITISH RULE

1800 ─┐

1818 British defeat the Marathas and become the effective rulers of India

1824 British begin conquest of Burma

1833 Death of Ram Mohan Roy (born 1772), father of modern Indian nationalism

1843 British conquer Sind

1850 ─ **1849** British conquer the Punjab
1853 First railway and telegraph lines in India
1857 Outbreak of the Indian Mutiny

1877 Queen Victoria proclaimed Empress of India

1885 Foundation of Indian National Congress

1900 ─

1920–2 Non-Cooperation Movement against the British

1935 Government of India Act; Indians gain provincial autonomy

1947 India partitioned; India and Pakistan independent
1950 ─┘

1818 the Governor-General, Lord Hastings, looked forward to 'a time not very remote ... when England will, on sound principles of policy, wish to relinquish the domination which she has ... unintentionally assumed over this country'. Nearly forty years later opinions had changed. The Indian Mutiny of 1857 had forced the British to realise that if they were not yet ready to grant independence to this most precious possession of theirs – and at that point in time they certainly were not – they had better grasp it more firmly. Immediately after the Mutiny, the Governor-General became 'Viceroy'. Nearly twenty years after that Queen Victoria became 'Empress of India'. The administration was strengthened: one Viceroy of India, Lord Mayo, told his staff to 'teach your subordinates that we are all British gentlemen engaged in the magnificent work of governing an inferior race'.

While the British paid lip service to the idea of Indian involvement in political affairs – they agreed to the foundation of the National Congress in 1885, which led eventually to the first government of the independent country – the reality was that this was a vassal state. When Lord Curzon became Viceroy in 1898, Britain was the most powerful nation on earth with imperial possessions that stretched across the globe. Curzon, the greatest political toff of his age, vowed that he would carry out a programme that 'would keep Britain in India for at least another hundred years'. In the event what he did had exactly the opposite effect. He decided to divide Bengal, creating a new province composed mainly of Muslims in the east. He did not consult public opinion and his actions, which were later reversed, created suspicion and resentment among the Indian population. The National Congress that had hitherto been an amenable sounding board for Indian opinion became stronger in its advocacy of self-rule.

At the end of the First World War, in 1919, the British seemed to take real steps towards granting India independence. It introduced eleven self-governing provinces and gave Indian ministers control over areas such as public health, education and agriculture. Many Indians wanted more. They had supported Britain throughout the war, they had suffered shortages, restrictions and rising prices. As protests broke out, the British government unwisely introduced measures that extended its wartime emergency powers – including giving judges the power to try political cases without juries. Agitation grew. In Amritsar in the Punjab, British banks were set ablaze and five Englishmen were killed. The local commander, Brigadier General Reginald Dyer, then carried out an act that was to stain the British record in India forever. He took the decision to break up a prohibited meeting. He marched fifty of his men into the Jallianwallah Garden where a crowd of unarmed men, women and children were gathered. His troops then opened fire on them, and kept firing for ten minutes: 379 people were killed and 1,200 wounded. The Amritsar Massacre was the blackest day for the British in the history of India since the army mutiny nearly sixty years before. From then on the movement for Indian independence would be unstoppable.

There are three great figures in the story of independence for India – Mohandas ('Mahatma') Gandhi, Jawaharlal Nehru and Muhammad Ali Jinnah. Between them these men led their people into the new countries that partition created. The greatest of all was Gandhi, the father of the Indian nation. He qualified as a lawyer in London and having failed to set up his own practice in India accepted a posting with an Indian company in South Africa. Appalled at the treatment of Indian immigrants by the South African government he led a twenty-year long campaign for their rights and won them many concessions before returning to India in 1915. Here he became leader of the Indian National Congress Party which gave him complete authority over its affairs in 1921 after he had successfully started his nationwide campaign of peaceful non-cooperation with the British authorities. His influence was drawn from his selflessness, his devotion to the cause of the Indian people, and his peaceful courage. The striking image of him dressed in a Hindu loincloth, the dress of the lowest caste, became a worldwide symbol of Indian nationhood. It could not be erased, even when he was imprisoned by the British authorities. In 1934 he handed over leadership of the Congress Party to Nehru, but he remained hugely influential in Indian affairs. His policy of non-violence, his simple way of life, his resolution, his energy and sheer humanity made him one of the most remarkable figures in the whole history of the twentieth century.

Nehru was hugely influenced by Gandhi. Educated at Harrow and Cambridge he abandoned Western dress once his political career in India began and led the Congress Party into socialism. He wanted to modernise India and favoured a programme of industrialisation, unlike Gandhi who saw the country developing through its love of the earth and its agrarian economy. Nehru failed to extract a promise from the British that they would grant independence to India in return for support during the Second World War. He therefore refused to support Britain's war aims and was imprisoned from 1942 to 1945. After the war he was the inevitable candidate to lead the country into independence and became India's first prime minister in 1947.

The third person, Jinnah – Pakistan's father of the nation – was, like Gandhi, a lawyer. He too qualified in London. He was not an observant Muslim and preferred to speak in English and wear Western dress throughout his life. He joined the Indian National Congress Party but gradually came to believe that the Muslim population needed their own separate state. In 1947 he became Governor-General of the new state of Pakistan but died from a combination of tuberculosis and lung cancer in 1948.

The move towards self-government in India gained pace dramatically once the Second World War was over. In Britain, Winston Churchill, no particular friend to Indian independence, had lost power and the new Labour administration was more inclined towards it. Britain, weakened by the war, knew that hanging on to India by force was simply not an option: public opinion would not have stood for it. In February 1947 Lord Mountbatten was sent to India as Viceroy with a promise from the British government that the country would receive full self-government by June of the following year. In fact, India was independent by

August. 'At the stroke of the midnight hour, when the world sleeps,' said Nehru in his famous speech, 'India will awake to life and freedom.' Britain was congratulated on its common sense and magnanimity in at last setting free its cherished imperial posses- sion. The post-war world, exhausted by conflict and anxious for peace, felt that the emergence of a great new democracy in Asia demonstrated the spirit of the age. Indeed it did. What people over- looked at the time was that something equally important – in terms of its subsequent effect on the world, more important perhaps – had also taken place. That was partition.

The idea of dividing the Indian sub-continent into two separate countries was not seriously adopted by any political party until 1940 when the Muslim League formally made it part of their programme. Even at that stage it seemed a rather unrealistic proposition and many Muslims appeared uninter- ested in it. Their position changed when in 1942 the British put for- ward constitutional proposals that made two separate nations a pos-

> 'At the stroke of the midnight hour, when the world sleeps, India will awake to life and freedom.' (Nehru)

sibility. From this moment on ultimate division was probably inevitable. The concept of Pakistan – in Urdu *pak* means pure and *stan* country or place of rest – became the driving force of Muslim independence. The religious and social differences between Hindu and Muslim would have been very difficult to accommodate in a single national entity. During the nineteenth century the Muslims had come to feel disenchanted. They no longer enjoyed the power they had had under the Mogul emperors whose supremacy had been destroyed by the British and the Hindus. They formed the Muslim League in 1906 in order to help secure positions in govern- ment. Many of them believed that life under the British would be preferable than a free country dominated by Hindus. Gradually, as it became clear that the dominant Congress Party would resist Muslim claims for greater equality, the campaign to create a

separate nation intensified until it became an unalterable requirement of the League led by Jinnah.

In 1946 there was bloody rioting in Calcutta, Bombay and
other cities as Muslims and Hindus fought against one another.
When Lord Mountbatten arrived in India the British were under
enormous pressure to find a solution. Mountbatten came up with
something simple and easy to effect. The Muslims would get
territories comprising Pakistan, albeit rather smaller than they
had previously argued for, the Hindus would get the rest, and the
whole plan would be put into effect quickly. The consequences
were disastrous. Britain's rule in India – a supreme example of a
few commanding order over many – shattered into violence and
mayhem. Britain had made its subjects free, but could not protect
them as it did so. The partition of India resulted in one of the greatest voluntary and involuntary mass movements of population in
modern history. Muslims fled from India into Pakistan. Hindus
fled from Pakistan to India. No one knows quite how many:
estimates of the number of people on the move between 1947 and
1951 range from 10 to 18 million. Hundreds of thousands died –
some just abandoned on the roadside as the fatigue of their long
journey overcame them; others the victims of religious violence.
A British army captain who witnessed these events reported that
'every yard of the way there was a body ... The vultures had become
so bloated by their feasts they could no longer fly.' The fragile fabric
of imperial control had broken and political destiny fulfilled. As an
act of policy it was applauded as a momentous achievement: its
human price was appalling.

'An eye for an eye,' said Gandhi, 'makes the whole world blind.'
In advocating his ideas of non-violence he also said: 'What
difference does it make to the dead, the orphans and the homeless,
whether the mad destruction is wrought under the name of
totalitarianism or the holy name of liberty and democracy?' The
words of the man who did more than almost any other of his
countrymen to create an independent India fell on deaf ears as the
newly created nation went to war in 1947 with its newly created

neighbour. Gandhi himself became the victim of the violence he deplored and was killed by a fanatical assassin in the year following independence.

There have been two further wars between India and Pakistan since 1947, one in 1965 and another in 1971. Pakistan itself has suffered a turbulent history. Originally it consisted of two countries – one in the West, the other in the East – separated by a thousand miles of Indian territory. In 1970 the people of the east, who had played second fiddle to their Western counterparts since independence, rose up and created their own new state of Bangladesh. India helped them in their fight. Today Pakistan is aflame as different forces, religious and secular, totalitarian and liberal, fight to control it. In January 2008, barely a fortnight after returning to the country she said she wanted to lead back into full democracy, the opposition leader Benazir Bhutto was assassinated.

The story of the independence and partition of India is the story of the British Empire. It is a story that is wonderful and sad, grandly heroic and stupidly wrong. The Empire grew out of the opportunity to create trade. The need to protect that trade developed into total political and military domination. When, inevitably, the time came to relinquish it all, the panoply of power crumbled overnight and Britain became a powerless bystander at the edge of the world it had ruled for so long.

CHAPTER 10

The Arrival of the SS *Empire Windrush* at Tilbury Docks
1948

In 1948 the SS *Empire Windrush* docked at Tilbury, Kent. Among its passengers were nearly 500 people from Jamaica and Trinidad, anxious for a taste of life in England, the 'Mother Country'. They were Britain's first Caribbean immigrants.

Britain was often equivocal in its attitude towards its empire. Nothing illustrates this better than the case of Edward Eyre who was Governor of Jamaica in the 1860s. Eyre had spent most of his life working abroad in the service of his country. In Australia he had become a hero by leading a dangerous expedition across 850 miles of previously uncharted desert, determined to complete what he intended to do or 'die in the attempt'. He befriended the local aborigines and introduced plans to help their education. Twenty years later he found himself in the West Indies, but here he seemed to abandon charity and compassion. When a local rebellion began in 1865 he imposed martial law, killed or executed more than 400 people, flogged about another 600 and burned their homes to the ground. He was recalled to England where public opinion was divided by his actions. Many eminent people, including the philosopher John Stuart Mill, called for him to be charged with murder: many others defended him claiming he had acted responsibly to restore control. He was never brought to trial and died peacefully in Devon at the age of eighty-six.

All this took place at a time when the British were getting weary of their 'West Indian responsibilities'. Anthony Trollope, who went there on a mission for the Post Office in 1858, wrote: 'If we could, we would fain forget Jamaica altogether ... It belongs to us and must in some sort be thought of and managed and if possible governed.' The islands were no longer of particular strategic importance and the value of their sugar, cotton and coffee crops had declined. By the end of the century a Royal Commission reported that 'pecuniary sacrifices by the Mother Country' would be necessary. In other words, Britain would have to make grants and loans to its islands in the Caribbean if it was to keep them going. The wheel had turned full circle: British possessions, once a lucrative source of wealth, were now becoming a drain on resources. In 1935 riots about working conditions broke out on several islands. The subsequent report into these described the 'deplorable conditions' in which many labourers lived. 'It would not be unreasonable,' it said, 'to expect anything but discontent in such surroundings.'

When the SS *Empire Windrush* docked at Tilbury in 1948, the British Empire was almost a thing of the past. India had gone, divided into two independent nations the year before. Over the next fifteen years Britain would dispense of most of its other imperial belongings, including the West Indies, and grant them independence. These were the last rites of Empire, the necessary duties of a once great power accepting with as much good grace as it could the need to grant freedom to those it had controlled for centuries. What the people of Britain did not realise at the time was that in relinquishing these obligations they would create enormous changes in their way of life at home. The West Indians who walked down the gangplank at Tilbury, black faces in a white world, were the first physical examples of that change.

Administering empires is not easy. Dismantling them is even more difficult. In wrestling with the complexities of managing its extensive foreign possessions Britain sometimes acted cruelly or insensitively. To a large extent, however, it tried to imbue its imperial activities with a sense of moral purpose. When the Empire collapsed, the commercial benefits collapsed too – but some of the moral purpose remained behind. In 1960, the British Prime

Left: Emmeline Pankhurst arrested by Superintendent Rolfe outside Buckingham Palace, London, May 1914. Mrs Pankhurst (1857-1928) was trying to present a petition to the King. *The Suffragette* newspaper reported that as she was driven away to Holloway Prison she called out: "Arrested at the gates of the Palace. Tell the King!" Pankhurst was jailed several times during the fight to get women the vote. Rolfe died of heart failure two weeks after the incident.

Below: 11th August 1966: The Beatles leave London's Heathrow Airport for a tour of America watched by a crowd of screaming fans.

Top left: Portrait of Geoffrey Chaucer (c.1342-1400).

Top right: John Harrison's masterpiece – the longitude watch, subsequently called H4. Harrison began work on it in 1755. Its very stable, high frequency balance proved successful in sea trials in 1761 and 1764 – but the authorities still refused to award Harrison the Longitude Prize.

Above: The Boyhood of Raleigh, painted in 1870 by Sir John Everett Millais. Millais was one of the founders of the Pre-Raphaelite Brotherhood, but left the group to become one of the most celebrated and fashionable painters in Victorian Britain.

Left: Gin Lane, 1751, (engraving) is a fine example of Hogarth's satirical style.

Below: An experiment on a bird in the air pump by Joseph Wright of Derby (1734 – 1797). This picture, painted in 1786, hangs in the National Gallery in London and is a masterpiece of British art. Wright uses *chiaroscuro* – the mixture of light and shade – to brilliant effect.

Top: The English watercolourists of the early nineteenth century made an important contribution to the development of British art. John Sell Cotman's *Greta Bridge*, Yorkshire, painted in 1810, is a particularly good example.

Bottom: Lucien Freud's *Girl with a White Dog* is a beautiful example of twentieth-century British portraiture. Like all great portrait painters, Freud seems to get right inside his subjects, stripping away their defences.

arwich 1938: an English Bobby escorts two young Austrian refugees on their way to safety in London.
ae world's first organised police force, the Metropolitan Police, was founded in 1829 by Robert Peel.

Top: 'Have nothing in your house that you do not know to be useful or believe to be beautiful.' William Morris was the principal founder of the Arts and Crafts movement in 1859. Through the design of his home, the Red House, he applied this – his golden rule – to his own life.

Bottom: : The Battle of the Somme lasted from 1st July to 18th November 1916. 125,00 soldiers from Britain and the Empire were killed. There were more than a million casualties on both sides.

Left: The reconstructed Shakespeare's Globe stands near to its original sixteenth-century site in Southwark on the banks of the Thames in London.

Below: The Monty Python team turn themselves into a multiplicity of Alan Whickers. The television show 'Monty Python's Flying Circus' offered British audiences a new type of humour which quickly became very popular.

THE
Declaration and Standard

Of the *Levellers* of *England;*
Delivered in a Speech to his Excellency the Lord Gen. *Fairfax,*
on *Friday* last at White-Hall, by Mr. *Everard,* a late Member of the
Army, and his Prophesie in reference thereunto; shewing what will
befall the Nobility and Gentry of this Nation, by their submitting to
community; With their invitation and promise unto the people, and
their proceedings in *Windsor* Park, *Oatlands* Park, and severall other
places; also, the Examination and confession of the said Mr. *Everard*
before his Excellency, the manner of his deportment with his Hat on,
and his severall speeches and expressions, when he was commanded
to put it off. Together with a List of the severall Regiments of Horse
and Foot that have cast Lots to go for *Ireland.*

Imprinted at *London,* for *G. Laurenson, April* 23. 1649.

The Levellers were a seventeenth-century Puritan sect which advocated a levelling of society to make it more equal. This is the sect's 'Declaration and Standard', published on 23rd April 1649.

Minister, Harold Macmillan, made a speech to the South African parliament that captured the agony of a nation trying to face up to the responsibilities of its imperial past. 'The wind of change is blowing,' he told his audience, 'and whether we like it or not, the growth of national consciousness is a political fact.' National consciousness, he went on, is something 'for which both you and we and the other nations of the Western world are responsible'. In saying this he formally cut off Britain from any future imperial ambition – even though there were many at home who still wished to see the country survive as a colonial power in some form. What Macmillan understood was that national aspirations had to be nurtured and supported. He wanted South Africa – where apartheid was growing ever stronger – to abandon or tone down its racial policies and support Britain in its efforts to bring independence to the African nations that it once owned. The fight for independence was happening in a world that had divided along communist-capitalist lines. 'What is now on trial is much more than our military strength,' he said. 'It is our way of life.'

By the time Macmillan made that speech many thousands of immigrants were coming to live in Britain. Bill Morris, who became general secretary of what was then the country's biggest trade union, the Transport and General Workers' Union, was born in Jamaica and came to Britain in 1954. Four years later he joined the union because, he says, everybody else did. 'It made us feel protected.' The singer, Joan Armatrading, came to Britain from St Kitts in 1957 when she was seven years old. She made the journey alone, and in an interview once described how frightened she felt arriving in the middle of winter and, like Bill Morris before her, seeing snow for the first time. Sir Trevor Macdonald, now one of Britain's most successful and famous broadcasters, was born in Trinidad in 1939. He did not come to England until 1969, seven years after Trinidad elected for independence, but his recollections of growing up in the Caribbean say a lot about how West Indians as a whole regarded the 'Mother Country'. All things English, he remembers, were much admired. At school the emphasis was on English language and culture and the colonial idiom was a way of life. His father would encourage him to 'play the game', saying such things as 'taking part is much more important than winning'. London was the ultimate destination. When he finally arrived he found it incredibly exciting. As one of many West Indians who have found success in Britain, Sir Trevor demonstrates the way in which British society has adapted to its post-colonial role. Others who came to Britain from the West Indies in those early years were forced to take labouring jobs. As a result, some moved into the trade union movement and took positions at the forefront of social change.

Immigrants soon started coming from other parts of the former Empire, particularly Asia. This inward flow of people was increased suddenly in 1972 when the Ugandan dictator, Idi Amin, expelled 55,000 Asians from his country. It was the British who had originally brought them there, hiring them as cheap labour to help build the railways. They were all British passport holders and the British government felt it had a moral responsibility to look after them. In the last thirty-five years the Ugandan Asians have created one of Britain's most prosperous and successful communities. 'I never fell back on the state,' one man, Manzoor Moghal, told BBC News in an anniversary programme thirty years later. 'I wanted to explode this myth that Asians were scroungers.' Today the growth of the European Union has created a third wave of immigration into Britain, this time from the countries of Eastern Europe.

The stories and recollections of Britain's immigrants are the human side of a social upheaval that has transformed the country since the end of the Second World War. It has been by no means an easy process. In 1968 it was the subject of another important political speech. This time it took place at the annual meeting of the West Midlands Conservative Association where the speaker was the MP for Wolverhampton South West, Enoch Powell. Powell felt that immigration was a national danger. He pointed to America where the assassination of the Civil Rights leader, Martin Luther King, two weeks earlier had led to terrifying race riots. 'Like the Roman,' he said in the most emotive phrase of the speech, 'I seem to see the River Tiber foaming with much blood.' He predicted that what was happening in America would happen in Britain 'by our own volition and our own neglect ... Only resolute and urgent action will avert it even now.' Enoch Powell's speech divided the nation. Some saw him as a visionary, others as a racist villain. He had undoubtedly touched a nerve in Britain's sense of belief. The concept of multi-culturalism – the idea of allowing different racial, social and religious groups to pursue their own ways of life within the umbrella of a national community – had become the official policy of dealing with the growth in immigration. This was a difficult idea for many people to grasp. British values, imperial values were being washed away without a moment of regret. Or were they?

It was a difficult idea for many people to grasp. British values, imperial values were being washed away without a moment of regret. Or were they?

The rivers of Britain have not yet foamed with blood, although many parts of Britain suffered race riots in the early 1980s, culminating in riots in Brixton – the most serious to affect London in the twentieth century – and Liverpool and Manchester. Today it is Britain's role as a member of the European Union as much as its old imperial past that presents it with problems of immigration and racial conflict. Multi-culturalism itself is being re-examined: tolerance and freedom, it is argued, do not necessarily require complete separation of belief and behaviour.

The almost 500 West Indians who decided to take a look at Britain in 1948 represented the moment when the pendulum of imperial expansion swung back to the country from which it had originated. The Empire disappeared in a sense of loss and guilt, combined with a belief in duty and responsibility, all overlaid by self-interest and a desire to get on with life in as comfortable a way as possible. Such complexity cannot find resolution quickly. Those optimistic West Indians, eager for a glimpse of the 'Mother

The Channel Tunnel 1994

The idea of building a tunnel under the English Channel was proposed by a French engineer, Albert Mathieu, in 1802. The first serious attempt to build one did not come until much later when, in 1875, the French and British decided to cooperate on its construction. By 1877 the French had managed to sink a shaft to a depth of 330 feet at Sangatte in France, but the British attempt, at Saint Margaret's Bay in Dover, had to be abandoned because of flooding.

In 1881 work got under way again. Sir Edward Watkin, Chairman of the South Eastern Railway, formed a company called 'The Submarine Continental Railway Company', and using new boring equipment capable of cutting under the sea at the rate of half a mile a month, expected to finish a tunnel by 1886. The government grew nervous. Sir Garnet Wolsey – the British general who arrived too late to rescue General Gordon at Khartoum – announced that a tunnel would be 'calamitous for England'. Sir Edward Watkin tried in vain to calm the government's fears – he pointed out that the tunnel could easily be flooded if there were a threat of invasion – and the plan was abandoned.

The present tunnel was started in 1987 and carried its first passengers in 1994. It is the longest undersea tunnel in the world and cost between £10 and 12 billion – up to twice the original estimate. The journey from London St Pancras to the Gare du Nord in Paris takes 2 hours 15 minutes, and to the Gare du Midi in Brussels 1 hour 50 minutes. The sea is no longer a source of Britain's isolation.

Country', could not have known they were the beginning of a process that would change forever the social structure of post-imperial Britain.

4 Freedom

The Pursuit of Liberty

Introduction

The South African cleric and anti-apartheid campaigner, Archbishop Desmond Tutu, was once interviewed on the BBC radio programme *Desert Island Discs*. He told a story about how he was allowed out of South Africa to visit London in the early 1960s. He and his wife would wander around the streets of the city until quite late – well past what would have been curfew time back home. They would then indulge in a little piece of theatre. Pretending to be lost they would ask a policeman for directions and listen in delight as he addressed them courteously and called them 'Sir' and 'Madam'. It was, said Tutu, an incredible experience. To be treated equally, indeed with deference, was a feeling that was quite impossible to describe to someone who, like many of his fellow countrymen in South Africa, had never known it.

This little story speaks volumes. In Britain we take for granted our everyday liberties. Our rights are part of us: we wear them as easily as we do our clothes. We rarely think about them and we rarely feel the need to question them. We are the free citizens of a free country – that is all there is to it.

The fact is, however, that these rights were hard won over several centuries. Many other countries in the world have not been as successful as Britain in establishing a system of fundamental, inalienable individual liberties. Britain's belief in personal freedom is one of its unique qualities. The story of the fight for that belief is a fundamental part of British history. It begins with Magna Carta – the Great Charter that the barons of England forced King John to sign in 1215. Some of the language it used has remained a basic part of British law ever since. After that comes the Peasants' Revolt of 1381, the first significant uprising of ordinary men and women seeking greater justice and freedom.

The story then takes a leap forward to the seventeenth century, a period that saw the biggest battles for liberty. The Gunpowder Plot of 1605, the foiling of which we commemorate each year on 5th November, was an attempt by Catholic conspirators to redress the wrongs they felt were being done to them. It set the tone for the religious and political conflicts that would dominate the rest of the century. The execution of King Charles I in 1649 was the supreme moment in those conflicts but another King lost his throne before they were completely over. James II fled from the country in the Glorious Revolution of 1688 and a new structure of monarchical government was established under the provisions of the Bill of Rights of 1689.

In the eighteenth century Britain consolidated the constitutional achievements of the bitter struggles that had gone before. Cabinet government and the principle of the monarch ruling with Parliament were first put into practice when Sir Robert Walpole became the country's first 'Prime Minister' in 1721. Ideas about liberty abounded. Some of the most important were set out in Adam Smith's *The Wealth of Nations*, published in 1776, which explained how a free market needed to work.

In the nineteenth century Britain began cautiously to give more of its people the right to participate in government and put the nation on the road towards becoming a full democracy. The Great Reform Act of 1832 was the first step. Women, however, still had to fight furiously to get their voices heard. The foundation of the Women's Political and Social Union in 1903 gave birth to the Suffragettes and one of history's most heroic struggles for liberty.

Britain's democracy and its liberties continued to expand throughout the twentieth century. The foundation of the National Health Service in 1948 married practicality to ideology by giving free men and women the right to free health care. It is a long journey from King John to the NHS. But the same language, the same ideas and the same hopes can be heard at its beginning and its end; and at each of its great summits along the way.

CHAPTER 1

Magna Carta

1215

In 1215 a group of English barons forced King John to sign Magna Carta, or the 'Great Charter', in which he agreed to certain limitations on his power. The document is regarded as the first important expression of individual liberty in Britain.

In December 2007 an edition of Magna Carta dating from 1297 was sold at auction in New York for $21 million – then equivalent to more than £10 million. It had changed hands from one American millionaire to another. Its new owner promised to return it to its place on display in the American National Archives in Washington, alongside the original copies of the Declaration of Independence and the American Constitution. The auctioneer described the document as 'the birth certificate of freedom'. The essence of it, he said, is that no one is above the law. In the twentieth century such glorious freedom so enthusiastically hyped came at a price – $8,528 per word to be exact. The price paid in the thirteenth century, when the document was first drafted, was rather different.

King John came to the throne after the death of his brother, Richard I, 'the Lionheart', in 1199. Both men are controversial figures in British history. Richard has been portrayed traditionally as heroic, courageous and true; John as mean, treacherous and shifty. Neither is probably entirely accurate. Richard was undoubtedly a great warrior but he neglected his native country, choosing to spend most of his time abroad, either on a Crusade or fighting the French. He died during the siege of a small castle in the Limousin. John, the youngest of Henry II's five sons, though only four survived infancy, does not appear to have been a particularly trustworthy character. He tried to seize the throne when Richard was out of the country, but was forgiven and eventually made Richard's legitimate heir. Once on the throne himself he precipitated a war with France by marrying Isabella of Angoulême when she was betrothed to a French noble. His French lands were seized by the King of France, Philip II, who gave them to John's nephew, Arthur. John then fell out with the Pope who excommunicated him for refusing to endorse his candidate for Archbishop of Canterbury. This was a serious matter. The excommunication was preceded by an interdict that meant all church services apart from baptisms and confessions were suspended and that the barons were absolved from their oaths of allegiance. Threatened by a papal crusade against his kingdoms, John reluctantly agreed to meet the Pope's candidate for Archbishop, Stephen Langton, in 1213 and the excommunication was rescinded.

John's troubles were by no means over. His own campaigns in France failed to recapture the land that he had lost and in 1214, in a final attempt to win back his territory from the French King, Philip II, John went on a campaign in western France, where most of the disputed territories were situated. His ally, Otto IV, the Holy Roman Emperor, invaded France from the east. Philip totally defeated Otto at the Battle of Bouvines south of Lille in northern France. John was isolated. He had no alternative but to return home. He had lost an empire: all his former lands in France apart from Aquitaine and part of Poitou were ceded to the French. John had found himself in conflict with one of the most successful French kings of the Middle Ages, and had been roundly defeated.

War, then as now, costs money. In order to pursue his territorial ambitions in France John had extended his monarchical powers to impose taxes and raise armies. For a man with so many enemies he had been remarkably successful at pursuing his own personal strategy against the wishes, and without the support, of those around him. He had managed to create an alliance against the French King, even if it had failed; he had managed to compromise with the Pope so that he remained on the throne with his support;

and he had kept the barons, on whom he depended for money, in their place. After the Battle of Bouvines, however, the tactics of this energetic medieval monarch began to unravel. The barons were restless and unhappy and in this recalcitrant mood they turned to the man John had finally acknowledged as Archbishop of Canterbury, Stephen Langton. Langton reminded them of legal precedent – and in particular the charter granted by Henry I when he had come to the throne in 1100. Henry I had seized the throne from under the nose of his brother, Robert of Normandy, and in order to keep it needed the barons on his side. He therefore agreed at his coronation to repeal the 'bad customs' that had grown up during the reign of his predecessor, William II. 'I take away all the bad customs by which the kingdom of England was unjustly oppressed,' he had declared. 'I restore to you the law of King Edward with those amendments introduced into it by my father with the advice of his barons.' King Edward was Edward the Confessor; Henry's father, William the Conqueror. So Henry I had agreed to return to the principles of a time when kings ruled in partnership with their barons. This, argued Stephen Langton, was exactly what King John should be made to do.

The barons needed little encouragement and once they received news of the Battle of Bouvines mobilised to press their case against their king. Early in 1215 they presented themselves before John and demanded redress. At first the King tried to resist but he soon realised this was useless. Exasperated and angry he called the barons to a meeting at the island of Runnymede, between Staines and Windsor, on the River Thames. The King camped on one side, the barons on the other while the discussions took place on the island itself. There was not much to discuss. John had nowhere to turn, and agreed to the terms of Magna Carta in a single day. The self-interests of a group of powerful nobles combined with the erratic intransigence of an unpopular king created the document that would be marketed nearly eight hundred years later as the 'birth certificate of freedom'.

It was no such thing, but it was, without question, a hugely important step in the development of the English constitution and the rights of the individual within the state. Magna Carta took the vague expressions of Henry I's charter of more than a century before and developed them into clear, written law. 'No freeman,' ran the article that lies at its heart, 'shall be seized or imprisoned, or dispossessed, or outlawed ... save by legal judgement of his peers or by the laws of the land.' The laws of the land were then given proper machinery through which to operate. County courts were to be held monthly and the King's court – the Court of Common Pleas – was no longer to follow the King on his travels, but to sit in a fixed place. Magna Carta also addressed the way in which the King could raise money. Both John, and Richard before

'No freeman,' ran the article, 'shall be seized or imprisoned, or dispossessed, or outlawed ... save by legal judgement of his peers or by the laws of the land.'

him, had been dismissive of the administrative systems for taxation that had grown up during the first decades of the twelfth century. Both had imposed fines and ransoms pretty much at their pleasure, grabbing money wherever they could to pay for their military exploits. These taxes – or *scutage* – were to be subject to baronial consent: 'no *scutage* or aid shall be imposed in our realm save by the common council of the realm'. Again, Magna Carta provided the machinery for this obligation. The common council had to be summoned properly. The greater barons were to be called by special writ, lesser landowners – 'the tenants-in-chief' – through the sheriffs and bailiffs at least forty days before. The custom and practice of a previous age was enshrined as a right, and the first faltering steps towards parliamentary government had been made.

The other important feature of Magna Carta is that it was in many ways a national document. Although the barons led opposition to the King, they were not strong enough to act entirely on their own. They needed the support of the Church and of the freemen – all classes in fact other than the villeins and serfs who remained bound in servitude to their masters. So the Church of England was to have 'all her whole rights and liberties inviolable'; London was to have restored 'all the old liberties and customs which it hath been used to have'; and all other cities, boroughs, towns and barons of the Cinque Ports and all other ports were to once more enjoy 'all their liberties and free customs'. Various other clauses demanded the restraint of the King's officers: there were also provisions for the management of forests and rivers.

King John, outwitted at Runnymede, was not a man to give in easily. Encouraged by the Pope, who disapproved of any attack on royal authority, John recruited an army of French mercenaries and turned against the barons. The Pope suspended Stephen Langton, the man whom he had originally forced on John as Archbishop, for supporting Magna Carta. The barons sought help from the French King who responded by sending an army under the command of his son Louis, and Magna Carta seemed forgotten as England went to war. Only John's sudden death in 1216 opened the way for peace to be restored. His infant son, Henry III, became King: he reigned for fifty-six years during which the barons continued to extend their powers in the land.

Magna Carta was reissued as soon as Henry became King and again when he turned eighteen in 1225. His son, Edward I, reissued it for the last time in 1297. By the end of the thirteenth century it had become a settled part of English law – although it fell into the background after that: Shakespeare's play about King John, written at the end of the sixteenth century, makes no mention of it. It was only when the gentlemen of England once more found themselves in opposition to their king that they turned to the document that was by then more than four hundred years old. One of the great lawyers who opposed both James I and Charles I in the seventeenth century, Edward Coke, referred to Magna Carta as the guiding light of English freedoms. 'Magna Carta,' he told Parliament in 1628, 'will have no sovereign.' In making that statement he placed the Charter that King John had reluctantly signed at Runnymede at the centre of the arguments for the rights of individuals under the law.

The colonists who went to the New World also revered the memory of Magna Carta and in the eighteenth century turned to its principles as they prepared to build a new nation independent of the British crown. The shaky promises of a cornered king became the founding principles of liberty across the world.

CHAPTER 2

The Peasants' Revolt
1381

In 1381 several groups of peasants and tenant farmers took up arms against their landowning masters. Their rebellion was short but violent. It was the biggest civil insurgency in medieval Britain.

The Peasants' Revolt of 1381 was the biggest social rebellion in England before the outbreak of the Civil War in the middle of the seventeenth century. Unlike the Civil War the actual event achieved very little. It was widespread and violent; it tested the mettle of the boy king, Richard II, and it spawned an outburst of radical, even revolutionary, demands. In a period of little more than two weeks, angry tenant farmers and peasants from the fields of the eastern and southern counties of England converged on London and elsewhere, causing mayhem and destruction. Although the revolt spread well beyond the boundaries of London it subsided quickly once the capital regained control. The rebel leaders were suppressed and England returned, more or less, to its usual routines. It was an extraordinary example of 'people power', but it demonstrated just how much the spontaneous cry for reform requires careful organisation if it is to be translated into something of lasting advantage.

In 1348 the bubonic plague had reached England. It had started in southern Europe the year before, brought there by ships trading between Sicily and Africa. Up until the outbreak of the plague – 'The Black Death' as it became known – Britain had been relatively free from deadly diseases. The population increased steadily and there were land shortages so the peasants had to work hard to feed themselves. The Black Death changed all that: in total it is estimated that it killed between 25 and 50 per cent of Europe's populations. In Britain it affected sections of the people in different ways. The old and the young were hardest hit – about 60 per cent of the elderly died – but adult men and women over the age of twenty had a lower mortality rate of around 40 per cent. The result was that by the time the epidemic passed – although in actual fact the plague in various forms returned to Britain every generation afterwards until it died out in the seventeenth century – the way of life in the countryside looked very different. Death had smashed the old system where plenty of labour and not much land had kept men bound to their lords on their estates for fear of being driven into starvation if they could not work. In its place it had put a system where labour was scarce and wages high. Villeins who, although they were given small strips of land to look after, remained the property of an estate and were not allowed to leave it without permission, took the opportunity to escape, safe in the knowledge that there was plenty of work and plenty of landowners only too happy to make it available. Landlords were forced to sell their land – sometimes to the men who had previously worked on it for them: times were getting very tough.

An extraordinary example of 'people power' ...

In 1351 Parliament passed an act called the Statute of Labourers – a sort of medieval pay act which sought to set wage levels and force work out of men who did not own land themselves. In looking for a remedy for their troubles the lords of the manor also fell back on their ancient rights and tried to enforce the rules of serfdom, creating resentment among the peasants whom these laws most affected. When Richard II came to the throne in 1377 Parliament complained at the way villeins were trying to withdraw their services. Worried by declining income from their land holdings, anxious to regain control over their workforce and additionally burdened by the cost of the continuing war with France, Parliament decided to impose a series of poll taxes. The first, imposed in 1377, was a groat (four pence) a head; the second, in 1379, was graduated in the interests of fairness; but the third, which came into effect in 1381, was a shilling and led to the Peasants' Revolt.

At the end of May two risings took place east of London, in Brentwood, Essex and in Gravesend, Kent. Although they were two separate incidents their timing and nature indicates that there was probably some sort of collusion. Villagers in Fobbing, near Brentwood, refused to pay the local tax collector and fought off a force called out by the Chief Justice of the Common Pleas. The men of Kent attacked Dartford and Maidstone and then set out for London with their leader, Walter, or 'Wat', Tyler, at their head. We know very little about Wat Tyler – but he obviously struck a bold figure as he led his men towards the capital. The rebels attacked the symbols of authority they hated most, in particular Church property. The great monasteries of Britain were unpopular because, as big landowners, they took a conservative attitude towards serfdom and villeinage: in this respect they were no better or worse than their secular brethren. At the same time the teachings of the Church were coming in for criticism from dissident priests who preached that its wealth had grown too great and that it was time to turn back to the true message of Christ and the lessons of the Bible. This was something ordinary people both recognised and understood, and it fuelled the vehemence of the Peasants' Revolt.

The rebels sacked the Archbishop of Canterbury's palace at Lambeth and then gathered together at Blackheath. Here they listened to another of the revolt's leaders, a dissident priest called John Ball. 'When Adam delved and Eve span, who was then the gentleman?' he asked them. In other words: there was no nobility in the Garden of Eden so why should it exist today? This was radical stuff and his audience responded by pouring across London Bridge, throwing open the prisons at Newgate and Fleet, sacking the lawyers' headquarters at the hospital at Clerkenwell and attacking John of Gaunt's Savoy Palace, where the Savoy Hotel and Theatre stand today. John of Gaunt was not at home: he had wisely disappeared into Scotland.

The young king, Richard II, then only fourteen years old, agreed to meet the rebels. He first spoke to the men of Essex at Mile End. They asked for the abolition of serfdom and for the annual rent of land to be no more than four pence an acre. The King listened carefully and then acceded to their demands. In the meantime the men of Kent, who had marched along the Thames from Gravesend, entered the Tower of London where Simon of Sudbury, the Archbishop of Canterbury and Chancellor of England, was captured and executed before a huge mob. The King then went to meet Wat Tyler at Smithfield. Tyler's demands were equally as large as those of his comrades from Essex. 'There should,' he is reported as demanding, 'be no bishop in England, but one, no prelate but one and all the lands ... of the possessioners should be taken from them and divided between the commons ... [and] there should be no villein in England or any serfdom or villeinage, but all to be free and of one condition.' This was heady stuff, a proposition for a total levelling of society, the sort of thing that in later ages would earn the name of revolution.

But at Smithfield in 1381 revolution was still a long way off. The boy king agreed to the rebels' demands as he had appeared to do at Mile End the day before. As the tension eased the Mayor of London, Sir William Walworth, who was riding with the King, pulled Wat Tyler from his horse and stabbed him. Tyler, severely wounded, was then executed at Smithfield. The King ordered the peasants to disperse and, as if the death of their leader Tyler had slain their hopes in an instant, they agreed to do so. The revolt was all but over. Within a few weeks the rebellions that had broken out in other parts of the country were suppressed; the King's promises, which had anyway simply been empty gestures to buy time, were withdrawn; and the drama of 'the English Rising' died away. John Ball was hanged, drawn and quartered in front of the King. In his speech at Blackheath he had used powerful language: 'now the time is come, appointed to us by God, in which ye may (if ye will) cast off the yoke of bondage and recover liberty'. His execution killed such hopes and his dreams of liberty evaporated into the ordered hierarchy of the Middle Ages.

The failure of the Peasants' Revolt did not mean that the problems of managing the manors and villages of medieval England went away. Villeins continued to flee from their masters, and there are many legends about men who decided to abandon their jobs and live as 'free men'. Some of them refer back to the story of Robin Hood who, although he dates from the time of King John, seems to have been something of an inspiration for those who decided to go it alone in subsequent times. The great landowners dealt with this problem by leasing their land rather than managing it directly themselves and, bit by bit, their great estates were broken up into smaller farms run by tenants. The wealth of the countryside began to be shared more widely: some peasants became rich as they managed to acquire land that their former masters could no longer manage on their own. With this change in land ownership came changes in social structure. The idea of villeinage was not formally abandoned until Henry VII ascended the throne after the Battle of Bosworth in 1485, but by then it had virtually died out of its own accord. It had become an economic albatross and the lords of the manor looked for other ways to make their estates pay. Wat Tyler and John Ball were not strong enough, or organised enough, to achieve anything more than a frightening and violent eruption but they lived in an age when great economic change, rather than individual action, brought about the results they marched and died for. The importance of this change cannot be underestimated because it was a true liberation of the working men and women of Britain. By the end of the fifteenth century, once the battles between rival noble houses came to an end and the country was united under a powerful Tudor king, Britain was ready to start the long climb towards free nationhood. It was a journey that could never have been undertaken without the steady emancipation of its people in the years before.

CHAPTER 3

The Gunpowder Plot
1605

In 1605 Guy Fawkes was discovered next to a pile of gunpowder barrels in a vault below the Palace of Westminster. He was one of a group of Catholic conspirators who had intended to blow up Parliament as it was being opened by the King. The plot was intended to strike a blow for the freedom of Catholics in Britain.

His mother was executed and his father murdered. He became King when he was just a year old, and assumed full royal power at the age of fifteen. For twenty-five years he governed his people, bullied by Presbyterian clergy and used as a pawn in the power struggles of the nobility. At the age of thirty-six he inherited the throne of his neighbouring kingdom and governed both until he died twenty-two years later. He kept both countries he ruled out of war abroad and, in an age of turbulent religious and political differences, managed to keep the peace at home as well. This was James VI of Scotland – mocked in history as 'the wisest fool in Christendom' – who in 1603 succeeded his cousin Elizabeth I, as James I of England. His is not a bad record for a fool.

It is not surprising that James learned the art of survival. He was twenty-one when his mother Mary, Queen of Scots, was executed, but he would not have remembered her. He was barely twelve months old when she fled to England and a life of imprisonment. His father, Lord Darnley, an immature and petulant young nobleman whom his mother unwisely married, had already been murdered by aristocratic rivals. Significantly Lord Darnley was killed as the result of a violent explosion at the house where he was staying: his son narrowly escaped dying in a similar attack only two years after he had assumed power in England.

James had never been officially proclaimed heir to the English throne. Elizabeth had promised him that she would not resist any right or title that he possessed, but that fell short of a full endorsement. James therefore lobbied the powers abroad to support his claim, but his biggest coup was in securing the backing of Robert Cecil, Elizabeth's most important minister. He was the son of William Cecil who, with Francis Walsingham, had been one of the political architects of Elizabeth's reign. These two men had taught Robert that ruling England required a combination of wise statesmanship and cunning espionage. He had proved adept at both and before his father died in 1598 had been raised to the position of the Queen's most trusted advisor. He was rather small and wiry, some say deformed. Elizabeth called him her 'elf' – and sometimes, less to his liking, her 'pygmy'. As the Queen grew old Cecil knew that her succession would be vital to the peace of England. He had first-hand experience of disruption and rebellion. The Queen's one-time favourite, the Earl of Essex, rounded on Cecil after being accused of treachery and accused him of exactly the same thing in an attempt to save his own skin. Cecil had had to appeal for witnesses to prove his innocence. Essex was convicted and executed in 1601.

Cecil then set about ensuring that when the Queen died the crown would pass peaceably to the King of Scotland, son of the cousin she had reluctantly sent to her death fifteen years before. He began a correspondence with James – a careful and secret correspondence in which his own name was disguised with the number 10, James with the number 30 and Elizabeth with the number 24. Cecil entered into this on two conditions. Firstly, an absolute respect had to be paid to the feelings of the elderly Queen: James was not to try to procure recognition from the English parliament or anywhere else of his right to succession. Secondly, everything had to be done with the utmost secrecy.

While Cecil worked meticulously to manage what he knew was

going to be a tricky transference of power, many Catholics in England began to hope that if James became King he would support them. He was after all the son of a Catholic Queen: surely he would begin to reverse the onward march of the Protestant Reformation that had made many of them virtual exiles in their own land. When Queen Elizabeth died in 1603 they began to hope for better times. As James progressed towards his coronation some Catholic leaders petitioned him and asked for toleration. The King responded by agreeing to suspend the fines they received for refusing to attend Church of England services on condition they continued to support him and his state. James was a man with a tolerant outlook and in his letters to Cecil had expressed the view that blood should never be spilled because of religious differences. What England's optimistic Catholics did not know was that he had also said that their numbers should not be allowed to increase. Gradually they came to realise how wrongly they had judged their man. Once James was on the throne resentment grew at his refusal to take up the Catholic cause. Two plots, both rather incompetent, were uncovered. Then a third one came to light: this was rather more serious.

The principal conspirator in the Gunpowder Plot was not Guy – or Guido – Fawkes, but Robert Catesby. He was a wealthy gentleman from Warwickshire, some of whose friends had been implicated in the Essex plot against Elizabeth towards the end of the old Queen's reign. He was an organiser, a man with sufficient charisma to get people to follow him. When in 1603 the King of Spain, Philip III, sent an envoy to congratulate James on his accession, Catesby and his friends knew that they were on their own. Even the country that had equipped and despatched the Armada was not prepared to protect England's Catholics: if they were to restore freedom of worship for their faith they would have to take the law into their own hands. The plotters began work in May 1604 after the first session of the new Parliament opened. One of them, Thomas Percy, had just managed to secure himself a place at court. The conspirators' plan was to use a vault beneath the house which

Percy rented next to the Palace of Westminster. The gunpowder would be ferried across the Thames at night from Robert Catesby's house in Lambeth. They later rented a more convenient place, a chamber located at ground level just below the House of Lords' meeting room in the Palace of Westminster. While they prepared for the attack they also discussed what to do once they had seized the reins of power. They intended to kill the King and his heir, Prince Henry, in the explosion, as the royal party attended the opening of Parliament and then capture the other two children, Charles and Elizabeth. Charles was rather sickly: Elizabeth, they imagined, would make a better monarch for their new regime. Over time they managed to stack thirty-six barrels of gunpowder beneath the House of Lords. They were ready for the opening of Parliament's next session that had been delayed and was now set for 5th November 1605.

Robert Cecil, now Lord Salisbury, had got wind of yet more plots during the summer of 1605. On 26th October, just as he was sitting down to supper with some fellow members of the Privy Council, a former Catholic called Lord Monteagle turned up with a letter. Rather like a warning about a modern terrorist attack it advised their lordships to 'devise some excuse to shift of your attendance at this Parliament' because, it said, 'a terrible blow' would be struck. Monteagle may have written the letter himself. He had been a follower of the Earl of Essex and was probably keen to demonstrate his loyalty to the new order. Having received information about a possible plot, he thought he would use it to improve his position. The Privy Council sat tight. The King was away hunting: Cecil decided to show him the letter when he got back.

On 1st November the King was shown the letter and the Lord Chamberlain, as the man responsible for the arrangements for the opening of Parliament, was ordered to search the vaults below the Palace of Westminster. Lord Monteagle went with him. On 4th November, as it was making its rounds, the search party came across Guy Fawkes next to a pile of brushwood and faggots that concealed the gunpowder. Satisfied with the explanation that it all belonged to the courtier Thomas Percy, the search party moved on, but once back at base Monteagle became suspicious. The King ordered a new search, and at midnight on the 4th Guy Fawkes was found booted and fully clothed next to the barrels of gunpowder with which he and his co-conspirators had planned to destroy the monarchy. He was arrested and brutally tortured. The other conspirators fled north but were tracked down and either captured or shot. It is believed that Robert Catesby and Thomas Percy were killed by a single bullet that passed through both of them.

The King was careful not to fan the flames. The plot, he told Parliament, had been the work of a few fanatics, not of the whole Catholic community. His determination to show tolerance and to try to heal the religious differences of the people he governed had not deserted him even in the moment when he might have been killed. What James did not realise was that it was not only religious controversy

James I had survived an act of attempted regicide. His son would not.

that was likely to unsettle England. Strong political convictions were also evident in a country that had grown more self-assured during the years before James came to power. Robert Cecil's careful management had persuaded the gentlemen of England to accept a Scottish king even though they remained deeply suspicious of Scotland and many things in it. While their new monarch seemed to be able to handle the issues of religion with reasonable skill they were not so sure about his policies in other important matters. James wanted to unite England and Scotland in one kingdom of Great Britain: England was not ready for that. More seriously he took a view of the role of the monarchy that began to disturb some of his subjects in Parliament.

James I believed in the divine right of kings. This theory of political absolutism was to prove one of the main factors in the misfortunes of the Stuart monarchy and James was the first to advance it. He believed that a king drew his authority directly from God and not from any power on earth. Only God could remove him:

no one else. James, perhaps because of his extraordinary childhood and upbringing, was able to pick his way adroitly through the minefield of English religious and political differences. In this one thing he resembled the Queen who had ruled before him and who had also known what it was like to have one of your parents executed. Such things presumably teach you how to protect yourself. In all other respects he was very different from her, but in none so much as his belief that his right to rule was God-given. Elizabeth had identified herself with the people she governed: James chose to stand apart. He wanted to be tolerant and learned – to a large extent he was – but he still set the monarchy on a course towards political disaster. He survived an act of attempted regicide. His son would not.

CHAPTER 4

The Execution of King Charles I 1649

The execution of Charles I was one of the most momentous events in British history. Monarchical government was abandoned and a republic created in its place. This revolutionary act was an historic turning point in the development of the British state.

At about ten o'clock on the morning of 30th January 1649, the King of England, Charles I, walked through St James's Park accompanied by his private guard. With colours flying and drums beating he made his way up the stairs of the gallery of Whitehall Palace and into the chamber that had once been his bedroom. He said his prayers and at about midday ate some bread and drank a glass of claret. From there, with musketeers on either side of him, he walked to the Banqueting House next door. The Banqueting House had been built for his father twenty-seven years before by the architect and designer Inigo Jones. It was one of the most magnificent buildings Britain had ever seen and since its completion had been used for grand royal occasions. In January 1649 it had been opened for a royal event once more: outside the large entrance that led onto Whitehall a scaffold draped entirely in black had been constructed. It was here that Charles was to be executed.

The King stepped out into the cold January air. He was wearing two shirts in case the weather made him shiver and appear as if he was afraid. On one side of the scaffold were both mounted and foot soldiers, on the other, the side where today Whitehall leads into Trafalgar Square, was a large crowd of onlookers. The King was anxious about the arrangements for his execution. He asked if the block could be made a little higher, but it could not. He urged the executioner more than once to take care with his axe: he wanted it to be sharp enough to cut off his head with one, clean blow. He also explained that he would want to pray briefly before he was killed and that he would thrust out his arms when he was ready for the axe to fall. He was very particular about this, and went through it with the executioner more than once. He also made a speech in which he protested his innocence. 'I never did begin a war with the two houses of Parliament,' he said. 'I do believe that ill instruments between them and me has been the chief cause of all this bloodshed.' As for the people, he continued, 'Truly I desire their liberty and freedom as much as anybody whomsoever.' He then added 'that their liberty and freedom consists in having of government', and went on to explain briefly what he meant by that. 'A subject and a sovereign,' he said, 'are clean different things.' If any of the crowd listening to him had thought that at the moment of his death he might have softened or changed his belief in his divine right to rule, those few words would have told them that he had not. Charles I left his kingdom as he had governed it, noble, gracious, incorrigible and misguided.

The trial and execution of Charles I was the culmination of developments in Britain that had been at work for more than a hundred years before it took place. Like many other important events in modern British history its fundamental causes can be traced back to the reign of Henry VIII at the beginning of the sixteenth century. When Henry broke with Rome and made himself head of the Church as well as head of state in 1534, he ushered in forces that he could not have foreseen. The Reformation was racing through Europe. Martin Luther had nailed his 'ninety-five theses' denouncing the practices of the papacy and the Catholic Church to the door of a church in Wittenberg in Germany seventeen years before, in 1517. His ideas, and the ideas of the other European reformers, were beginning to enjoy acceptance all over Germany and Holland, helped by the recent invention of the printing press. Henry's break with Rome opened Britain to these ideas in a far more powerful way than would have been possible if the Pope had remained head of the English Church. In an age when religion dominated everything and when belief in God was unarguable, the liberation of thought provided by the Reformation was intense. It empowered people: they looked at themselves anew.

By the time Charles's father, James I, came to the English throne in 1603 Britain was a Protestant nation, but its Protestantism took many forms. At the centre was the Anglican Church, essentially modelled on previous Catholic lines but with some changes to the liturgy and no Pope at its helm. Around it was a conglomeration of other interpretations of the Gospel – generally referred to as Puritan but in fact divided into Presbyterian, Anabaptist, Calvinist and so on – all fervently supported by their followers. Britain was a religious hothouse, and Parliament was the place where the ideas spawned by the creativity of the new religions spilled over into politics. When men talked about 'liberty' they meant on the whole the liberty to pursue the religion of their choice, but it was not a big step from religious freedom to political freedom and the right to have a say in how the country was governed. When Charles I became King in 1625 he faced a country seething with religious argument, emboldened by the growth of parliamentary representation and unafraid of its opinions. This fervent and excitable nation was given a monarch who preferred the ways of the old religion to those of the new, believed in his divine right to rule and preferred to govern on his own rather than through a parliament with whom he disagreed. Catastrophe was inevitable.

After his defeat at the Battle of Naseby in 1645, Charles fled to Scotland where, under an agreement negotiated with the help of the French, he hoped he might emerge in a stronger position than if he were the prisoner of the English Parliament. The Scots used their prize to try to do a deal with the English, offering to return the King in return for the reformation of the English Church on Presbyterian lines. Charles, who did not want to see Presbyterianism introduced into England any more than many English members of Parliament, tried to play one side off against the other. He would do this more than once in the period leading up to his death: his unshakeable belief in the divinity of his appointment gave him the confidence to try to negotiate from a position of weakness. The Scots, realising that the King was not really supporting their ambitions, returned their captive to England. Charles was held at Hampton Court Palace from where he escaped. He made his way to the Isle of Wight where he believed the governor, Colonel Hammond, to be sympathetic to his cause. He had written a letter to the House of Lords on his escape in which he appealed to them for an audience. 'Let me be heard with Freedom, Honour and Safety,' he wrote, 'and I shall instantly break through this Cloud of Retirement and shew myself really to be "pater patriae".'

The would-be father of the nation was in fact planning his return to the throne through another alliance with the Scots. The Governor of the Isle of Wight did not turn out to be as supportive of the Royalist position as Charles and his attendants had hoped and confined his royal visitor in Carisbrooke Castle. Charles, however, aware that Parliament and the army were divided about how to conduct the future government of the country, continued his intrigues. Having failed to keep the support of the Scots before, he this time secretly agreed to their new proposals for the introduction of Presbyterianism. On this condition a Scottish army invaded England with the intention of returning him to the throne but in 1648 was heavily defeated by Cromwell at Preston. Cromwell and other leaders of the army had by now lost all patience with the King. Cromwell's son-in-law, Henry Ireton, organised an army coup in which Parliament was purged of all those who might be inclined to continue negotiations with Charles and in 1649 the King was brought to trial. These fast-moving events took place against a background of furious national debate about the future direction of Britain's government. The idea of killing the King was far removed from the minds of many, including those who thoroughly disapproved of him and his policies. The trouble was that Charles, by always trying to extricate himself from a hopeless situation by subterfuge, played into the hands of the real power in the land – the army. The army, dominated by the righteous

Puritanism of Cromwell, Ireton and their fellow commanders, was an implacable enemy unforgiving in the pursuit of its beliefs. Once he had lost its trust, Charles I had lost his life.

Charles I was brought to trial in the Painted Chamber of the Palace of Westminster on 20th January 1649. The President of the Court, John Bradshaw, read out the charges. 'The Commons of England,' he announced, 'being sensible of the great calamities that have been brought on this nation, and of the innocent blood that hath been shed in this nation,' was bringing the King before them as the person responsible for it all. Charles refused to recognise the jurisdiction of the court. In this he was legally correct – no court at that time had the automatic power to put a King on trial – but it was not a defence that would help him win support. Events had by this time moved beyond that point. As Bradshaw argued: 'There is a contract and a bargain made between the King and his people, and your oath is taken: and certainly, Sir, the bond is reciprocal: for as you are the liege lord so they liege subjects.' In other words the sovereign had a bond with his subjects to protect them, and in this Charles had failed.

Where Charles was on stronger ground was when he answered Bradshaw's assertion that he was arraigned before a 'Court of Justice'. 'I see I am before a power,' was the King's shrewd retort. This was the nub of it. The trial of Charles I was by no measure a real trial at all. It was a piece of Puritan theatre, a relentless demonstration of the power of an army which, victorious in its righteous struggle against the forces of wickedness, was at last able to wreak revenge upon its enemies. Charles, having refused to recognise the jurisdiction of his accusers, was allowed little opportunity to defend himself. Within a week his fate was sealed and he was accused of high treason. He was guilty of a 'wicked design to erect and uphold in himself an unlimited and tyrannical power to rule according to his Will, and to overthrow the Rights and Liberties of the People'. He was a 'Tyrant, Traitor and Murderer ... a public and implacable Enemy to the Commonwealth of England'. For all his faults it is hard to think of Charles I as a monster of these proportions. The little King – he was only about 5 foot 4 inches tall – found himself caught up in events the magnitude of which he did not understand. He thought that all his strength came from just being a king: in fact this was his greatest weakness.

This was an extraordinary moment in the history of Britain. With the King dead, the monarchy and the House of Lords were abolished and England became a republic governed by a Council of State. In the middle of the seventeenth century, in a Europe dominated by great monarchical families, where power was concentrated in the hands of the traditional authorities of the monarch and the Church, England was governed by a small group of Puritan gentlemen led by a tough Cambridgeshire squire. The so-called 'Interregnum' – the eleven years between the execution of Charles I and the restoration of his son in 1660 – was the biggest political experiment ever carried out in the

The little King found himself caught up in events the magnitude of which he did not understand.

country. It took place more than 120 years before the revolutions that engulfed France and America at the end of the eighteenth century and before ideas of individual liberty had become common currency. It changed the course of British political history and set the country on a different course from its continental neighbours.

Liberty is elusive. The small group of MPs who, under the watchful eye of a powerful standing army, executed the King, did so in the name of the people. But the government that they introduced afterwards was no more representative of the people as a whole than Charles I's had been. That is the nature of revolutions. In England in 1649, as in France in 1789, or Russia in 1917, a general uprising led eventually to the concentration of power in the hands of the most determined and best organised group which was then free to pursue its own agenda. In mid-seventeenth century England that agenda was about the moral reform of the nation.

At the end of 1653 Oliver Cromwell became Lord Protector. As the head of the army, he had stamped the authority of the new

Seventeenth-Century Dissenters

During the English Civil War and Cromwell's interregnum there were a number of dissident groups, some with stranger beliefs than others. Here are a few of them:

Levellers

The Levellers wanted a social 'levelling' and a more egalitarian society. Though not one cohesive group, their demands included suffrage for all freemen. They believed that the ownership of property should not play such a significant part in law, and that the monarchy and House of Lords should be abolished. They also sought welfare reform and argued for medical care and schooling for all. When the Levellers were crushed by Cromwell in 1649, dissidents began to look for other outlets for their disaffection, and often turned to groups like the Diggers and Ranters.

Diggers

The Diggers, or 'True Levellers', were a more radical group who again demanded social reform (including equality for women), but hoped to achieve this partially through the development of self-supporting communes and cultivation. Leading Digger Gerrard Winstanley wrote in 1649 that: 'In the beginning of Time, the great Creator Reason made the Earth to be a Common Treasury ... but not one word was spoken in the beginning that one branch of mankind should rule over another.'

Ranters

Much of what we know of the Ranters comes from their opponents' writings. They do not seem to have been a structured, unified organisation; contemporaries criticised them for immorality, and Winstanley wrote that they believed only 'in the outward enjoyment of meat, drink, pleasures, and women'. They refused to accept the authority of the scriptures, and believed in pantheism, the idea that God is present in nature.

Fifth Monarchists

Basing their beliefs on a prophesy of King Nebuchadnezzar in the Old Testament, Fifth Monarchists were convinced that Christ's Second Coming was imminent and that they were the elect. Though they were early supporters of Cromwell, the Fifth Monarchists felt betrayed when he dissolved the Nominated Assembly in 1653.

Muggletonians

In 1652, John Reeve and Lodowick Muggleton claimed to be the two witnesses of *Revelations* 11.3 ('And I will give power unto my two witnesses, and they shall prophesy a thousand two hundred and threescore days, clothed in sackcloth' – *King James Bible*) and to be able to bless and curse others according to God's wishes. They made good use of these powers, and cursed around a thousand people in their first ten years. One of the stranger Muggletonian beliefs was that all people would become male on entering heaven. Incredibly, the sect lived on after this period and the last Muggletonian is believed to have been Philip Noakes of Kent, who died in 1979.

government on all parts of the country, defeating Royalist rebellions in England and Scotland and smashing any opposition in Ireland. As Lord Protector he wanted to allow complete freedom of religion saying he would prefer to allow 'Mahometanism' than the persecution of 'one of God's children'. His puritanical Parliament was less sure about such licence so Cromwell simply dissolved it. He invented a new system with eleven major generals each ruling a different region of the country. Immoral behaviour was outlawed: drinking, gambling and sports on a Sunday were all repressed. When he died in 1658, England had had enough of republicanism. His son, Richard, who was named his successor as Protector, had no stomach for it either and England reached out for the monarchy once more.

Like Charles I, Cromwell found the business of governing much more difficult than the idea. He achieved power because he was a brilliant general utterly convinced of his opinions and his interpretation of the Gospel. He also wanted to be tolerant, or as tolerant as his rather severe God would allow him to be. The regime Oliver Cromwell forced on his country was flawed in all sorts of ways, not least because it tried to marry ideas of individual liberty with strict religious observance. But, by temporarily destroying the monarchy and demonstrating the passion and strength of English opinion under duress, he laid down the foundations of British democracy.

In 1660 Charles II came to the throne. The Stuarts were back. But the English Revolution was not over yet.

CHAPTER 5

The Glorious Revolution and the Bill of Rights
1688–1689

In 1688 James II was forced to abandon his throne when the nation grew worried that he planned to reintroduce Catholicism to Britain. This was the so-called 'Glorious Revolution'. Britain welcomed a new Protestant monarch, William III, who with his wife Mary ruled the country as King and Queen under the terms of a new constitutional settlement set out in the Bill of Rights.

Observing James II while he was in exile in France, the aristocrat Madame de Sévigné said: 'When one listens to him one realises why he is here.' Another lady of the French court, Madame de la Fayette, had this to say: 'Our dear King James,' she wrote, 'is good and honest but the most incompetent man I have ever seen in my life. A child of seven would not make such silly mistakes as he does.' The four Stuart Kings of England were good at silly mistakes. They veered between survival and disaster, sometimes steering a reasonably successful course through the treacherous territory of the country's religious and political conflicts, or else walking proudly into disaster. James II was the last of the four. He ruled for nearly four years before crisis forced him into exile at the court of Louis XIV in France. As an individual he was rather unimportant but his brief period of power encompassed supremely important events.

In December 1688, a Protestant Englishman, Roger Morrice, watched as Dutch soldiers paraded through the streets of London.

In Fleet Street he saw women shaking the troops' hands. 'God bless you,' they cried. 'You come to redeem our religion, our laws, liberties and lives.' A few months later he strolled through Westminster Hall with what he described as 'true liberty'. The observations of Roger Morrice were written in his 'Entring Book', a huge diary a million words long in which he revealed his secret fears about the state of the country in which he lived. Like many of his fellow citizens he hated Catholicism – or 'popery' to give it the name he preferred to use. He believed that it was hell-bent on destroying the Protestant Church in Britain and everywhere he looked he saw evidence of this. His fears were confirmed when, in 1685, Charles II died and his brother James, Duke of York, became King. James was a Catholic. He had resigned from his position as Lord Admiral after refusing to take Anglican communion as the provisions of the Test Act, passed by Parliament in 1673, required. Between 1679 and 1681 some MPs, aware of James's religious sympathies, had tried to pass legislation to prevent him from succeeding to the throne but had been thwarted by Charles who dissolved Parliament more than once to prevent it being passed. His brother's deft manoeuvrings secured the British throne for James: his own clumsiness lost it before his reign had barely begun.

James seemed remarkably insensitive to the fears and passions of his people from the very first moment that he inherited the throne. On the day of his coronation – the crown almost fell off his head when it was placed there by the Archbishop of Canterbury – he also took communion with his Catholic confessor. The discomfort that many were feeling was masked momentarily by the uprising led by one of Charles II's illegitimate sons, the Duke of Monmouth. He returned from exile in the Netherlands and laid claim to the throne. Having landed at Lyme Regis he raised an army in the West Country, but was defeated by the King's forces at the Battle of Sedgemoor in 1685. He was brutally executed. His followers were rounded up and brought before Judge Jeffreys who, in the notorious 'Bloody Assizes', dispensed the justice of the times with enthusiastic violence. Having hanged or deported hundreds of people in Monmouth's tattered army, the King rewarded him with the post of Lord Chancellor.

The rebellion briefly strengthened James's position. He had acted as a King should and suppressed insurrection. But he was not a man to take advantage of the opportunities life gave him. His personal preferences and beliefs overrode any skills he possessed as a ruler and, reinforced by the House of Stuart's conviction of its absolute right to govern, set about unpicking anti-Catholic legislation. In November 1685 he was criticised by the House of Commons for appointing Catholic army officers in contravention of the Test Acts. He ignored their attack and appointed other Catholics to public office, granting them dispensation from the provisions that would have previously prevented their appointment. In April 1687 he issued a Declaration of Indulgence which suspended the Test Acts altogether and removed other laws that forbade Catholic worship and education. He followed this up with a second Declaration the following year. He demanded that it be read out in all the country's churches and when seven bishops refused, they were put on trial for sedition. The situation had grown very tense: Huguenots, French Protestants fleeing from Louis XIV's persecution of their religion, brought with them stories of atrocities. For many in Britain there was little doubt that their nation too was about to be enslaved by popery. In June 1688, James's second wife, Mary of Modena, gave birth to a boy. A healthy Catholic heir was the last thing she had been expected to produce: she had already lost ten children, either at birth or in infancy. The King's son was his enemies' last straw and they looked across the sea for a Protestant saviour.

Waiting for them in Holland was William of Orange. He was married to Mary, the daughter of James by his first wife, Anne Hyde. Mary, like her husband, was a Protestant. Her mother had been the daughter of the Earl of Clarendon, one of the architects of the restoration to the throne of Charles II and a Lord Chancellor of England. Their combined pedigree made them an ideal couple to inhabit the country's troubled throne and in 1688 seven noblemen sent William a letter in which he was invited to invade because there were 'nineteen parts of twenty of the people throughout the kingdom ... desirous of a change'. William needed no second bidding. England would give him the power base he needed to challenge the aggression of France. He issued a declaration criticising James's advisors for having 'overturned the religion, laws and liberties' of the kingdom and, reassuring the people that his expedition had no other purpose but 'to have free and lawful Parliament as soon as possible', landed at Torbay in Devon with his troops on 5th November. James, who seems to have possessed a curious mixture of obstinacy and indolence, took the view that this time he was powerless to resist. His other daughter, Anne, had deserted to her sister's cause and his troops, including his best commander, the Earl of Marlborough, had defected to the invader. He fled to France.

The King had gone, but it was not yet time to crown his successor. The Parliament that met in the wake of James's departure decided on two courses of action unique in the history of Britain. Firstly, it offered the crown to William and Mary jointly; secondly, it came on condition that they agreed to a Declaration of Rights. This was the first and only time that the country was ruled by a King and Queen together and, more importantly, the moment when the monarchy was required to accept limitations on its power before being granted the right to rule. This was the Glorious Revolution. The battles, bloodshed and arguments of seventeenth-century Britain culminated in the historic agreement made between William and Mary and the Convention Parliament in 1689. The Declaration, enshrined as a Bill of Rights in the same year, upheld the supremacy of the Protestant religion by preventing Catholics, or those married to a Catholic, from becoming monarch. It also set out the constitutional framework within which the monarchy was expected to operate. It stated that the suspension or creation of laws without Parliament's consent was illegal; that taxation by royal prerogative was illegal; that subjects had the right to petition the monarch without redress; that a standing army was illegal, unless approved by Parliament; and that 'for the amending, strengthening and preserving of the laws, Parliaments ought to be held frequently'. Some of this sounds like Magna Carta four hundred and seventy-four years on. All of it expounds the inalienable rights of the British people, through their Parliament, which have formed the basis of their freedom ever since. Edmund Burke described it as an event 'made to preserve our ancient indisputable laws and liberties'. Macaulay made it the starting point for his *History of England*. He believed that although we give it the name of 'revolution', it was actually an historic act of preservation, providing Britain with a constitutional security that would prevent it falling prey to destructive revolution later. A later leader, Margaret Thatcher, called it 'the first step on the road [which] led to the establishment of universal suffrage and full parliamentary democracy'.

The Revolution of 1688 was glorious because in many ways it was not a revolution at all, but simply the ideal point in time to reaffirm the rights and liberties for which men and women had been fighting since the century began.

There are some who would take issue with this interpretation of the events of 1688–1689. James II, they argue, was trying to introduce religious toleration by supporting Catholics. The Bill of Rights was a conservative document that reinforced the status quo rather than celebrated the liberties of the future. It was for the most part a re-statement of existing law, not an argument for anything new. It is true that the noblemen who invited William of Orange to invade their country were seeking to return to a situation where Catholicism was outlawed and where the King would respect the established religion of the country. But the fact remains that by using the opportunity of his removal to refashion and restate the relationship between monarch and people, the Convention Parliament provided Britain for the first time with a strong basis for governmental partnership.

Gin Craze

Binge-drinking is nothing new. In London in the 1720s the consumption of gin reached epidemic proportions. It was sold in 'dramshops' which promised their customers that they could be 'Drunk for a Penny. Dead drunk for twopence' – adding, for those wanting to sleep off their booze: 'Straw for Nothing'. With heavy drinking came an increase in violent crime and higher mortality rates. In 1729 the government, concerned that the country was degenerating into an excess of vice, attempted to tax gin production. The producers complained and the law was repealed four years later. After that, the craze for gin got steadily worse. William Hogarth's famous engraving, *Gin Lane* (1751), provides a terrifying picture of what life was like in a city that consumed 11 million gallons of gin a year. In the middle of the picture a gin-soaked mother abandons her baby while in the background a man and a dog fight for possession of a bone. Another man is pawning his coat, his wife her kitchen utensils; the only people making money in this desperate scene are pawnbrokers, coffin-makers and, of course, distillers.

Hogarth's engraving appeared at the height of the gin craze. New, harsher legislation introduced in the 1750s gradually led to a downturn in the gin industry and the craze for immoderate consumption died out. Gin – or Geneva as it was originally called – was invented by the Dutch in the seventeenth century as a form of medicine, and began to reach Britain in the wake of William of Orange's accession to the throne. William, determined to penalise France, raised taxes on French brandy, but reduced them on alcoholic drinks made from British corn. He also removed constraints on spirit sales and production, cancelling a monopoly which the Company of Distillers had enjoyed for fifty years. The result was that spirits such as gin, aniseed water and 'plague water' became enormously popular. Britain's appetite for cheap booze has always been part of its history.

James II, like his brother, father and grandfather before him, believed in the absolute nature of his royal prerogative. Because he was a Catholic, he tried to introduce Catholic toleration. But that was not what his people wanted: they would not in fact accept Catholic emancipation for another hundred and forty years. The Revolution of 1688 was glorious because in many ways it was not a revolution at all, but simply the ideal point in time to reaffirm the rights and liberties for which men and women had been fighting since the century began.

James II threw his insignia of office, the Great Seal, into the River Thames as he ran away to France. But he still made one effort to recover his throne. He raised an army in Ireland, but was defeated by William – 'King Billie' – at the Battle of the Boyne in 1690. He returned to France where, free to indulge in his taste for mistresses, he died in 1701. The country he left behind settled into comparative domestic peace at last. From now on its wars would be fought abroad, on the continent of Europe, and the world beyond.

CHAPTER 6

Sir Robert Walpole Becomes Prime Minister

1721

In 1721 Sir Robert Walpole became the King's chief minister. Although he never officially held the title of 'Prime Minister' he was to all intents and purposes the first politician to hold that position. His long tenure of power marked the time when the government of Britain by cabinet, through Parliament, was consolidated and enlarged.

Life in Britain during the first quarter of the eighteenth century was very different from what it had been a hundred years before. At the beginning of the seventeenth century the country seethed with religious and political turmoil. The unrest led to the execution of one King and the dethronement of another. When George I, the German Elector of Hanover, discovered that he was to be the next King of England in 1714, the turbulence delivered one final jolt to the system before it died away. The son of James II, James Edward Stuart, landed in Scotland with the support of a few Tory noblemen, but his expedition collapsed, the French support upon which it was relying never materialised and the Jacobite rebels were rounded up and executed. This was the last gasp of a cyclone of discontent: the country, as if exhausted by its internal struggles and the factious politics they had created, gradually began to roll along more calmly to the stately rhythms of a landowning oligarchy. From splendid palaces, dignified manors or elegant townhouses, the gentlemen of England smoothly proceeded to extend their hold over the nation. Into this equable, if unashamedly selfish, landscape stepped one of the most remarkable politicians in British history – Sir Robert Walpole.

Robert Walpole was chief minister to both George I and George II for twenty-one years, from 1721 to 1742. He was above all a man of appetites. He liked money, he liked fine food and wine, he liked collecting valuable treasures, and he liked women. But more than anything else he liked the fountain from which these good things flowed – power. He understood better than any of those around him that to hold power in Britain in the first part of the eighteenth century you needed to do two things that modern politicians regard as second nature: you had to network, and you had to spin. He knew that without the confidence of the King he would be lost, but he was also aware that he needed the confidence of the House of Commons too. His unique skill was to make himself the conduit between the

Sir Robert Walpole was one of the most remarkable politicians in British history.

heart of the body politic, the King, and its nerve ends – the bewigged gentry watching his every move with glistening concentration from the benches of the House of Commons. He enjoyed the power of patronage and he was not above bribery and corruption: in looking after the country he made sure that he looked after himself. But by exercising the art of survival for so long he consolidated the relationship between the monarchy and its people and helped create a stable system of government capable of weathering the most tempestuous storms.

Robert Walpole was born in Norfolk and throughout his life adopted the earthy manners and plain speaking of a country squire. He was in fact much more than that. Educated at Eton and Cambridge he became an MP at the very beginning of the eighteenth century. In 1705 he was made a member of the Council of the Lord High Admiral, and three years later 'Secretary at War'. His political ascent was interrupted in 1712 when he was imprisoned in the Tower of London for 'a high breach of trust and notorious corruption', but his Whig friends stuck by him and after only six months he was released. This was a time in British politics when the labels 'Whig' and 'Tory' had begun to be applied to supporters of different interests – although they were still a long way from forming political parties as we understand them today. A 'Tory' tended to be a High Anglican traditionalist who disliked religious dissent and disapproved of the war with France; a 'Whig' supported the war and was in favour of religious toleration. The failure of the Jacobite rebellion in 1715, which had been supported by some important Tory peers, severely reduced the influence they had enjoyed under Queen Anne and cleared the way for the Whigs to gain the ascendancy under the Hanoverian kings.

It was the South Sea Bubble that floated Robert Walpole to the top. When in 1720 the crisis broke, Walpole seized the opportunity to advance his personal position. He was by this time Paymaster General. An investor in the scheme himself – he was never a man to turn down an opportunity to make fast money – he had nevertheless warned of its dangers when it had been first proposed. He was therefore able to give the impression that he had been critical of it all along and was given a free hand to introduce measures to alleviate its disastrous effects – meting out harsh treatment to the company's directors and taking control of its affairs. Most important of all, he protected the King and some of his ministers from their involvement in the scandal. His skill earned him the title of 'Skreen Master' from his critics and the position of First Lord of the Treasury and Chancellor of the Exchequer from his everlastingly grateful monarch.

Walpole then made the decision that earns him his place in history. He chose to remain in the House of Commons rather than move to the House of Lords as tradition would have expected him to do. He knew that if he was to retain power he needed to maintain influence over the country's MPs – and it is this innate understanding of the nature of power in British politics that makes him such an important figure. Having gained power, he held on to it. Both the kings that he served, George I and George II, were happy to trust him with the running of the country, and by using his influence over them – or their wives and mistresses – Walpole was able to secure the appointments he wanted to build around him a team of ministers with whom he could work. He never enjoyed the power of appointment himself – that still resided with the King – but he was trusted sufficiently to obtain the results he wanted. Mastery of the House of Commons, an ability to manage the King, his boss, and the creation of an efficient ministerial team – 'a cabinet' – are the qualities that allow Walpole to be called Britain's first 'Prime Minister'. A courtier of the period, Lord Hervey, said of him that George II and his Queen 'were possessed with an opinion that Sir Robert Walpole was, by so great a superiority, the most able man in the kingdom, that he understood the revenue, and knew how to manage that formidable and refractory body, the House of Commons, so much better than any other man, that it was impossible for the business of the Crown to be well done without him'. The King gave his clever minister Number 10, Downing Street, which Walpole decided should be made available for the use of all successive First Lords of the Treasury – another example of how he gathered around him the status and trappings of prime ministerial office.

The other reason why Walpole stayed in power for so long was that his policies appealed to the British squirearchy. He kept taxes low. He supported a tolerant approach to religious dissidence. He liked peace and avoided war. But no one, however clever, can walk the tightrope of British politics forever and eventually, after twenty-one years in power, even Sir Robert Walpole was forced out of office. The reason was war. Although he always preferred to 'let sleeping dogs lie', Walpole found himself at war in the Caribbean with Spain in 1739 because of tensions over trade rights. He knew it was wrong. 'They may ring the bells now,' he said when the nation responded joyfully to news of its declaration, 'but soon they will be wringing their hands.' Nevertheless, he acquiesced to popular demand and allowed it to go ahead. It went badly: Spain prevented a massive British fleet from capturing their port of Cartagena in what is now Colombia, and Walpole's enemies pounced.

'It was not,' said a Victorian commentator, George Cooke, of Walpole, 'the minister who corrupted the age; his crime was that he pandered to the prevailing depravity.' But Walpole's success owed much more to his extraordinary ability than it did to lining the pockets of those who would support him. As he battled to save his career and reputation he made a defiant speech to the House of Commons. 'My great and principal crime,' he told them, 'is my long continuance in office; or, in other words, the long exclusion of those who now complain against me.' There was definitely some truth in that. 'I will not shrink,' he went on, ' from the responsibility which attaches to the post I have the honour to hold; and should ... any one step taken by government be proved to be either disgraceful or disadvantageous to the nation, I am ready to hold myself accountable.' He had a point here too. The manner of his administration might not have been to everyone's liking, but its effectiveness was beyond doubt.

But his time had passed. A new breed of politician was coming on to the scene – 'the patriots' as Walpole scornfully called them. Among them was William Pitt the Elder, who led the charge against the 'prime minister' in the House. 'The people may become disaffected as well as discontented,' he sneered, 'when they find the King continues obstinately to employ a minister who, they think, oppresses them at home and betrays them abroad.' In later life Pitt changed his views of Walpole's time in office, but that would come far too late to save the First Lord of the Treasury's career. Walpole's support was draining away. In February 1742 he resigned from all his offices and died three years later.

In his home county of Norfolk, Walpole built one of the greatest houses of the period: Houghton Hall is an exquisite Palladian-style villa. The most distinguished architects of the time – William Kent and Colen Campbell among them – worked on its design. The local village was knocked down and moved a bit further away to provide its halls and salons with better views. It was hung with the finest paintings and decorated with the rarest *objets d'art*. It was a provincial palace, a splendid symbol of the aspirations of the age, a great, quiet monument to English rural wealth. In its peaceful and secure setting it represents much of what Robert Walpole was all about. In the seventeenth century the liberties of Britain were fought for – noisily, violently and passionately. In the eighteenth century they gradually came to be quietly accepted, in no small part the pleasant fruits of Walpole's masterly management of government.

CHAPTER 7

The Publication of Adam Smith's
The Wealth of Nations
1776

In 1776 the Scottish writer and philosopher Adam
Smith published his two-volume work, *An Inquiry into
the Nature and Causes of the Wealth of Nations* – known
throughout the world by its shorter title *The Wealth
of Nations*. His ideas provided the basis for the
development of a free-market economy in Britain.

Adam Smith published *The Wealth of Nations* almost exactly four
months before the American colonists issued their Declaration of
Independence. Smith's book was 900-pages long – the life's work
of a learned mind. The colonists' Declaration was just a little over
1300-words long, the resounding rallying cry of revolutionary
politicians. Despite these differences they had many things in
common. Both were central products of the Age of Enlightenment;
and both changed the world. In fact Adam Smith was very much
alive to the issues confronting Britain and her American possessions. 'The discovery of America,' he wrote, 'and that of a passage
to the East Indies by the Cape of Good Hope are the two greatest
and most important events recorded in the history of mankind.'
He was quite sure that the colonists ought to be allowed to go
their own way. Britain needed to leave behind its 'golden dream' of
imperial power and marry its 'future views and designs to the real
mediocrity of her circumstances'. Such radical foresight was typical
of a man whose ideas as a whole influenced the future of Britain
profoundly.

Adam Smith had an acute understanding of what made the

world tick. In his everyday life, however, he was notoriously absent-minded. Once, when making tea, he used bread and butter instead of tea leaves. During a visit to a Glasgow factory he became so involved in his explanation of his theories on labour that he fell into a tanning pit. He was a dedicated scholar who collected a library of over three thousand books, but he was not remotely stuffy. His lectures at Glasgow University were enormously popular. 'He has nothing of that stiffness and pedantry,' wrote James Boswell 'which is too often found in professors.' He enjoyed cards, though does not seem to have had much luck with women. He seems to have fallen in love with women on one or two occasions, and to have been pursued by a French noblewoman on another, but he remained a bachelor, close to his mother whom he outlived by only six years. It was his mind that people admired. He was a member of Dr Johnson's Literary Club, the most influential intellectual gathering in Britain during the second half of the eighteenth century, where, at the Turk's Head tavern in Soho's Gerrard Street, he could discuss his ideas with men like Edmund Burke, Richard Sheridan, Edward Gibbon and Oliver Goldsmith. Europe was wakening to new ideas. The liberty of the individual and the rights of man were concepts under constant discussion. Within a few years they would crystallise into political action, sweeping away the French monarchy in bloody revolution and cutting the American colonies adrift from their British masters. Adam Smith, with his odd manners and well-stocked mind, was one of those who fuelled the forces of change.

By the middle of the eighteenth century the British economy was different from other countries in Europe in quite a few respects. The Industrial Revolution was beginning to get under way and trade and commerce were booming, providing employment for huge numbers of people. London was already a world shopping centre. According to one observer: 'every production of art, and every effort of industry', could be seen in The Strand, which was then its main commercial highway. Adam Smith was born far away from London, in Kirkcaldy in Fife, but here too, in this port on the

Firth of Forth, evidence of Britain's business as a trading nation was everywhere to be seen. Daniel Defoe, who visited the town about the time Smith was born in 1723, reported that 'it has some considerable merchants in it, I mean in the true sense of the word merchant. There are also several good ships belonging to the town … the traders in Kirkcaldy have really a very considerable traffic, both at home and abroad.' The author of *The Wealth of Nations* grew up with evidence of global wealth all around him.

He also grew up in a country that was embarking on a period of security following the Act of Union with England in 1707. Although it had lost its parliament, Scotland was enjoying social stability, and, as the century advanced, its intellectual and artistic life began to blossom. Artists, writers and philosophers helped to build Scotland into an important intellectual centre – men like the architect Robert Adam, who was born in the same town as Adam Smith, or the philosopher and historian David Hume, who became his lifelong friend. In the gracious terraces and elegant public buildings of Edinburgh's New Town, where the thinkers of the age looked back to classical antiquity for inspiration, Adam Smith and his contemporaries questioned everything in the world around them. This was the 'Scottish Enlightenment' – the northern branch of a movement that absorbed all Europe at this time. The Scottish Enlightenment had a particular interest in exploring human nature. Its members wanted to find ways to improve the lives of ordinary Scots whose standard of living was much lower than their English counterparts. Living in a country with historic universities, a strong academic tradition and close ties with France, where many of Europe's greatest minds could then be found, they were well equipped to explore solutions to the problems of mankind.

In 1759, Adam Smith published *The Theory of the Moral Sentiments* in which he examined how we tell the difference between right and wrong. This was an important intellectual debate of the time. Some argued that the only standard that mattered was that set by the law and the sovereign who made it; others believed that moral principles could be worked out on a rational basis. Smith took a different view altogether. He argued that people are born with a moral sense: their understanding of right and wrong is instinctive, not decided for them by lawmakers. He also came up with the idea of sympathy. We have, he said, a natural sense of conscience, of belonging to society, and we automatically step into the shoes of an 'Impartial Spectator' to judge or assess our actions. In other words human society is not subject to any form of design: it is dependent on the randomness of human action. This concept of human freedom, of unfettered behaviour, is something that Smith would go on to develop further in *The Wealth of Nations*. Meanwhile *The Theory of the Moral Sentiments* was very well received. Edmund Burke called it 'one of the most beautiful fabrics of moral theory that has ever appeared ... Rather painting than writing.' This literary success led to him to being asked to accompany the young Duke of Buccleuch on his Grand Tour of Europe, an offer so generous – it included a guaranteed income of £300 a year for life – that Smith could not turn it down. Between 1764 and 1766 he travelled throughout France and visited Geneva, where he met Voltaire. The death of the Duke's younger brother brought the tour to an end, but not before Smith had had the opportunity to meeting some of the country's most important intellectuals. He also found time to begin work on *The Wealth of Nations*.

France in the 1760s was a grand, hidebound nation full of beauty, culture and brilliant ideas, imprisoned within the sclerotic structure of the *ancien régime*. The King, Louis XV, great grandson of Louis XIV, had already been on the throne for nearly fifty years. He was an absolute monarch, but his failure to reform the government of his country meant that his successor, his grandson Louis XVI, would eventually go to his death in the French Revolution twenty-five years later. Adam Smith in his tour of France could already see the telltale signs of decay. France, he observed, was 'a museum of economical errors', and would do well to take the advice of François Quesnay, one of its most influential thinkers, who argued that the price of products, goods or services could not be fixed. 'Competition alone,' he said, 'can regulate prices with equity.' Back home in Kirkcaldy, his £300 a year safe and sound, Adam Smith spent the next ten years in quiet study. He thought about what Quesnay had said, watched the ships in his home port plying their trade, and, marrying theory to practice, finally came up with the book that would form the basis of modern economic thinking.

Adam Smith was not an economist. The word as we understand it today did not exist in the middle of the eighteenth century. He was a moral philosopher: his main aim was to understand human actions so that he could provide them with a moral frame-work. In *The Wealth of Nations* he did this by starting from the premise that self-interest was at the heart of society, but that this was not something we should be worried about. The self-interest of different groups was not mutually exclusive. In a typically pithy phrase he observed: 'It is not from the benevolence of the butcher, the brewer, or the baker, that we expect our dinner, but from their regard to their own interest.' Competition, he believed, was essential to the health of society because it forced people to produce goods and services that would be of value to others. The producer, he explained, 'intends only his gain, and he is in this, as in many other cases, led by an invisible hand to promote an end which was no part of his intention'. He also laid out his ideas about the division of labour, explaining it through the example of pin-making. In the eighteenth century the hand-made pin, used for fastening pieces of cloth or paper, was a luxury item exported all over the world. Adam Smith argued that an individual worker could probably make only twenty pins a day. But if ten workers divided up the eighteen parts of the pin-making process between them, their combined output would increase dramatically. He said he had seen a small factory where ten men, although poor and lacking the best machinery, had, by dividing their labour in the way he described, produced as many as 48,000 pins in a day.

Smith then went on to discuss how the surplus created by such a process led to opulence, allowing the worker to exchange his surplus for other things. From this he moved to a discussion of the laws of supply and demand. The 'natural' price of a commodity, he wrote, was the cost of producing and supplying it; but the 'market' price can only be determined by demand. These two price levels must be kept in equilibrium, he said. The introduction of taxes or monopolies that unnaturally depressed or inflated the one against the other 'diminishes opulence'. This analysis led Smith to the conclusion that free trade was the only way to operate the market. Britain, he argued, 'should by all means be made a free port, that there should be no interruptions of any kind made to foreign trade, that if it were possible to defray the expenses of government by any other method, all duties, customs, and excise should be abolished, and that free commerce and liberty of exchange should be allowed with all nations and for all things'. Even Adam Smith's most devoted followers have never been able to introduce economic policies as radical as that!

Smith would have been horrified at the thought of his studious reflections being used as the manifesto for rapacious commercial self-interest.

Adam Smith's belief in the natural forces of the market became the principles upon which the capitalist economies of the West built their fortunes in the nineteenth and twentieth centuries. He became an icon. In 1984 in the United States, President Ronald Reagan's supporters at the Republican Convention wore badges bearing his image. In March 2007 his picture replaced that of composer Sir Edward Elgar on the British £20 note, together with an illustration of the division of labour in pin manufacturing. Prime Minister Gordon Brown – also MP for Kirkcaldy – evoked the memory of Adam Smith in a speech in January 2007. 'The Wealth of Nations,' he said, 'explained the foundations of the world's first industrial revolution starting here in Britain.'

Adam Smith himself would probably have found these claims exorbitant. He certainly would have been horrified at the thought of his studious reflections being used as the manifesto for rapacious commercial self-interest, even if he was the first person to explain how the dynamics of a free market needed to work. He simply wanted to explain how human beings needed to behave to make themselves freer and therefore happier. The idea that the study of economics in itself could become a philosophy would never have occurred to him: the mechanics of the market were inseparable from the mechanics of man.

Perhaps it was inevitable that Adam Smith's work would become a capitalist bible. After *The Wealth of Nations* was published the President of the Royal Society criticised its author for writing a book on trade when he had never experienced the world of business himself. Samuel Johnson, perspicacious as ever, leapt to Adam Smith's defence. 'There is nothing that requires more to be illustrated by philosophy,' he said, 'than does trade.' For that remark every modern student of business studies should give thanks. They owe more than they may realise to the quiet contemplations of Adam Smith and the other intellectual giants of the eighteenth century.

CHAPTER 8

The Great Reform Act
1832

In 1832 Parliament passed an act of parliamentary
reform that greatly extended men's right to vote in
Britain. The act was bitterly opposed by many sections
of society and the number of people enfranchised
was still very small. Despite this the 1832 Act, and the
subsequent Reform Acts of the nineteenth century,
helped build Britain into the democracy it is today.

William Thackeray's novel, *Vanity Fair*, is set in the Britain of
the early nineteenth century. Among its vivid cast of characters is
Sir Pitt Crawley, a mean, boozy baronet who owns the borough of
'Queen's Crawley'. The population of Queen's Crawley, Thackeray
tells us, had declined over the years and had reached 'that condition of borough which used to be denominated rotten'. A rotten
borough was a constituency entitled to send two members to
Parliament even if its population was tiny or non-existent. Usually
under the control of the local landowner or lord of the manor,
it was a profitable, corrupt and entirely undemocratic method of
selecting the representatives of the people. It was, however, a privilege which its owners were not inclined to give up lightly. In *Vanity
Fair*, Sir Pitt is heard to say 'with perfect justice in his elegant
way: "Rotten! be hanged – it produces me a good fifteen hundred
a year."'

Queen's Crawley was a product of Thackeray's imagination,
but it did not differ from many places that really existed. Typical
of these was Old Sarum, the ancient early settlement outside
the city of Salisbury. By the early part of the nineteenth century no
one lived there anymore, and yet it was still entitled to send two

members to Parliament. The fact that a constituency did not need to have any inhabitants at all was only one of the extraordinary features of the way Parliament recruited its members. In some places it was enough to have lived there for six months before a man could vote (women, of course, were still entirely disqualified). In others only members of a local corporation were allowed to do so. Some boroughs were only open to 'freemen', although the definition of a 'freeman' varied from place to place. Then there were boroughs where the right to vote was inherited; yet others where voting was permitted for those who paid the local poor rate. The boroughs produced the majority of the House of Commons' 658 members, but there were also a number of county seats. Here too inequality was rife. Each county was, like the boroughs, entitled to return two members whatever the size of its population. At the beginning of the nineteenth century the growing towns of the Midlands and the North of England had virtually no representation at all. The right to vote was based on ancient, semi-feudal procedures that restricted the number of electors to something between 400,000–600,000 people out of a population of 16.5 million. Democracy did not exist.

There had been calls for reform throughout the second half of the eighteenth century. An early advocate was William Pitt, Earl of Chatham, who had first entered Parliament as a member for the defunct village of Old Sarum. Speaking in 1766, he coined the word 'rotten' to describe the state of the constitution. 'It cannot continue a century,' he said. 'If it does not drop, it must be amputated.' In 1780 the Duke of Richmond presented a bill for establishing annual parliaments, universal manhood suffrage and equal electoral districts but a proposal so radical was rejected without a division. The argument for reform was then taken up by the Earl of Chatham's son, Pitt the Younger, who both before and during his time as Prime Minister tried to abolish rotten boroughs and increase the number of county and large borough seats. Outside Parliament there was increasing pressure for change. Britain's growing middle class, empowered by the new-found affluence of the Industrial

Revolution, felt frustrated by its lack of representation in the affairs of state. Catholics, who were still excluded from voting, were looking for change as well. The demand for reform took place against the background of the ideas of the Enlightenment where concepts of individual liberty were at the forefront of men's thinking. The radical writer and thinker, Thomas Paine, who had a huge influence on both the American and French Revolutions published his most famous work, *The Rights of Man* in 1791. 'Can anything be more limited, and at the same time more capricious,' he wrote, 'than the qualification of electors is in England?' Paine was able to explain the ideas of the Enlightenment in a way that ordinary people could understand. His book became very popular among working men. Constitutional societies sprang up all over the country, publishing pamphlets to spread their beliefs.

Then, in 1792, the temperament of the British people changed. In September they began to hear the news of the massacres in Paris where a violent mob had murdered hundreds of Catholic priests. The following year they listened fearfully to the stories of the execution of the French King and Queen and Robespierres's great Terror. For many of them Tom Paine was no longer a radical friend, but a dangerous revolutionary whose advocacy of a republic sounded alarmingly like the bloodthirsty ambitions of the French mob. The French Revolution may have smashed to pieces the antiquated, medieval practices of the *ancien régime* – but it held back the development of democracy in Britain by nearly forty years. The forces of liberalism are always at their weakest when fear stalks the land. Within a few years Britain was at war with France where a young general called Napoleon Bonaparte had seized the initiative and, claiming that he was carrying the spirit of the Revolution to all parts of Europe, set about building a new French Empire. By the end of the 1790s even William Pitt was concerned that radicalism might lead to revolution. In 1795 the Seditious Meetings and Treasonable Practices Acts clamped down on dissent, despite fears from some Whigs that this stifling of debate could be more dangerous than the evil it was trying to defeat. Such concerns have an echo in our own time when people worry that measures to defeat terrorism will only result in the erosion of our civil liberties. In one final attempt to carry out reform Charles Grey, who had tried before to bring the issue before Parliament, proposed changes – but his efforts failed. All thought of reform drained away as the nation huddled together to protect itself from the devilish activities of the power across the Channel.

As the war against Napoleon drew to an end nearly twenty years later, a new radical spirit emerged in the country. The long fight against France had had a damaging economic impact. In the north of England, still growing rapidly as the engine of Britain's Industrial Revolution, men started to campaign for better conditions. Unemployment and food prices were high. In 1817 cotton workers from Manchester tried and failed to march on London. Two years later the city's appetite for protest led to a terrible disaster.

On 16th August 1819, a large crowd gathered in St Peter's Field in Manchester. The meeting had been organised by the Manchester Patriotic Union Society to draw up a petition for parliamentary reform. Shortly after one o'clock in the afternoon, as it got under way and the speeches began, the local magistrates decided to stop it. Presumably they were worried by the slogans on some of the banners in the crowd, although by modern standards they seemed harmless enough, calling for things like 'Annual Parliaments' and 'Universal Suffrage'. They were also concerned that the first speaker on the platform was one Henry 'Orator' Hunt, well known as an activist in radical politics. The local yeomanry – mainly tradesmen completely inexperienced in crowd control – were ordered to arrest him. As they made their way through the thousands of people gathered for the meeting they were jostled and drew their sabres. A company of hussars, whom the magistrates had put on standby, were sent in to rescue them and in the ensuing panic eleven people were killed and about four hundred injured, many trampled by the soldiers' horses. The event passed into history as 'The Peterloo Massacre', an act of brutal repression against the growing demand for greater liberty among the people of Britain.

The government showed no remorse. Hunt was arrested and imprisoned. The 'Six Acts' passed later that year gave magistrates increased powers to search and seize weapons, shorten the period in which defendants could prepare for trial, and limited public meetings outside the parish boundary to no more than fifty people. Britain in the early part of the nineteenth century was modernising fast. Railways, mills, coal, iron and cotton were transforming the country and preparing it for a period of wealth the like of which it had never seen before. But to begin with these great developments did not carry with them a movement for intellectual and social change. Fear of radicalism remained the principal preoccupation of the governing class, and its fears seemed justified when, in 1830, France fell prey to revolution once more. Even William Gladstone, the great liberal reformer of nineteenth-century British politics, who was then a young man at Oxford, took fright at the thought of parliamentary reform. 'If,' he said, 'the nobility, the gentry, the clergy are to be alarmed, overawed or smothered by the expression of popular opinion ... the day of our greatness and stability is no more.'

Fear of radicalism remained the principal preoccupation of the governing class.

In 1828 the victor of Waterloo, the Duke of Wellington, became Prime Minister. The stern, unbending qualities that had served him so well as a soldier were of less benefit to him as a politician. The Tories had been in power since 1812. Wellington was determined to continue their resistance to reform, but the pressure for change was at last becoming irresistible. Unrest in the country was growing and the more liberal wing of the Tory Party began to feel that some sort of change was inevitable. In 1830, Charles Grey, now Earl Grey and the leader of the Whigs in Parliament, asked the Duke whether he planned to introduce any measure of parliamentary reform. The Duke said he did not. Indeed he went further, and

The Factory Act 1850

In the nineteenth century children were used mercilessly as cheap labour, and conditions in factories were as bad or worse than many third-world countries today. A series of Factory Acts passed between 1802 and 1891 regulated the hours for children and women, although conditions remained harsh. The 1802 Act, for instance, said that children were not allowed to work for more than twelve hours a day. The Act of 1833 prevented the employment of children under the age of nine, and a further Act in 1844 restricted eight- to twelve-year olds from working more than six and a half hours a day.

The 1850 Act was more far reaching. One of its proponents was Lord Shaftesbury, the philanthropist and social reformer who, although disliked by many of his contemporaries for his reliance on religion rather than reform, kept the idea of improvement in factory conditions alive. The statue of Eros in Piccadilly Circus in London is a memorial to him.

The 1850 Act ruled that women and young people could only work in factories between 6 a.m. and 6 p.m. in the summer and 7 a.m. and 7 p.m. in the winter. Work had to finish by 2 p.m. on a Saturday, and the British weekend was born.

added that he 'should always feel it his duty to resist such measures when proposed by others'. It was the death knell of his ministry. He was forced to resign and Grey became Prime Minister. At last Britain could begin to change.

It would still be a gradual process. Lord Grey's government was as temperamentally opposed to radicalism as the Tories had been. When the Reform Bill was presented to Parliament by a member of the cabinet, Lord John Russell, he announced with astonishing complacency that 'there is no one more decided against annual parliaments, universal suffrage and the (secret) ballot than I am. My object is not to favour, but to put an end to such hopes and projects.' The bill that finally went into law increased the number of people entitled to vote by 80 per cent, but it was still only the equivalent of one in five of the male adult population. The parliamentary seats were redistributed and rotten boroughs were abolished. The large industrial towns were given much fairer representation. All this amounted to fairly reluctant legislation. The King, William IV, who had tried to get Wellington back as Prime Minister before Grey's ministry introduced the 1832 Reform Act, forbade all celebratory firework displays. The Duke himself was of the view that 'the Government of England is destroyed'.

The 1832 Reform Act was more important for what it indicated than what it did. In real terms it did not extend the franchise by very much: Britain remained a country under the control of wealthy landowners. But by accepting the principle of reform it had started a process that would continue throughout the rest of the century. In 1866 Lord John Russell, by then the Liberal Prime Minister, introduced a further Bill for reform which, although typically cautious, split his party and forced him to resign. The Conservatives under Benjamin Disraeli then picked up the torch and in 1867 drove through a measure that doubled the existing franchise. In 1884 Gladstone, by then long converted to the cause, widened the right to vote even further, extending the franchise to about two out of three of the adult male population. In long, slow, stages Britain began to evolve as a true democracy. The right to vote, however, remained a male prerogative. Women would have to fight another battle all on their own.

CHAPTER 9

The Foundation of the Women's Social and Political Union

1903

> In 1903 six women, including mother and daughter
> Emmeline and Christabel Pankhurst, founded the
> Women's Social and Political Union to campaign
> for women's right to vote in Britain. They and their
> followers became known as the 'Suffragettes'.

In 1999 the Labour MP, Tony Benn, told the BBC about a secret memorial he had placed in a House of Commons broom cupboard. It was a photograph of a woman called Emily Davison, draped in suffragette colours. Emily Davison was one of the most famous campaigners of the Suffragette movement. In 1911 she had hidden in the cupboard during the national census so that when she was discovered she could give her address as the House of Commons when she filled in the census form. Two years later she ran in front of the King's horse during the Epsom Derby and attempted to seize its bridle. She was seriously injured and died without ever regaining consciousness. Tony Benn called his tribute 'one of the very few monuments to democracy in the whole building'. It was, he said, 'a modest reminder of a great woman with a great cause'. Today, when we look at photographs of the women at the forefront of the campaign for women's votes, they seem to be rather unlikely radical militants. With their big hats and bustle skirts they look like natural members of Edwardian society. In fact their battle was fought with a determination and fierceness deliberately designed to disrupt the complacency of the age. The grand, quiet world of the last days of the British Empire would not be disturbed by reasoned argument alone. It needed the passion and self-sacrifice of the Suffragettes to bring about changes to the injustices of the political system.

Emmeline Pankhurst was one of the most influential women in the history of Britain in the late nineteenth and early twentieth centuries. She was born in Manchester in 1858 and twenty-one years later married a barrister, Richard Pankhurst. She came from a radical background and she married a radical man. After he failed to win a seat in Parliament the family moved to London where, based in a large house in Russell Square, they mixed with the forward-thinking people of the day, including William Morris and members of the Arts and Crafts movement. They were involved in the formation of the 'Women's Franchise League' in 1889, and at about this time Emmeline gave an interview to the paper *Women's Herald* in which she is reported as saying: 'I am a radical, devoted to the politics of the people, and to progress, especially where the education, emancipation and industrial interests of women are concerned.' This was the Pankhurst manifesto. In her manner and dress she was, as her daughter Christabel described her, 'a woman of her class and period'. In her thinking she was very much more than that.

The Pankhursts returned to Manchester in the early 1890s where Richard died suddenly in 1898. From this moment Emmeline devoted herself entirely to politics. The motto of the 'Women's Political and Social Union' was 'Deeds not Words', but to begin with the actions its members took were fairly peaceful and mainly revolved around interruptions at meetings of the Manchester Liberal Party. Mrs Pankhurst was by this time an experienced public speaker very much at ease in the world of political campaigning. In 1905 she and other members of the movement persuaded a Liberal MP to present a private member's bill in support of votes for women. The bill was talked out and Emmeline and her supporters held a demonstration outside Parliament in protest at the procedures of the House of Commons. She later said that this was the moment when the militant tactics of the Suffragettes began. For the moment, however, their hopes rested on the outcome of the impending election and back in Manchester the Pankhurst household was, according to one of their supporters, 'a home of love, unity and confusion' as Emmeline and her daughters, Christabel, Sylvia and Adela, canvassed in support of MPs allied to their cause. Despite the Liberal victory of 1906, no legislation for women's right to vote appeared in the King's speech. 'We must take a more militant attitude,' Emmeline told a big meeting in London, and from that moment on the fight was no longer just an intellectual one: it was a brutal, physical battle too.

For the next eight years, up until the outbreak of the First World War in 1914, the Suffragettes fought with a fury to get their message heard. They smashed windows in West End shops – 'a window can be replaced; a woman's body cannot' – said Emmeline; poured corrosive liquid into pillar boxes; and cut down phone and telegraph wires. They attacked golf clubs – bastions of male privilege then as now – and used acid to burn slogans on their greens: 'No Votes, No Golf' proclaimed one.

The Suffragettes fought with a fury to get their message heard.

They damaged works of art, including 'The 'Rokeby Venus' by Velásquez, and attacked public buildings. They set off a bomb at Oxted Station and fired an old cannon near Dudley Castle setting off an explosion. They started fires, ripped up flowerbeds and threw eggs. 'Those of you who can break windows – break them,' said Emmeline. 'Those of you who can still further attack the secret idol of property … do so.'

Violence on such a scale did not endear the Suffragettes to those in power or to many ordinary men and women in the country either. But the authorities were also to blame for how the campaign developed. When arrested many women went on hunger strike. They were often force fed in a brutal manner, and stories of their treatment only further inflamed their supporters. One Suffragette said that she had not been incited to action by anything any of the Pankhursts had said but 'by the government's treatment of

Mrs Pankhurst'. Working-class women tended to be dealt with more roughly than their middle-class or aristocratic colleagues who sometimes disguised themselves to prove the point about inequality of treatment. In 1913 the government introduced the so-called 'Cat And Mouse Act' under which prisoners suffering from the effects of a hunger strike could be temporarily discharged and then re-arrested once they had recovered.

There is an engaging story about Emmeline Pankhurst practising stone-throwing on a secluded part of Hook Heath in Surrey. Determined that she should be seen to be able to practise what she preached, but aware that her accuracy at missile despatch was completely untested, she and her friend, the composer Ethel Smyth, took themselves off to the countryside for a trial run. Choosing a large fir tree as a target, Emmeline picked up a handful of stones and began to throw them. The first flew backwards out of her hand and narrowly missed Ethel Smyth's dog. Only on the third attempt did she manage to hit her target. But such gentle, comparatively harmless, activity hardly captures the intensity and the courage with which the Pankhursts and their supporters fought for what they believed. Mrs Pankhurst went on hunger strike twelve times. During one of her last periods in prison the officers at Holloway decided she should be searched in case she was concealing an emetic to prevent her holding down food. She was forcibly stripped. Afterwards, refusing any help to dress her again, she lay on the floor lambasting those who had carried out the search. The image of this elegant, almost dainty, Edwardian lady lying stark naked on a prison floor watched by a group of officials is a much more accurate image of the nature of the battles which the Suffragettes fought.

In 1913 Emmeline Pankhurst travelled to America to try to win support for her campaign there. She made a speech at Hartford, Connecticut in which she described herself 'as a soldier who has temporarily left the field of battle'. But the battle, she said, would go on. 'It has come to a battle between the women and the government as to who shall yield first, whether they will yield and give us

Five Remarkable Women

Lady Mary Wortley Montagu (1689–1762)

One of the most influential women of the eighteenth century, Lady Montagu's extraordinary life saw her elected, by the age of eight, to the all-male Kit-Kat Club and later elope and marry Edward Wortley Montagu. Lady Montagu was responsible for the introduction of smallpox inoculation to Britain from Turkey, where her husband briefly served as ambassador. Her eloquent travel correspondence remains an important part of British literature.

Elizabeth Fry (1780–1845)

Social reformer Elizabeth Fry became a devout Quaker in 1798, and her religion had a profound impact on how she led the rest of her life. Having first witnessed the inhumane conditions of Newgate prison in 1813, she became one of the leading European campaigners for penal reform, particularly with regard to women prisoners. Education was another priority for Fry, and she co-founded schools both within and outside prisons. In 2002 Fry became one of only three women – the others being the Queen and Florence Nightingale – to appear on English banknotes.

Lady Florentia Sale (c.1790–1853)

Dubbed 'the Grenadier in Petticoats' by her husband's fellow officers, the formidable Lady Florentia Sale travelled with her husband, British army officer Sir Robert Henry Sale, to Mauritius, Burma and India,

---

the vote, or whether we shall give up our agitation. Well, they little know what women are. Women are very slow to rouse, but once they are aroused, once they are determined, nothing on earth and nothing in heaven will make women give way.'

The way the battle continued, however, was not quite as Emmeline expected. As has often happened to reforming movements in British history, it was a war that changed everything. In 1914, as the First World War began, militant feminists were released from prison and the Pankhursts joined Britain's patriotic

and proved herself more than capable of handling the privations of the life of an army wife. Lady Sale was taken hostage, together with other women, soldiers and children, during the Afghanistan Massacre of 1842, though they later succeeded in bribing their way to freedom. Her remarkable journal recounting these events was published in 1843 to great acclaim.

Grace Darling (1815–1842)

The daughter of a lighthouse keeper, Grace Darling helped save the lives of nine survivors of a shipwreck off the Northumbria coast in September 1838. Victorian society delighted in this story of female heroism, and Grace became so famous that her notoriety became something of a trial. It was said that so many people requested locks of her hair that she almost went bald, and five weeks after the rescue her father wrote to the newspapers to complain of the interminable portrait sittings that she had had to endure.

Edith Cavell (1865–1915)

Nurse Edith Cavell became a modern-day martyr during the First World War, after being executed by a German firing squad in October 1915. Cavell had been head nurse at a Red Cross hospital in Belgium where she helped hundreds of Allied prisoners of war escape. After being betrayed, she was interrogated, tried and shot.

upsurge, campaigning against pacifism and Bolshevism and renaming the 'Women's Social and Political Union' the 'Women's Party'. From becoming furiously anti-government, Mrs Pankhurst and Christabel became positively jingoistic, even handing out white feathers, the symbol of cowardice, to men who had not enlisted for the fight. War against Germany helped achieve their aims more rapidly than their war against the British Establishment. Women took on men's jobs as more and more troops were summoned to the Western Front and by the war's end even the former

Prime Minister, Herbert Asquith, who had not supported women's suffrage before, was heard to say: 'How could we have carried on the war without them? ... I find it impossible to withhold from women the power and the right of making their voices directly heard.' In 1918 the Representation of the People Act not only widened the right to vote to all adult men in Britain, but gave it to all women over the age of thirty – as long as they met minimum property qualifications. Ten years later, in March 1928, a bill was introduced that gave women the right to vote on the same terms as men. It became law the following July, two weeks after Emmeline Pankhurst had died.

All great movements require great leaders, and Emmeline Pankhurst was one of those. She was dictatorial. She fell out with two of her daughters, one of whom went to Australia in 1914 and never saw her mother again. She put principles before people. She was prepared to sacrifice everything for the cause in which she believed – even her life. The woman who nursed her through most of her hunger strikes, Kate Pine, said that she often worried that Emmeline would not last the night and gave her saline injections to save her. During the last period of her campaign Mrs Pankhurst was a middle-aged woman of fifty-six, and yet she still put herself through the privations of arrest, imprisonment and hunger strike. She had extraordinary charisma and a good nose for publicity: her marketing skills were excellent. Most importantly, by advocating militancy she made sure that her mission would not be ignored. Women's right to vote might not have been included in the Reform Act of 1918 if the issue had not been at the forefront of the public's mind. On its own, the role of women in the war effort would not necessarily have been enough to achieve it. Mrs Pankhurst knew that. 'The wrongs and the grievances of those people who have no power at all,' she said in her speech in Connecticut, 'are apt to be absolutely ignored. That is the history of humanity right from the beginning.' Emmeline Pankhurst had faults and she made mistakes. But she was never ignored.

CHAPTER 10

The Creation of the National Health Service 1948

In 1948 the British government announced the creation of the National Health Service. The NHS is now one of the most admired and cherished features of British national life.

I was born in 1946, just after the Second World War had come to an end. I grew up in a world of peace without plenty. Rationing still existed and everything was divided and apportioned – even the occasional Mars Bars, which my mother cut into slices before handing round to the family. We lived in Cricklewood in North London, and I can remember queuing for free orange juice in the local welfare clinic in the Kilburn High Road – it came in corked medicine bottles with prescription labels – and making a cautious visit to the horse butcher in West End Lane where the meat was cheap. I think we only tried it once. We were perfectly active, healthy and well fed, but a feeling of shortage, of indefinable deprivation, somehow pervaded the atmosphere. At school, to which we were never sent without having been dosed with cod liver oil, we were forced to drink a third of a pint of milk during our morning break. I have disliked drinking cold milk ever since. It reminds me of the days when nearly everything you drank or ate had to be good for you: food as a pleasure in its own right was a luxury to be enjoyed only occasionally. This was Britain in the age of austerity, the age when slowly and stoically it re-equipped itself after the long struggle of the war. At the heart of this process was the foundation of the National Health Service.

'The health of the people,' said Disraeli, 'is really the foundation upon which all their happiness and all their powers as a State depend.' He himself never showed much interest in social reform – even though his second ministry was responsible for the Public Health Act of 1875. Between 1870 and the outbreak of the First World War in 1914 a lot of legislation was introduced which extended the responsibility of government for the health and well-being of the nation. The reforming Liberal administration of 1906–1914 was its main architect: it gave schools permission to provide meals for underfed children, school medical examinations were introduced and in 1911 the National Insurance Act, designed to protect workers from sickness and enforced unemployment, was passed. As the war ended, in 1919, the Ministry of Health was created. The nation's health had become a government matter: it was recognised that a healthier country was not only happier, but likely to be more prosperous too. Of this there can be little doubt. Academic studies in America have since reached the conclusion that 50 per cent of Britain's economic growth since the start of the Industrial Revolution can be attributed to better nutrition.

One of the government's principal advisers when it passed the National Insurance Act was a lawyer and writer called William Beveridge. He became a senior civil servant and then left politics to pursue an academic career, first as Director of the London School of Economics and then as Master of University College, Oxford. A Liberal economist who combined great scholarship with a strong belief in social reform, Beveridge provided the intellectual foundation for the formation of the Welfare State and the National Health Service after the Second World War. At a time when men and women were looking to government to increase their prosperity and improve their lives – no one talked of the 'nanny state' in those days – Beveridge's ideas of how to maintain full employment and how to look after people became the accepted wisdom of the day. During the Second World War the government turned its attention to how the country would be rebuilt when the hostilities ended, and once again turned to Beveridge for advice. The Prime

Minister, Winston Churchill, his mind and efforts concentrated entirely on the need for victory, thought Beveridge was a 'windbag and a dreamer', but the report he produced in 1942 was one of the most influential documents written in Britain in the twentieth century.

It was called 'Social Insurance and Allied Services' – hardly a title to make the blood race, but it sold 600,000 copies. The reason was partly because it did not confine itself to the sober language of government reports: it was a manifesto for comprehensive change. 'A revolutionary moment in the world's history,' it announced, referring to the fight to the death against Nazi Germany, 'is a time for revolutions, not for patching.' He called what he proposed 'a British revolution', a natural development from the past that would build on the measures already in place to make far-reaching improvements to the nation's welfare. At the heart of this was an attack on 'Want'. 'Want', said Beveridge, was 'one of only five giants on the road of reconstruction and in some ways the easiest to attack.' The others he described as 'Disease, Ignorance, Squalor and Idleness'. The method of attack would be to create a national system of social security in which compulsory payments would pay for health and unemployment insurance, child benefits, maternity support and state pensions. The report also recommended the establishment of a National Health Service. In one document it laid out the intentions, structure and operating systems of Britain's post-war welfare state.

In 1945, to his horror and dismay, Winston Churchill was defeated in the general election, and it fell to the new Labour government to begin the work of national reconstruction. In 1946 it introduced the National Insurance Act that levied compulsory contributions from employers and employees to insure against periods of ill health, unemployment and maternity. At the same time it turned itself to the problem of how to provide proper health care for the nation as a whole. The wartime coalition government, which had ruled Britain during the war and of which the Labour Party had been a part, promised to create a health service that would be comprehensive and free. The trouble was that nobody quite knew how to do it and the man that the Prime Minister, Clement Attlee, had put in charge of the task did not inspire universal confidence.

Aneurin Bevan seemed an unlikely choice to be made Minister of Health. He was a passionate ex-miner who had known periods of un-employment in his youth and had served as MP for the South Wales constituency of Ebbw Vale since 1929. This was his first time in office. During the war he had been vociferous in his criticism of the national government's plans to introduce censorship: Churchill is supposed to have called him 'a squalid nuisance'. In carrying out the task of creating the National Health Service, however, 'Nye' Bevan, as he was known, proved remarkably vigorous and effective. Essentially he created a two-tier system. At its core was a national unified hospital system divided into regional divisions. This was supported by medical services such as ambulances and specialised clinics managed by local authorities. Crucially, he decided that the cost of all this should be paid for, not by national insurance, but by general taxation. A grateful nation paid up and took possession of prescription glasses, false teeth and hearing aids in their millions.

A grateful nation paid up and took possession of prescription glasses, false teeth and hearing aids in their millions.

Nye Bevan described it as 'the biggest single experiment in social service that the world has ever seen undertaken'. This was more than political hyperbole – except for the fact that it soon lost all trappings of an experiment and became an established fact. He won the support of the medical profession, many of whom were highly sceptical of the plan; he furnished men and women with desperately needed medical items; and he brought a common standard to the country's hospitals designed to let them offer equality of service and keep pace with medical developments. He claimed that some of what the government had introduced was based on the healthcare system which operated in his home town of Tredegar in the 1920s. 'We are going to Tredegarise you,' he said. Rather more grandly he claimed that 'we now have the moral leadership of the world ... we shall have people coming here as to a modern Mecca, learning from us in the twentieth century as they learned from us in the seventeenth'. In saying this he was more prescient than perhaps he knew, although the complaint often heard today is that they come not to learn, but to take advantage.

When the NHS was invented the population of Britain was 50 million. Today it is over 60 million and rising. With population growth have come great strides in medical care and higher expectations from patients. Between the end of the 1970s and the mid-1990s the number of operations for things like hip replacements or renal transplants doubled. When the health service started only 30 per cent of babies were born in hospital: by the end of the twentieth century hospital birth had become the norm. As a result the National Health Service today is a vast organisation that consumes £90 billion a year of public money and costs British citizens the equivalent of nearly £1,500 each per year. Its structure, efficiency and costs are discussed, criticised and analysed more often and in more detail than any other branch of government. Aneurin Bevan and some of his colleagues resigned from the government in 1952 when one-shilling prescription charges were first introduced. They saw it as a betrayal of the founding principles of the organisation. Since then successive governments have struggled with the intractable problem of funding it and nearly all administrations have been criticised for the way they manage it. It is a national obsession, a marvellous British innovation that we take for granted and grumble about without a second thought. We use it as the whipping boy for our liberties and enjoy nothing more than flogging it half to death. Despite all this it has given the country an enormous amount: every citizen has the right to free health care whether simply feeling under the weather or very seriously ill, and most of them exercise this right at some point in their lives.

When the Labour government agreed in 1948 to fund the National Health Service from taxation rather than from social insurance it opened the floodgates for continually increasing expenditure. It knew that the system it was creating would call for a constant replenishment of resources, and it took the risk that successive governments would be prepared to find the money necessary to keep the service going. That is what has happened, although not without a great deal of hand-wringing and complaint. The NHS has struggled on. As Aneurin Bevan, who died in 1960, predicted: 'It has now become part of the texture of our national life. No political party would survive that tried to destroy it.' He also talked about the principle that lies at its heart: 'The essence of a satisfactory health service is that the rich and poor are treated alike, that poverty is not a disability, and wealth is not an advantage.' There can be few better explanations of British liberty than that.

Five British Disasters

The Great Fire of London 1666

In the early morning of Sunday 2nd September 1666, a fire broke out in the King's bakery on Pudding Lane. Most of the nearby buildings were made of timber and a strong wind fanned the flames. The fire soon destroyed many streets of houses, commercial premises and churches. Despite the efforts of local people, the fire continued to rage for four days, and was only fully extinguished on the night of Thursday 6th, by which time over 13,000 houses had been destroyed and 20,000 people had been left homeless. Only four people were reported to have died in the inferno, but the real death count is likely to have been much higher. Though it was probably started accidentally, at the time Catholics and foreigners were blamed for the fire, and the Spanish Ambassador opened his house as a safe haven for those who feared for their lives in the hysteria of the aftermath.

The 'Mighty Landslip' 1839

On Christmas Day 1839, a huge landslip took place at Bindon, on the Dorset coast by Lyme Regis. A great chunk of land now known as Goat Island was left separated from the rest of the coast by an immense chasm. The dramatic landscape that was created became a great tourist attraction, although some people were too frightened to visit the area. In 1840 a guide to the site was published. It warned that: 'Many are breathless and bewildered at the sight. One individual from Honiton, was taken home to a sick bed from which he was with difficulty recovered.'

The Tay Bridge Disaster 1879

On 28th December 1879, two years after it had been built, the Tay railway bridge at Dundee collapsed in a storm, and a train carrying over seventy passengers fell into the river below. There were no survivors. The Scottish poet William Topaz McGonagall was inspired by the tragedy to write *The Tay Bridge Disaster*, acclaimed for being one of the worst poems ever written in the English language. It comes to a delightful climax with the following lines:

... I must now conclude my lay
By telling the world fearlessly without the least dismay,
That your central girders would not have given way,
At least many sensible men do say,
Had they been supported on each side with buttresses,
At least many sensible men confesses,
For the stronger we our houses do build,
The less chance we have of being killed.

The Spanish Flu Epidemic 1918–1919

The Spanish Flu Epidemic of 1918–1919 killed over 225,000 British people and probably more than 50 million people worldwide, a higher total than the death toll for the entire First World War. It was highly contagious, and the living conditions of trench warfare on the Western Front meant that it spread even more quickly amongst soldiers. Unusually, it was young adults – those in their twenties and thirties – who seemed most likely to catch 'Spanish Flu'. Many died from pneumonia caused by the disease. Recent studies have shown that it may well have passed directly from birds to humans.

The Aberfan Disaster 1966

On 21st October 1966 a whole generation of children from the South Wales village of Aberfan and the surrounding area was, in the words of the Minister of State for Wales, 'wiped out'. The Merthyr Vale Colliery coal slagheap above the village slid down the mountainside, burying houses, a farm and the local junior school. Local firefighters dug villagers from the rubble, some knowing their own sons and daughters were probably lying dead in it: 144 people, 116 of them children, were killed in the tragedy.

5 Ingenuity

Britain's Innovations

Introduction

Wigan Pier was an old music-hall gag used to describe the grimy jetty on the Leeds-Liverpool Canal where coal barges unloaded. George Orwell used it in the title of his book, *The Road to Wigan Pier*, in which he described the appalling living conditions of many of the people living in Britain's northern industrial towns just before the Second World War. Alongside the jetty is a cotton mill which houses one of the world's largest steam engines – the Trencherfield Mill engine – whose appetite for coal kept the barges busy. Today it is being developed as a glossy tourist attraction, a magnificent example of what we like to call 'Britain's Industrial Heritage', but when the engine was built at the beginning of the twentieth century it was a desperate place, dank and unhealthy, where hundreds of men, women and children worked long hours in terrible conditions.

The Trencherfield Mill engine is a last, late product of the Industrial Revolution that transformed Britain in the early nineteenth century. It is a period of history we view with pride and dismay. On the one hand it helped make Britain the most powerful nation on earth, on the other it caused social and economic hardship on a vast scale. That is often the nature of change. A nation needs ingenuity and invention to survive, but it often brings with it unforeseen consequences.

This chapter explores the ingenuity which provided the inventions and changes which gave Britain some of its most important discoveries, ideas and institutions. It starts in the fourteenth century with Geoffrey Chaucer, the first person to use the English language as an effective and entertaining method of communication. Language was also the weapon used by the translators of the *Authorised Version* of the Bible at the beginning of the seventeenth century to help create a doctrinal foundation for the Church of England.

At the end of the seventeenth century, ingenious financiers invented the Bank of England to help the government pay for its wars and other expensive activities. Shortly afterwards that government turned to its people to find someone clever enough to discover a way of fixing a longitude at sea.

In the middle of the eighteenth century, James Watt invented the machine which would power the Industrial Revolution. Early in the nineteenth, Robert Peel created a police force to help manage a growing and increasingly unruly population. Charles Darwin's discovery of evolution through natural selection changed the way the whole world thought about where it came from. Not long afterwards the publication of 'The Laws of Football' tamed the animal instincts of the nation and encouraged it to participate in a sport in which loyalty and teamwork were the most important attributes.

In the twentieth century, the invention of the television and the foundation of the BBC brought football, entertainment and much else besides into people's homes. In the world outside, the jet engine announced the beginning of easy, far-flung travel.

In every period, in all circumstances, the British have resorted to their ingenuity to survive and progress.

CHAPTER 1

Chaucer's *The Canterbury Tales*
1387

In about 1387 Geoffrey Chaucer began writing his most famous work, *The Canterbury Tales*. He was the first person to use the English language expressively and is often called the 'Father of English Poetry'.

Borough Market in the London borough of Southwark has become one of Britain's most fashionable places for buying food. You can find almost anything you want to eat there – Spanish hams, Orkney lamb, English oysters, Lincolnshire sausages and Italian olives, oil and truffles. People in search of good food and a good time visit it from all over England, and from abroad: it is a centre of epicurean pilgrimage. In that sense it is continuing a tradition which has existed in that part of London for more than 600 years. It was at the Tabard Inn on Borough High Street, close to where the market stands today, that Chaucer's pilgrims gathered for their journey to Canterbury. They, too, seem to have been a jolly, lively crowd – twenty-nine (thirty including Chaucer himself) different men and women from all walks of life thrown together for a few days to ride to Thomas Becket's shrine in Canterbury Cathedral.

Chaucer would have been familiar with the people he decided to write about. He was born in London in the early 1340s, the son of a wine merchant, who first started work in the household of the Countess of Ulster, wife of Lionel, one of the sons of Edward III. From this position he worked his way up to become one of Lionel's attendants and went on a campaign with him to France where he was captured and ransomed. His master bought him back for £16 in 1360. Growing up in England during the Hundred Years' War clearly carried a number of risks with it. He then moved into the service of John of Gaunt, the wealthiest of the King's sons and a man of enormous power and influence, and from this into the service of the King himself. He travelled to Italy – he had already been to Spain – to negotiate commercial agreements between England and Genoa and visited the court of the unpredictable and violent Viscontis, the rulers of Milan. He became a Controller of Customs in London, where he would have witnessed the Peasants' Revolt of 1381. As one of John of Gaunt's employees this might have been a dangerous time for him since the peasant mob attacked the prince's palace on the River Thames.

After the Peasants' Revolt, Chaucer moved to Kent where he was appointed a Justice of the Peace and 'Knight of the Shire'. He was not actually a knight as such, but was given the status so that he could sit in Parliament. He became Clerk of the King's Works and returned to London towards the end of the 1390s where, in 1399, Henry Bolingbroke deposed Richard II and took the throne for himself as Henry IV. Chaucer died the following year in 1400. A full life of government duty was not without other incident. In the late 1370s he was accused of 'raptus' by a woman called Cecily Champaign. We do not know precisely what the charge meant: it could have been rape or some other form of sexual assault, or may even have been a trumped-up accusation in order to extort money. In any event, Chaucer was cleared of the charge in 1380. We also know that he was robbed on three separate occasions in 1390, perhaps because as someone in royal service he was known to be carrying money. Throughout all these times he wrote poetry. His first important work, the poem 'The Book of the Duchess', appeared some time around 1370. *The Canterbury Tales*, which he never finished, was his last.

The written English language's first important practitioner was obviously a shrewd and sophisticated individual. He fought in a military campaign, he visited the capitals of Europe and he carried out high-ranking duties for a monarchy which was going through a turbulent time. He was a survivor, someone who mixed easily in the fast-moving world which was London at the end of the fourteenth century. It was not a big city – its population was about 50,000 – so Chaucer would have been able to get to know it well. The pilgrims he describes in *The Canterbury Tales* are a lively, cosmopolitan lot. There is a knight who seems to have fought all over the world – in Russia, Spain and Turkey. His son, a squire, has seen service in Flanders and northern France. There is a monk who has apparently given up the rule of Saint Benedict because he found it a bit too strict, and a prioress who speaks French beautifully, but after the school of Stratford-at-Bow: Parisian French is completely unknown to her. There is a swarthy sailor from Dartmouth; a merchant whose name Chaucer cannot remember and a doctor for whom money is the best medicine of all. These are just some of the colourful characters who have got together in a Southwark pub and whom their host, the innkeeper, persuades to tell each other stories to pass away the time on their pilgrimage through Kent. The best story-teller, he tells them, will win a free meal.

Chaucer was writing at a time when European literature was beginning to blossom. Its roots were in Italy, in the writings of Dante, who died in 1321, and Petrarch and Boccaccio, both of whom died in the mid-1370s. Chaucer might have met Petrarch while he was visiting Florence. There is no evidence of this, but there can be no doubt that he read and was influenced by the work of all three men. He used Boccaccio as the source for his poem 'Troilus and Cressida' and for 'The Knight's Tale' in *The Canterbury Tales*. But Dante would have been his most important inspiration because he had been the first person to write, as Chaucer wrote, in his own native tongue. Up until this time nearly all written work – mainly the chronicles of monks and official documents – was in Latin. Dante's *Divine Comedy* is regarded as the first post-classical great achievement of European literature, a masterpiece as important as anything before or since. In the Florence which Chaucer visited, Boccaccio – who added the word *Divine* to Dante's original title of just *Comedy* – was also writing in this new language, called Italian. Chaucer wanted to do the same for English, to take his language

Ten Great British Novels:

The History of Tom Jones, A Foundling (1749)   Henry Fielding (1707–1754)

'I think the *Oedipus Tyrannus*, *The Alchemist*, and *Tom Jones*, the three most perfect plots ever planned. And how charming, how wholesome, Fielding always is!'

Samuel Taylor Coleridge

Pride and Prejudice (1813)   Jane Austen (1775–1817)

'Also read again and for the third time at least Miss Austen's very finely written novel of *Pride and Prejudice*. That young lady had a talent for describing the involvement and feelings and characters of ordinary life which is to me the most wonderful I ever met with ... What a pity such a gifted creature died so early!'

Walter Scott in his diary

Hard Times (1854)   Charles Dickens (1812–1870)

'Of all Dickens's works [*Hard Times*] ... is the one that has all the strength of his genius, together with a strength no other of them can show – that of a completely serious work of art.'

Literary critic F. R. Leavis, The Great Tradition

Middlemarch (1871)   George Eliot (1819–1880)

'One of the few English novels written for grown-up people.'

Virginia Woolf

The Mayor of Casterbridge (1886)   Thomas Hardy (1840–1928)

'A Plot, or Tragedy, should arise from the gradual closing in of a situation that comes of ordinary human passions, prejudices and ambitions, by reason of the characters taking no trouble to ward off the disastrous events produced by the said passions, prejudices, ambitions.'

Thomas Hardy, in his notebook, April 1878

To the Lighthouse (1927)   Virginia Woolf (1882–1941)

'... you can't help my thinking it the best thing you've ever done ... You're no longer bothered by the simultaneity of things and go backwards and forwards in time with an extraordinary enrichment of each moment of consciousness.'

Fellow Bloomsbury Group member Roger Fry,
in a letter to Virginia Woolf

Decline and Fall (1928)   Evelyn Waugh (1903–1966)

'It is really screamingly funny, & I think there is a good chance of its being a success if not a bestseller ... I don't think our mothers will approve of it, certainly mine won't!'

Evelyn Gardner, who married Waugh in 1928

Lady Chatterley's Lover (1928)   D. H. Lawrence (1885–1930)

'Ask yourselves the question: would you approve of your young sons, young daughters – because girls can read as well as boys – reading this book. Is it a book that you would have lying around the house? Is it a book you would wish your wife or servants to read?'

Prosecution counsel, Mervyn Griffith-Jones, at the 1960 obscenity
trial involving Penguin Books, who sought to publish Lawrence's
novel for the first time in Britain

Nineteen Eighty-Four (1949)   George Orwell (1903–1950)

'Orwell's *Nineteen Eighty-Four* is one of the few dystopian visions to have changed man's habits of thought. It is possible to say that the ghastly future Orwell foretells will not come about, simply because he foretold it: we have been warned.'

Anthony Burgess, author of another novel with a bleak vision
of our future: A Clockwork Orange

Midnight's Children (1981)   Salman Rushdie (1947–)

'It was written in a new voice. It had the complexity of the great European novels by which it was influenced; it was equally full of the freewheeling, folkloric voice of Indian storytelling and legend. It was politically aware, but wonderfully fantastic.'

Malcolm Bradbury, novelist and chair of the panel that awarded
the Booker Prize to Rushdie for Midnight's Children

and shake the stiffness out of it until it flowed like a melody. The result was what some critics have called Britain's first novel, *The Canterbury Tales*, written at a time when the country's national identity was in its infancy and just beginning to grow. The author, G. K. Chesterton, one of the most influential British writers of the first half of the twentieth century, said: 'There was never a man who was more of a maker than Chaucer. He made a national language; he came very near to making a nation.'

Chaucer's nation is in full view on the road to Canterbury. But today he is not much read, mainly because the English he used is no longer ours. It is Middle English containing words and spellings that are often difficult to understand. We cannot even be sure how many of them were pronounced. To get to know him, and to begin to appreciate his wit and portrayal of character, it is a good idea to read him in translation so his description and observations are not obscured. For instance, Chaucer obviously had an eye for women. One of the last things he wrote, but never finished, was a poem called 'The Legend of Saint Cupid', or 'The Legend of Good Women'. A friend of his said later that Chaucer failed to complete it because it encumbered his wits to think of so many 'good women'. Here is his most famous woman of all, the Wife of Bath, as described in the famous translation of *The Canterbury Tales* by Neville Coghill:

Chaucer wanted to take his language and shake the stiffness out of it until it flowed like a melody.

> A worthy woman all her life, what's more
> She'd had five husbands, all at the church door,
> Apart from other company in youth;
> No need just now to speak of that, forsooth.
> And she had thrice been to Jerusalem,
> Seen many strange rivers and passed over them;
> She'd been to Rome and also to Boulogne,
> St James of Compostella and Cologne,

> *And she was skilled in wandering by the way.*
> *She had gap-teeth, set widely, truth to say.*
> *Easily on an ambling horse she sat*
> *Well wimpled up, and on her head a hat*
> *As broad as is a buckler or a shield;*
> *She had a flowing mantle that concealed*
> *Large hips, her heels spurred sharply under that.*
> *In company she liked to laugh and chat*
> *And knew the remedies for love's mischances,*
> *An art in which she knew the oldest dances.*

She sounds a bit of a well-travelled terror, a medieval version of the sort of person you might easily run into on a continental holiday today.

Chaucer also describes people belonging only to the age in which he lived. At the end of the fourteenth century, Britain was beginning to feel the first stirrings of resentment against the Catholic Church. The Oxford theologian, John Wycliffe, who attacked the Roman Catholic Church for its idolatrous religious practices, was a direct contemporary of Chaucer's, supported, when he first started writing and preaching, by one of Chaucer's employers, John of Gaunt. His followers were known as Lollards – a word taken from the Dutch word to mutter, probably because of the way they read their scriptures – and their movement became very popular, particularly in London, during Chaucer's lifetime. One of their main targets of attack was the sale of phoney holy relics and pardons. Those who bought them thought they would save their souls. Chaucer includes one of these clerical salesmen, the pardoner, on his Canterbury pilgrimage. In the Neville Coghill translation he is a man with hair 'as yellow as wax' hanging 'in driblets' behind his head:

> *He sewed a holy relic on his cap;*
> *His wallet lay before him on his lap,*
> *Brimful of pardons come from Rome all hot.*
> *He had the same small voice a goat has got.*

His chin no beard had harboured, nor would harbour,
Smoother than ever chin was left by barber.
I judge he was a gelding, or a mare,
As for his trade, from Berwick down to Ware
There was no pardoner of equal grace,
For in his trunk he had a pillow-case
Which he asserted was Our Lady's veil.
He said he had a gobbet of the sail
Saint Peter had the time when he made bold
To walk the waves, till Jesu Christ took hold.
He had a cross of metal set with stones
And, in a glass, a rubble of pigs' bones ...

And by his flatteries and prevarication
Made monkeys of the priest and congregation.

From this we can safely assume that Chaucer had a lot of sympathy for the teachings of Wycliffe and his followers. His eye for detail combined with his descriptive powers have given us a perfect picture of someone whose business has long ago disappeared from the world, but whose character we still recognise.

The English language today is one of the glories of civilisation. It is spoken everywhere. Its idioms and oddities are a delight to those who speak it and a source of endless frustration to those trying to learn it: it can be both starkly simple and bewilderingly complicated. A lot of the world's chatter is English chatter, first heard and enjoyed in the bustle of the Tabard Inn in Southwark, where, under the watchful eye of Geoffrey Chaucer, a bunch of busy pilgrims began their journey to Canterbury.

CHAPTER 2

The *Authorised Version* of the Bible 1611

In 1611 a new English translation of the Bible appeared. It was commissioned by King James I and created by a group of specially chosen scholars. In the centuries that followed it became a centrepiece of British family life.

The internet site eBay is a colossal global auction house. Everything you could possibly want is for sale inside it, from art treasures to dismal household tat. Sellers invite bids for their goods whose value, they hope, will be increased in the excitement of the chase. It is a brilliant idea, the car boot sale par excellence, a market place which demonstrates perfectly the ceaseless energy of supply and demand. Among the goods you can find for auction are family Bibles. For over 300 years the family Bible stood at the heart of many British households, both rich and poor. Often beautifully bound and richly illustrated, they were the repository of the family's delights and disappointments, a place round which it grouped in worship and where it kept records of births, marriages and deaths. Today, these once loved relics of a more devotional age are money-spinners: '2 volume Bible with family details (very sad)', read one recently advertised on eBay. 'Wonderful, wonderful bible (the leather is practically untouched by the hands of man),' proclaimed another; while a third announced: 'I have weighed this Bible and the weight is 21lbs/1.5 stone unpackaged.' History for sale. The *Authorised Version* of the Bible once sustained the nation's spirit, but not any longer. The language is too rich for modern tastes and the family Bible, once so precious and so loved, is just another piece of profitable flotsam on the internet.

The historian, G.M. Trevelyan, once wrote that James I had an 'over-busy brain'. It is a good description of a King whose studious energy led him on the one hand to propose the disastrous concept of the divine right of kings, and on the other to commission the process which created a book that inspired a nation. When James came to power in 1603, Britain's different religious groups all had high expectations that his policies would favour them over the others. The Catholics thought that the son of Mary Queen of Scots would be a natural ally, and their subsequent disappointment led directly to the Gunpowder Plot of 1605. The Puritans also saw him as a friend because he had suffered the power of the Presbyterian Church in Scotland during his reign there. In fact James was only too glad to be rid of the Presbyterians who, in his view, undermined royal power. 'A Scottish Presbytery,' he said, 'agreeth as well with a monarchy as God with the Devil ... Then Jack, Tom, Will and Dick shall meet and at their pleasures censure me and my council.'

James wanted to steer a middle course through the conflicting sea of opinion on which he found himself launched as King of England and Scotland. One of his first acts was to summon the Hampton Court Conference in which senior members of the established Anglican Church, together with some of its moderate Puritan reformers, were invited to debate the future. In terms of religious policy the conference achieved very little. The radical Puritans, who had not been allowed to attend, realised that the King was not prepared to move from his support of the ritual and ceremony of the Anglican Church, still based on Catholic teaching. They remained dissatisfied. But in its efforts to address some aspects of religious interpretation the Hampton Court Conference did produce one enduring legacy – the *Authorised Version* of the Bible. The leader of the Puritan delegation, John Reynolds, proposed the idea of a new Bible translation during one of the conference sessions, and James seized on the idea with enthusiasm. A new version, he believed, would help resolve religious controversy and unite the conflicting opinions of his new country.

The first person to tackle seriously the task of translating the

Bible into English was John Wycliffe. In the 1380s he and his followers produced manuscript versions of the English Bible as part of their campaign against the Roman Catholic Church. They believed that the true teachings of the Scriptures were hidden from the people because the Bible, the source of truth, was only available in Latin, a language incomprehensible to most of them. 'God's word must always be true if it is to be properly understood,' said Wycliffe, but his activities infuriated the papal authorities. In an age which did not yet possess the means of mass communication that would be facilitated by the invention of the printing press, his translations from the Latin struggled to survive. One of his strongest supporters, John Hus, who took Wycliffe's ideas back to his native Bohemia, was burned at the stake in 1415. In Britain his translation was suppressed.

It would take a hundred years before another English translation of the Bible appeared. In the early sixteenth century the scholar, William Tyndale, who was fluent in eight languages, tried to persuade the authorities that a new translation based on the original Greek and Hebrew was necessary. He was unsuccessful: the rising tide of the German Reformation, led by Martin Luther, was not something the English Church wanted to see washing up along its shores. Tyndale went abroad never to return, but in 1526 published in Worms in Germany an English version of the New Testament. It became one of the most influential books ever written. He aimed to write something both popular and scholarly, and informative and truthful. He was not particularly concerned with style, but in his ambition to carry out his mission eloquently, he produced a great literary work. 'It is God's Scripture,' he said, 'written for thy learning and comfort.'

Comfort is an important word. When people were able to read Tyndale's English sentences for the first time they understood the Christian message in a language that touched their deepest senses. They felt enriched and uplifted. Tyndale's Bibles were smuggled into England from their German printing presses and he himself was hounded and pursued by the Catholic Church. He managed to publish the first five books of the Old Testament, the Pentateuch, before he was arrested in Antwerp and taken to a prison near Brussels. In 1536 he was strangled and then burned at the stake. His last words were: 'Oh Lord, open the King of England's eyes.'

His prayer was heard. Three years later Tyndale's follower, Myles Coverdale, published a full version of the Bible which the Archbishop of Canterbury, Thomas Cranmer, authorised for use in all churches. Coverdale was not a scholar like Tyndale and he used translators to help him with his work. *The Great Bible*, as his edition was called, was not enough to satisfy the reformers and in 1560 another version prepared by supporters of another religious reformer, John Calvin, was published in Calvin's home town of Geneva. This bible – the so-called *Geneva Bible* – was the first to have numbered verses and also contained notes and explanations in the margin. It was enormously popular and remained the Bible of choice in most British households up until Cromwell's Protectorate in the middle of the seventeenth century.

James I was not fond of the *Geneva Bible*, whose Calvinistic footnotes reminded him of the Scottish Presbyterians who had made life difficult for him while he was their King. It was unlikely that yet another translation would, on its own, be able to solve the doctrinal differences of his subjects, but he became convinced that it was necessary. One Bible, one Church, one King seems to have been his approach. It was a highly organised and enormously ambitious project. Forty-seven translators were appointed, divided into six committees. Each committee was responsible for a continuous section of the bible – with one translating from 'Genesis' to '2 Kings', another from '1 Chronicles' to the 'Song of Solomon' and so on. The committees spent about four years preparing their versions, which were then reviewed and amended by a further General Committee of Review. The King set out clear rules for them to follow. They were to use a revised version of the *Great Bible* which had been re-published in an amended form in 1568 and was known as the *Bishop's Bible*. Old ecclesiastical words were to be kept: the word 'church', for instance, was not to be translated as 'congregation'. There were to be no marginal notes. The authors of the *Authorised Version* were to build on what had gone before: they had to revise rather than originate. Their job was to give the country a centre to its religion and a permanent resting place for its beliefs.

To a large extent they succeeded. By the eighteenth century the *Authorised Version* of the Bible had become the accepted text and as restrictions on printing it were relaxed, new editions with decorations and illustrations became increasingly popular. But it still managed to find its detractors. In 1768 a doctor of divinity called Edward Harwood published his *Liberal Translation of the New Testament* in which he attempted to replace 'the bald and barbarous language of the old vulgar version' with 'the elegance of modern English'. The result was a hideously florid piece of work, including this 'translation' of part of the Lord's Prayer: 'May the glory of thy moral development be advanced and the great laws of it be more generally obeyed.' Harwood, like the notorious Thomas Bowdler who in the early nineteenth century edited Shakespeare's plays to make them more suitable for women and children, was obviously one of those Englishmen who believed that he lived in the best of all possible worlds and that the fashions of his age were eternal. He failed to understand that what already existed had a far stronger claim to eternity than anything he might produce.

The authors of the Authorised Version were to build on what had gone before. Their job was to give the country a centre to its religion and a permanent resting place for its beliefs.

Today organised religion is no longer part of most people's everyday lives and it has become fashionable to view the *Authorised Version* of the Bible as a glorious piece of literature rather than a sacred text. Even those who never go to church complain when they hear that it has been replaced by a modern edition. But very few people read the Bible for 'literary' reasons: it is, and always will be, a work of Christian worship. It is because Christianity was a mainstay of British civilisation for so long that it still has an effect on those who are Christians no longer. Its strength was that it gave its readers undiluted and emotional access to that which they revered above all else – their religious beliefs. It deepened and reinforced their faith. That is what its originator, James I, wanted above all else. He could not contain his pleasure and excitement as he sat before the clergy at Hampton Court in 1604. 'Blessed be God's gracious goodness, who hath brought me in to the Promised Land,' he declared, 'where religion is purely professed, where I sit among grave, learned and reverend men – not as before, else-where, a King without a state, without honour, where beardless boys would brave us to the face.' Away from the difficulties of his Scottish kingdom he was going to be able to build afresh and rule a united country joined under its absolute monarch in one religion. It was not to be: religion would be the principal source of conflict in Britain throughout the seventeenth century. The dream of King James lives only in his Bible.

CHAPTER 3

The Foundation of the Bank of England
1694

The Bank of England was established in 1694 to act as the government's banker and debt manager. Today it is a state-owned institution. What started as a piece of private enterprise has become Britain's central bank.

There could not be a more appropriate time to discuss the history of the Bank of England than the year 2008. Since late 2007 the world's financial markets have been in turmoil. The crisis started in the American market where big banks had lent money to help people buy cheap houses. Because property prices were rising the loans looked secure, but as the American economy weakened house owners found themselves unable to repay their debts. This contributed to a worldwide feeling that consumers were over-stretched and were relying too heavily on credit. Banks which needed to borrow in order to continue paying their customers' loans could no longer find the lenders they needed. In Britain, Northern Rock, a bank which had lent heavily to help fund house purchases, faced a run on its reserves as anxious depositors queued up to withdraw their funds. In September 2007 the Bank of England stepped in to support Northern Rock saying that in its role as 'lender of last resort' it stood ready to support any financial institution in 'comparable circumstances'. These roller-coaster events, which are still unravelling as 2008 advances, are not un-like the hurly-burly of debt and confusion which surrounded the creation of the Bank of England more than three hundred years ago.

London at the end of the seventeenth century was big, busy and insanitary. It had developed into a bustling centre of commerce, a warren of dirty streets where tradesmen jostled with prostitutes and criminals, presided over by wealthy merchants growing rich on the fruits of expanding trade. It was the London of Samuel Pepys and Daniel Defoe, both highly observant men on the make, whose descriptions of the capital are a vivid record of a country returning to normality after the long internal wars of the previous years. Returning home one March evening a few years after the Restoration of 1660, Samuel Pepys, in relaxed mood after a very jolly dinner, wrote: 'In our way the coach drove through a lane by Drury Lane where abundance of loose women stood at the doors, which God forgive me, did put evil thoughts in me, but proceeded no further, blessed be God.' Puritan England had been banished. The great experiment in moral certainty was over. The theatres were opening again, and all was well with the world.

But the years of political conflict were not quite over yet. As his reign continued, Charles II drew around him a court of Tory supporters who distrusted the Whig interests in London's commercial centres. They wanted to see the return of a monarchy free from the constraints of a Parliament dominated by critical businessmen. Their hopes were dashed when Charles' brother, James II, succeeded him on the throne and provoked the crisis which led to his deposition in the Glorious Revolution of 1688. Parliament summoned the Dutch William of Orange and his wife, Mary, to be King and Queen. In so doing they brought to the throne a man who understood extremely well the advantages of a nation with a strong, commercial infrastructure.

The Netherlands, too, had enjoyed prosperity and growth during the seventeenth century. Its wealth had been managed in part by the formation of the Dutch East India Company which had developed into a colossal, worldwide trading enterprise, but also by the establishment in 1609 of the Bank of Amsterdam. The bank had originally been founded to protect the city's coinage which, like the coinage of some other city states in Europe, became debased as it got worn and mixed up with the money of the neighbouring places with which it traded. This was at a time when the metal value of the coinage – normally gold or silver – was an actual value and not a representative one, as it is today. The freshly minted coinage was estimated to be worth about 9 per cent more than the worn out currency in everyday circulation, with the result that whenever it was released into the market it was melted down and used for other purposes. The Bank of Amsterdam, backed by the city, accepted deposits of all this coinage which it called 'bank money', and, after deducting a small amount as a management fee, retained it at its true, intrinsic value – not at the debased value. In this way it created an exchange rate which maintained the value of the city's money. Over time this operation produced beneficial side-effects because people were happy to leave their money in a place where they knew it was safe and where it was likely to be worth more because it was always held at the intrinsic, not the actual, value of the coinage. The bank's deposits, increased by the fees it charged, became capital of value to the city as a whole and helped fund its activities.

London possessed no such institution. It was the capital of a rich country. It stood at the centre of a Britain enjoying vigorous commercial growth. But the government had no reliable means of taking advantage of all this. If it needed money, officials from the Exchequer had to go cap in hand to the men with money in the City. There was no instrument available to fund public debt or to finance any new requirements. The monarch could always ask Parliament for money which might then decide to provide it through taxation – but this, as the Stuart Kings had discovered to their cost, was very much a hit-or-miss affair. Britain's financial fortunes depended entirely on private enterprise: those who had money could lend it or withhold it as they pleased.

William III needed money badly. One of his reasons for accepting the British throne was that he wanted an ally in the Dutch war against France. He needed Britain to be part of a 'Grand Alliance' against the predatory activities of Louis XIV. Wars cost money. The American banker Harvey Fisk once estimated that from 1688 until the end of the First World War the cost of wars accounted for more than 85 per cent of the total expenditure of the British nation. When William of Orange came to the throne, Britain's debts were a little over £1 million. His wars cost £18 million. Those of Queen Anne, who succeeded him, cost £33 million. The subsequent wars throughout the eighteenth century, including the American War of Independence and the Napoleonic Wars, brought the total cost to £850 million. These huge sums were incurred by Britain principally because of its wars against France and her allies – a series of battles for European and global supremacy which shaped the whole future of the country. It is unlikely that they could have been financed without a strong central system for managing public debt. The Bank of England was created for just such a purpose.

The Bank of England was the idea of a Scotsman called William Paterson. He was born in Tinwald in Dumfries but moved to England before leaving for the West Indies where he began to make his fortune. Returning to Britain he came up with a scheme in 1691 to organise a national bank so that there could always be a safe means of borrowing money at proper rates of interest. His idea was supported by London merchants who could see how well their counterparts in Amsterdam had done out of the bank there. Parliament was wary, but as the King's military ambitions against France took shape and money began to get tight, it set up a committee to listen to Paterson's ideas. What he proposed was that in return for the right to receive deposits, issue demand notes, lend funds and buy and sell bills of exchange a corporation would lend the government £1.2 million. The new institution would be called 'The Governor and Company of the Bank of England'. The loan would be offered for an annual return of about 8 per cent – £100,000 – plus £4,000 for management costs. Parliament, hard pressed, agreed to the terms and in 1694 under the provisions of the Tonnage Act, the Bank of England was granted a charter and allowed to begin business. 'The bank,' said Paterson, 'hath benefit of interest on all moneys which it makes out of nothing.' But his clever idea did not in the end benefit him particularly well. A few years after the foundation of the Bank he resigned to return to his native country where he became the principal champion of the disastrous Darien scheme, Scotland's first and last attempt at colonial expansion.

The Bank of England, meanwhile, went from strength to strength. Only three years after its invention, Daniel Defoe remarked: 'Banks, without question, if rightly managed are, or may be, of great advantage, especially to a trading people, as the English are.' And he added, 'in time of a war our preparations for any expedition need not be in danger of miscarriage for want of money'. Britain had created a system of legitimate debt: the cornerstone of capitalism was in place.

Britain had created a system of legitimate debt: the cornerstone of capitalism was in place.

The bank grew in importance and prestige throughout the eighteenth century and when its charter was renewed in 1781 it was referred to as the 'public exchequer'. It was by then so big that had all it depositors decided to withdraw their money at the same time it would have failed, but it always kept enough gold to pay its notes on demand. Its founders had realised that the right to issue bills would be an enormous privilege, and so it proved. As the government grew more dependent on the bank's loans, referred to as the 'national debt', it became the natural manager of the nation's currency and the arbiter of its monetary policy. The bank and the government became mutually dependent on one another: it had become the 'central bank' – a model which other countries would later adopt.

In the twentieth century the scale of its operations increased even further. The national debt rose to £7 billion during the First World War, and the bank helped manage the borrowing. But when Britain came off the gold standard in 1931, abandoning the principle of having its currency fixed to the value of gold, its gold reserves were transferred from the Bank of England to the Treasury. In 1946 the Bank of England was nationalised and came under public control, in effect an integral part of the government's centralised control of the economy. This position was loosened a little in 1997 when it was granted operational independence in the management of monetary policy and was allowed to set interest rates without reference to government.

The history of the Bank of England is the history of a capitalist economy. Its foundation and expansion are inseparable from Britain's development as a nation state. It came into being at a time when the country was expanding fast but needed credit to fund further growth; it became the manager of a national debt without which the country might not have been able to pay for the protection of its empire and its wars against France; and it provided the basis of a stable currency which all trading nations need. Like the East India Company, which managed Britain's interests around the world for 250 years, it was born out of the spirit of enterprise. Britain is not a capitalist country by decree, but by choice: its survival has been the result of commercial opportunism as much as anything else. Banking, and the Bank of England in particular, have been an essential part of this. 'A bank,' wrote Daniel Defoe in 1697 as he laid out a vision for the establishment of a bank in every important town in England, 'is only a great stock of money put together, to be employed by some of the subscribers, in the name of the rest, for the benefit of the whole.' Simple really: but then the best and most enduring ideas often are.

CHAPTER 4

The Longitude Act
1714

In 1714 Parliament established the Board of Longitude
and announced a prize for the person who came up
with the most practicable method of fixing longitude
at sea. Longitude was essential for the safe navigation
of shipping, but the search for a solution took nearly
sixty years.

Sir Cloudesley Shovell was one of the most popular and admired
seamen of his time. He rose through the ranks to become one of the
commanding officers of the Royal Navy and from 1695 a Member of
Parliament as well. His men liked him; his fellow officers respected
him. His tactics helped win the Battles of Barfleur and La Hougue
in 1692, when a French fleet swept into the English Channel to support the restoration of James II to the throne. He had a practical
attitude towards fighting. 'The misfortune and vice of our country,'
he once said, 'is to believe ourselves better than other men.'

In late November 1703 Shovell managed to survive 'the Great
Storm' – the worst in two centuries – when winds of 150 knots sank
four ships of the line and a hundred merchantmen. Ten thousand
sailors lost their lives on the Goodwin Sands off Kent. Four years
later he was not so fortunate. Summoned to return home after an
unsuccessful mission to try to capture the French Mediterranean
port of Toulon, he and the ships under his command found themselves entering the western approaches of the English Channel in
late October. British admirals often complained about keeping
their ships out at sea beyond the end of August because after that
autumn and winter currents made negotiating this treacherous
stretch of water extremely taxing, even to sailors who were familiar

with it. The Admiralty ignored their concerns. Britain had no winter base in the Mediterranean and its navy had to stay on duty until the last possible moment. Shovell and his squadron had no means of fixing their longitude. In the darkness they lost their direction and smashed into the reefs off the Isles of Scilly. Shovell's ship, *Association*, and three other ships of the line sank and he was drowned along with 1,400 of his men. His body was later washed ashore, and buried in Westminster Abbey. The nation was shocked. A good and popular admiral had lost his life, and the lives of the men under his command, returning home. He had died because he did not know where he was. He had been killed, not by war, but by his own native waters.

A longitude gives the location of a position east or west of a line running north to south called the Prime Meridian. In theory early sailors should have found establishing a longitude quite easy. They knew that for every 15 degrees that a ship travels east the local time advances by one hour. Therefore, if you knew the local time at two points – where you were and where you had come from – you should be able to calculate the distance between them. The trouble was that no clock had been built which could withstand the motions of a ship at sea, often buffeted by storms and subjected to frequent changes in temperature and humidity. As a result those in search of an answer turned to astronomical methods, but these too failed to provide an answer. In 1714 Parliament proclaimed that: 'The Discovery of Longitude is of such Consequence to Great Britain for the safety of the Navy and Merchant Ships' that a prize of £20,000 would be offered 'for such person or persons as shall discover the Longitude.' They were not the first people to come up with the idea of a prize of this kind, although the money they offered for the winner was far in excess of anything that had been suggested before: £20,000 was a huge sum at the beginning of the eighteenth century. In 1567 Britain's old enemy, Philip II of Spain, offered a prize for the discovery of longitude which was later handsomely increased by his son, Philip III, in 1598. The lure of this encouraged Galileo to carry out experiments in which he discovered and recorded the orbital periods of the planet Jupiter's four brightest satellites. Their positions, he believed, could be used to create a universal clock with which sailors would be able determine longitude, and he invented several devices for this. The problems of using them at sea were the same as clocks so they were only ever used to establish longitude on land.

Throughout the seventeenth century astronomers and mathematicians looked heavenwards for an answer to the longitude problem. In Britain, Charles II founded the Royal Observatory at Greenwich in 1675 with the specific purpose of finding 'the so-much desired longitude of places', and appointed John Flamsteed as the first Astronomer Royal. Britain at the time seethed with learned minds in search of solutions to everyday problems. Fifteen years before, in 1660, many of them had come together to found the Royal Society which to this day remains one of the most prestigious and admired centres of intellectual discovery in the world. Isaac Newton was a member, as was Christopher Wren, a distinguished astronomer as well as a famous architect. Another was Edmond Halley who gave his name to the comet he identified. Robert Boyle, whose experiments proved fundamental laws of physics and chemistry, was also interested in planets and stars, and as a young man studied 'the paradoxes of the great star gazer' Galileo. The engineer and architect Robert Hooke, who was also curator of experiments of the Royal Society, assisted both Boyle and Wren and came up with scientific discoveries of his own. These men debated often, quarrelled sometimes and thought constantly. Their discoveries and ideas laid the foundation of scientific development in Britain. But they could not discover the practical answer to the problem of longitude at sea. They knew how to calculate it in theory, but they could not translate their ideas into a workable solution.

The man who came up with the answer was not a high-powered mathematician or distinguished astronomer, but a Yorkshire carpenter and clockmaker called John Harrison. When the Board of Longitude was established, pendulum clocks were considered to be the most accurate form of timekeeping. John Harrison had started making these in his spare time. He claimed that although they were made mainly of wood his clocks were accurate to better than one second a month. He had achieved this astonishing precision by introducing new ideas to his design, including a pendulum which used a brass and steel wire grid to ensure that it withstood any changes in temperature and moving parts that had a rolling contact which did not need any oil. Most clocks of the period used an oil made out of animal fat which tended to deteriorate into a gummy mixture. Harrison's design was unique. No one before had ever made a mechanical clock which worked without oil. In 1728 he began to develop what he had learned in the manufacture of pendulum clocks into what he called 'sea clocks' – later called marine chronometers – and in 1728 went to London to present his findings to the Astronomer Royal, Edmond Halley. Halley took Harrison's work seriously and introduced him to Britain's leading clockmaker of the time, George Graham, who in 1730 lent the Yorkshireman money to build a model of his chronometer. There then began an extraordinary process of discovery, development, argument and resentment that lasted until just before Harrison's death forty-six years later.

The man who came up with the answer was not a high-powered mathematician or distinguished astronomer, but a Yorkshire carpenter and clockmaker.

John Harrison built five chronometers in his lifetime, subsequently classified as H1 to H5. Each one is a triumph of construction. Taken together they can be seen to climb the ladder of scientific achievement with masterly precision. The first, built between 1730 and 1735, was tried out on a voyage to Lisbon in 1736. It did not perform particularly well on the outward journey but on the return leg the captain and crew of the ship were very impressed with it, and praised Harrison's design. The Board of Longitude gave him £500 to continue his work. His next design, H2, was abandoned after two years and he threw all his efforts into a third, highly complex, creation. It took him nineteen years to complete and contained several important inventions. One was a bi-metallic strip of copper and brass that automatically adjusted the clock when the temperature changed – a design still used in thermostats for household appliances today. Another was an anti-friction device, a form of caged ball-bearing, which regulated the swings of the balances to ensure they took the same time whatever their length. This was essential to maintain accurate timekeeping in a ship which was always tossing and swaying. Harrison was convinced that H3 would win him the Longitude prize. It was made up of over seven hundred parts and so impressed Britain's scientific community that he was given the Royal Society's highest honour, the Copley gold medal. But the clock was still not accurate enough. For his next design, H4, Harrison changed tack altogether and in 1759 came up with his masterpiece.

H4 was not a clock at all, but a large pocket watch – about the size of a soup plate. While building H3, Harrison had begun to realise that watches, which have a fast-beating balance, are capable, if properly constructed, of keeping time far more accurately than portable clocks. This was a big step forward in the eighteenth century when watches were on the whole far more unreliable than clocks and not considered suitable for precision measurement. A thing of beauty as well as great craftsmanship, H4 was sent on a trial to the West Indies in 1761 where it performed magnificently. The Board of Longitude was still not convinced and eventually ordered a second trial in 1764. This time Harrison's chronometer had to compete with a rival – the lunar calculations devised by the Reverend Dr Nevil Maskelyne who on his return to London was appointed Astronomer Royal and placed on the Board of Longitude. There was no doubt Maskelyne's calculations worked, but they were far less accurate than Harrison's timekeeper. They had the added disadvantage of being so complicated that they could only be worked out by Maskelyne himself. Harrison became the victim of personal rivalry and political skulduggery.

The Board of Longitude agreed to give him half the prize

money – £10,000 – on condition that he disclosed all the details
of his invention. He complied and started work on his last design,
H5, but in the meantime the board ordered another clockmaker,
Larcum Kendall, to make a copy of H4. His work was shown to
Harrison and his son, who both agreed that Kendall's timepiece
was even more beautifully made than their original version.
Kendall's creation, known as K1, was sent with Captain Cook on his
second voyage around the Pacific between 1772 and 1775. Cook
praised the watch highly, and used it to help draw the extremely
accurate charts he produced during his journey. Harrison meanwhile, feeling cheated by the Board of Longitude, petitioned
George III for help. The King tested H5 himself and found it to
be astonishingly precise. He advised its inventor to appeal to
Parliament, which in 1773 agreed to grant Harrison a special sum of
£8,750. He was then eighty and lived for only another three years.
He never received the rest of the Longitude prize.

Like their inventor, Harrison's wonderful creations also
suffered at the hands of the authorities. He was forced to give them
his four prototypes – H1 to H4 – when he accepted the £10,000
award. The instruments were loaded into an unsprung cart and
taken off to the Greenwich Observatory where, neglected and forgotten, they fell into disrepair. In 1920 they were found by a retired
naval officer called Rupert Gould who spent many years restoring
them. It was he who gave them their 'H' designations. Today H1 to
H4 can be seen at the National Maritime Museum in Greenwich. H5
belongs to the Worshipful Company of Clockmakers and is on
show at their museum in London's Guildhall. In March 2002, H4 –
described by the National Maritime Museum as 'probably the most
important timekeeper ever made' – was wound up and made to
start again as part of Britain's Science Week. The rough and tumble
of eighteenth-century politics, when a dogged Yorkshire carpenter
had to overcome the self-regarding scepticism of his political
masters before he could prove his genius, is a story which still
ticks on in the intricate mechanisms of John Harrison's clocks.

CHAPTER 5

James Watt Patents His Steam Engine Condenser
1769

In 1769 James Watt received a patent from Parliament for his invention of a separate condenser for steam engines, designed to greatly improve their efficiency. Britain was catapulted into the age of steam.

In 1768, Joseph Wright of Derby painted one of the finest pictures in the history of British art. Called 'An Experiment on a Bird in the Air Pump' it shows the reactions of a group of people as they watch a 'natural philosopher' – a sort of showman cum scientist – withdraw the air from a glass bulb in which is trapped a white cockatoo. The scene is candle-lit and the balance of light and shade creates a beautifully still, macabre effect. You can almost feel the onlookers holding their breath as they wait to see if the bird will die. Among them are two girls whose father seems to be explaining what is happening. The older one cannot bear to look and has covered her eyes, but her younger sister is transfixed by the fate of the cockatoo and watches spellbound. The lighting of the scene is so well judged that it evokes an atmosphere of ceremony, as if some secret rite were being performed. In this provincial household the rituals of science have for the moment supplanted those of religion as people gather to worship at the altar of invention. The picture, which hangs in the National Gallery in London, gives us an insight into Britain at the beginning of the Industrial Revolution. The popular image of that period is one of great wealth created on the back of poverty, pollution and despair, but that was not how it began. It grew out of a thirst for knowledge and a love of invention, the enlightened aspirations of the men and women of Britain's thriving provinces.

Britain's first steam engine was invented at the end of the seventeenth century by Thomas Savery, who advertised 'An Engine to Raise Water by Fire' and announced that his invention could be made large enough to do the work of 'eight, ten, fifteen or twenty horses'. It was rather like an enormous pressure cooker and had no moving parts. It was designed to pump water out of mine shafts – Savery called it 'The Miner's Friend' – but although its principles were sound, its efficiency was poor. The first inventor of a proper engine was Thomas Newcomen who in partnership with Savery built a machine with a piston that could continue pumping for hours at a time and was capable of drawing water from a depth of more than 150 feet. The first Newcomen engine went into operation in a mine in Worcestershire in the Midlands in 1712 and by the middle of the eighteenth century more than a hundred of them were being used around the country. They were used solely for pumping water, mainly out of mineshafts. Then, in 1763, James Watt had the opportunity of taking a close look at how they worked.

James Watt was a mathematical instrument maker who ran a shop within the precincts of Glasgow University. He was a friend of three of the university's professors, Joseph Black, John Anderson and John Robison, all of whom were interested in the power of natural phenomena. In his lectures Anderson used a model of a Newcomen steam engine and when it went wrong it was suggested that James Watt have a look at it to see if he could repair it. He managed to get it working again, but in doing so he realised that the machine was desperately inefficient. It wasted a huge amount of energy because its cylinder needed to change temperature from hot to cold and then back again in order drive the piston up and down. Constantly changing the temperature meant that all the heat which had been built up for one part of the process was lost in order to provide cold for the other. Watt estimated that 80 per cent of the steam created by the engine was in fact wasted. Solving the problem took him two years of thought and study. In 1765, in the course of a

Sunday stroll, he came up with the solution. The engine needed a separate condenser which could be kept cold, allowing the cylinder itself to remain hot.

The road from theoretical invention to commercial reality is often a long one, and so it proved for James Watt. He came up with a working model of his idea within a few weeks, but it took far longer to develop it into a working machine. His experiments were funded by John Roebuck, an entrepreneur and inventor who owned and ran ironworks in Stirlingshire. Roebuck took a two-thirds share in the patent which Watt was finally granted in 1769, but his factory proved unsuccessful at developing the machine to the high specifications required. Eventually he ran out of money and sold his share in Watt's patent to a Birmingham manufacturer called Matthew Boulton. Watt, who had been forced to earn his living as a surveyor and civil engineer, was still no nearer seeing his invention come to fruition after nearly ten years of waiting and experimenting. In 1774 he packed his bags and left Scotland for the Midlands. It was the move which changed his life. Matthew Boulton was far more than just another Midlands manufacturer. He and Watt had become acquainted several years before Watt's move south, and he was interested in using a steam engine to improve the efficiency in his factory. He was the ideal partner. He was wealthy, he was interested in ideas, he was patient and he had a generous outlook. Perhaps most important of all, his factory was used to making works of craftsmanship out of steel and his workforce was therefore much more capable of developing the complicated valves and other pieces of equipment required by his new partner's invention.

If you wanted to pick one date in which modern capitalism whirred into life you could do worse than the year 1776. Three of its most important components came into existence that year. Adam Smith published his *Wealth of Nations*, which became the handbook of laissez-faire economics; the American colonists issued their Declaration of Independence and set in train the process by which their new country would become the global centre of capitalist enterprise; and James Watt's first steam engine began commercial

Five British Paintings

Gin Lane (1751)   William Hogarth (1697–1764)

Hogarth was a radical. He believed that art should reflect the
contemporary world around it and his pictures were popular with all
classes of British society. *Gin Lane* is a fine example of his satirical
style: this and other engravings of moral subjects allowed him to
reach a wide audience. Hogarth also wanted to start a 'British' school
of art to reject what he saw as the artificiality of European painting of
the time. He was opposed to the idea of a Royal Academy – eventually
founded in 1768 – which he thought would encourage patrician
domination of the arts.

An Experiment on a Bird in the Air Pump   Joseph Wright of Derby
(1768)   (1734–1797)

Joseph Wright never worked in London. He spent his life painting
the lives and times of Britain's provincial middle class – the men and
women who were prospering from growing trade and the beginning
of the Industrial Revolution. In this painting, a masterpiece of British
art, Wright uses *chiaroscuro* – the mixture of light and shade – to
brilliant effect.

Greta Bridge, Yorkshire (c.1806)   John Sell Cotman (1782–1842)

Watercolours from the nineteenth and twentieth centuries hang in
homes throughout the land. They depict landscapes and rural scenes
providing a romantic, contemplative view of Britain and British life.
The watercolourists of the early nineteenth century made an

---

operation and provided the power which drove Britain's Industrial Revolution. The simple steam pump grew into a glorious
multi-faceted machine. Within a few years Watt had developed his
original invention so that it had a rotary action capable of turning
machinery. He then modified the piston mechanism to give it
greater power. After that he introduced a regulator which made the
whole thing smoother and easier to operate.

By the mid-1780s Watt's steam engine was beginning to trans-
form the life of the nation. The engine was no longer a piece of

important contribution to the development of British art. One of
the most admired was John Sell Cotman who spent most of his life in
London, but made frequent trips to Yorkshire to paint. This picture
is a beautiful example of his work.

The Boyhood of Raleigh   John Everett Millais
(1869–1870)   (1829–1896)

Millais was one of the founders of the Pre-Raphaelite Brotherhood, a
group of nineteenth-century painters who adopted a revolutionary
approach to art by trying to break with the conventions of the past.
As his career developed he left the Brotherhood behind and became
highly successful and fashionable. He was the first British artist to be
awarded a hereditary title when he became a baronet in 1885. This
picture explains his popularity – a typical example of the imaginary
historical scenes his Victorian audience loved.

Girl with a White Dog (1951–1952)   Lucian Freud (1922–)

Lucian Freud was born in Germany but he became a naturalised
British citizen after his family fled to Britain to escape Nazi
persecution. He is the grandson of the founder of psychoanalysis,
Sigmund Freud. He paints mainly portraits – friends, lovers or people
he just knows – all of them represented in a raw, realistic style. His is
very much a twentieth- and twenty-first-century view of portraiture
in which people's defences – often including their clothes – are
stripped away.

remote machinery belonging to coal and tin mines, but a central
feature of the factory or workshop, the busy, tireless companion
of labour in all its forms. It represented the greatest revolution in
the generation of power since the invention of the medieval wind-
mill. No longer dependent on water to drive their machinery,
manufacturing centres of all kinds could be built anywhere with
their workers grouped around them. They could operate for as
long as they liked and their great machines adapted and expanded
to suit the particularities of their needs. In the early nineteenth

century the steam engine was transferred to transport and drove the growth of the railways and international shipping. Matthew Boulton is reported to have told Samuel Johnson's biographer, James Boswell: 'I sell here, Sir, what all the world desires to have – power.' He was right. His partner had harnessed it and would ultimately give his name to its measurement: power and Watt became synonymous.

Steam began to drive everything. In 1768 a barber from Preston called Richard Arkwright invented a spinning frame for producing strong, serviceable yarn from imported cotton. He was a very different character from James Watt – more hard-headed businessman than reflective scientist. He turned to textile manufacturing when his previous source of income, wig-making, declined and by 1771 had established a spinning mill at Cromford in Derbyshire. He recruited his workforce locally and housed them in specially built cottages, favouring large families with lots of children who could be set to work in his mill. To begin with he used horse- or water-power, but by the mid-1780s he had adapted the James Watt steam engine to his manufacturing processes. A few years later, on Christmas Eve 1801, Richard Trevithick allowed a group of passengers to take a spin along Camborne Hill in Cornwall in his steam-powered road locomotive which he called the 'Puffing Devil'. In 1804 a locomotive built to his design hauled 10 tons of iron, five wagons and seventy men over 9 miles along the Merthyr Tydfil tramroad. The journey took four hours and five minutes. The time did not matter. Steam had once again proved its power and also won 500 guineas for a local ironmaster who bet a rival businessman that Trevithick's engine would complete the task. A quarter of a century later, George Stephenson's 'Rocket' became the most famous steam engine ever built when it reached a speed of 29 miles per hour and won the Rainhill Trials organised by the directors of the Manchester and Liverpool Railway. When the railway was officially opened a year later, the 'Rocket' knocked down and killed one of the leading politicians of the day, William Huskisson, as he stepped forward to meet the Duke of Wellington. Steam was unstoppable. Its strengths and dangers were an integral part of Britain's new industrial world.

When James Watt and Matthew Boulton were not busy designing and building the mighty engines of a new age, they enjoyed meeting with a group of friends in the Midlands known as the Lunar Society. Their club met every month on the Monday nearest to the full moon, not out of any ritualistic notion, but for the highly practical reason that it gave them more light with which to travel home. They held their meetings at one another's houses – often at Matthew Boulton's house in Soho, Birmingham – where they discussed the great issues of the day. Josiah Wedgwood, pottery manufacturer and anti-slavery campaigner was part of the group, so was Joseph Priestley, the minister of religion and amateur scientist who discovered oxygen. Another prominent member was Erasmus Darwin, grandfather of Charles, and himself a botanist as well as a poet and inventor with a considerable reputation. The 'Lunaticks', as they liked to call themselves, were thinkers – men whose energy, imagination and ingenuity were shaping the future of the world. They were liberal-minded, tolerant and optimistic: they believed that what they were doing would

James Watt and his fellow members of the Lunar Society changed the country forever. They started a revolution.

bring great benefit to mankind. They were the soul of the Industrial Revolution, an intellectual cooperative of mainly self-taught men who helped each other socially and financially and rejoiced in the love of science, art and ideas. Between 1788 and 1791, Erasmus Darwin published a long poem in two parts written in heroic couplets called 'The Botanic Garden'. Heavily annotated with erudite notes it is an extraordinary fusion of learning and poetry. His verses extol the beauty of invention – as with this description of a steam engine:

> Press'd by the ponderous air the Piston falls
> Resistless, sliding through it's iron walls;
> Quick moves the balanced beam, of giant birth,
> Wields his large limbs, and nodding shakes the earth.

His notes expand on this poetic theme:

There is reason to believe it (the steam engine) may in time be applied to the rowing of barges and the moving of carriages along the road ... As the specific levity of air is too great for the support of great burthens by balloons, there seems no probable method of flying conveniently but by the power of steam, or some other explosive material; which another half century may probably discover.

From stately verses to an astonishing vision of the future, 'The Botanic Garden' embraced the ambition of Britain at one of the most important turning points in its history. James Watt and his fellow members of the Lunar Society changed the country forever. They started a revolution. They did it from the best of motives, but the better world they dreamed of brought hardship and despair at the same time as it delivered prosperity and hope. Revolutions, as the world knows to its cost, are often like that.

CHAPTER 6

The Metropolitan Police Act
1829

In 1829 the Home Secretary, Robert Peel, created a new organisation to tackle crime on the streets of London. It was the world's first organised police force.

One Saturday night in July 1749 a riot broke out in the Strand in London. Three sailors, believing they had been robbed by the prostitutes they had visited in 'The Crown' pub, returned a little while later with a gang of mates to smash the place up. They beat up the people inside, threw the furniture into the street and set fire to it. A crowd gathered and joined in. Guards were called in from Somerset House at the top of the Strand and in the early hours of the morning the riot subsided with a few arrests. The following night another riot broke out. The crowd wrecked a couple of houses and rescued two of the prisoners who had been captured the night before. The disturbance was still going on Monday when the local magistrate returned from a weekend at his country place in Ealing. He was Henry Fielding who had recently published the novel for which he is most famous, *The History of Tom Jones, a Foundling.* It is one of the great works of English literature, a breathtakingly colourful account of a young man's struggle to be good in a rotten world, full of characters some of whom would not have been out of place in that weekend's events in the Strand.

What Fielding wrote about in his books he had seen at first hand, and as he began to sort out the consequences of the riots, he realised that firm measures would have to be introduced if London were to become a safer place. A lot of the magistrates were corrupt and disinclined to control a population which, in Fielding's view, had succumbed to 'a vast torrent of luxury' created by wealth from trade. Those in debt robbed others to find the money they needed while the poor were in 'a scandalous condition'. He decided that the best way to control crime was to license places of entertainment and, in 1753, to hire professional 'thieftakers' to hunt down the gangs who were making life intolerable for London's citizens. Matters came to a head that year because there had been five murders within the space of a week. Fielding proposed to the government that he could recruit men of 'known and approved fidelity and intrepidity' and was given £600 to carry out the task. The little force, known as 'The Bow Street Runners' because they operated out of Fielding's court in Bow Street, were very successful and were expanded and improved by his blind half-brother, John Fielding, who succeeded him as magistrate for the area.

The Fielding brothers were energetic in tackling the problems of crime in their local areas, but a system which relied entirely on the enthusiasm of the incumbent magistrate was unlikely to prove very successful in the long term. Anyway, the idea of a regular, well-paid police force was not something the British warmed to: it smacked too much of a government method for interfering with their everyday liberties. Meanwhile the London of *Tom Jones* grew into the city of *Oliver Twist*, the biggest urban conglomeration in the world, rich, dirty, violent and dangerous. Oliver and Bill Sikes walked through Smithfield Market on their way to commit robbery across ground 'nearly ankle-deep with filth and mire'. An enormous throng, made up of every conceivable kind of threatening individual swirled around them: 'Countrymen, butchers, drovers, hawkers, boys, thieves, idlers and vagabonds of every low grade, were mingled together in a mass.' William Cobbett, the journalist, radical MP and social reformer called the city 'the great *wen*' (*wen* meaning boil or pustule). London was magnificent: a thriving centre of the growing British Empire, but it was beginning to balloon out of control. When he became Home Secretary, Robert Peel said he wanted 'to teach the people that liberty does not consist in having your home robbed by an organised gang of thieves and by leaving the streets of London in the nightly possession of drunken women and vagabonds'. The liberties of England had become an excuse for licentious exploitation. It was time to create a police force to encourage people to conform to their civic responsibilities.

Sir Robert Peel was one of the most influential British politicians of the first half of the nineteenth century. He became Home Secretary in Lord Liverpool's administration in 1822 and for the next five years carried out a huge number of reforms when more than a hundred and fifty outdated statutes were either partially or wholly repealed. He removed the Combination Laws introduced at the end of the eighteenth century which prohibited all trade union activity. The Combination Act of 1825 permitted trade unions' existence, although it curtailed their activities. He also removed the death penalty as punishment for more than a hundred different crimes. In later life he would go on to lead the Conservative Party and serve as Prime Minister twice. Many people regard him as the founder of the modern Conservative Party, and in a letter he wrote to his constituents in 1834 it is easy to see why. He supported, he told them, 'a careful review of institutions ... undertaken in a friendly temper combining with the firm maintenance of established rights, the correction of proved abuses and the redress of real grievances'. In many ways these were the ideas upon which he had relied when, five years before, he founded the Metropolitan Police.

> *The liberties of England had become an excuse for licentious exploitation.*

Peel laid down nine principles for the creation of an effective police force. Its first duty was to prevent crime and disorder; 2: it had to recognise that its ability to perform was dependent on public support; 3: it needed the willing cooperation of the public in the voluntary observance of the law; 4: its ability to earn cooperation diminished in direct proportion to its need to use physical force; 5: its own impartial observance of the law was paramount and had to override public opinion; 6: it should use force only when its powers of persuasion were exhausted; 7: it should always be aware that the police are the public, and the public are the police; 8: it should never be seen, or thought to be seen, usurping the powers of the judiciary. The police are simply carrying out in a full time capacity what all members of the public need to do. And 9: it had to recognise that the absence of crime, not the enforcement of the law, was its greatest test. It is a long list, but a good one. On the whole those are still the principles by which we still expect our police forces to operate.

Today the idea of having police officers on our city streets is something we take for granted, but the London public looked warily on the group of men whom Peel ushered into its presence in 1829. There were just over a thousand of them altogether – 895 constables, 88 sergeants, 20 inspectors and 8 superintendents. They wore black stovepipe hats and blue swallowtail coats. The recruits – under the overall control of two commissioners – had to be under thirty-five, at least 5 foot 7 inches tall, literate and of good character. This last characteristic was, at the very beginning, in rather short supply. In its first few years the police seem to have lost quite a few men because they turned out be drunk, or were dishonest and ill-disciplined. Little by little the 'Peelers' or 'Bobbies' – both nicknames are derived from their founder – were fashioned into a respectable force. Within a year it had grown to 3,000 men organised into seven divisions and was capable of tackling the violence which still plagued the streets of the capital. Their first officer killed on duty was in 1830 when he tried to stop a fight between two drunks near King's Cross. In 1831 they were called out to stop the riots outside the Duke of Wellington's house on Hyde Park Corner.

In 1834 their efforts were rewarded by the comments of a Parliamentary Select Committee which reported that London's police force 'as respects its influence in repressing crime, and the security it has given to persons and property, is one of the most valuable modern institutions'. Valuable it certainly was, but dangerous too. London's rapidly expanding middle classes were only too grateful to have policemen around, but some of their fellow citizens from the rougher parts of town were not so welcoming. Henry Mayhew, who chronicled the lives of London's poor in the 1840s, reported how boys laid in wait for unsuspecting policemen and hurled stones and bricks at them. Many of those who lived and worked in London had no fixed place of work and nowhere to live. Some of them combed the sewers to find bits and pieces valuable enough to sell; others were on the constant look-out for something to steal and were prepared to fight, or even kill, to get it. The police officer, armed only with a truncheon and a rattle to raise the alarm – kept in the breast pocket to protect the heart in the event of a knife attack – was always vulnerable.

By the end of the nineteenth century the population of London had grown to 7 million, and the Metropolitan Police from a force of 3,000 to 16,000. Other forces were now established all over the country – and with them came the problems of policing a modern industrial democracy. Cases of drunkenness, and even corruption, tarnished the image of the Metropolitan Police; one Commissioner, Sir Edmund Henderson, was forced to resign in 1886 after riots in Trafalgar Square; and in 1898 there were calls for the police to be armed after a constable was murdered. An all too familiar picture was beginning to take shape.

Robert Peel understood that a strong police force depended primarily on an unbreakable bond between it and the people it was recruited to serve. He knew that no police force could ever be perfect, but he knew, too, that it was better than nothing. His nine principles explained with great clarity how a strong police force should operate as an integral part of a democratic nation. In a democracy the people get the police, as they get the government, they deserve.

The Red House

The Red House in the hamlet of Upton near Bexleyheath in Kent was built by William Morris, the founder of the Arts and Crafts movement, in 1859. It represents a landmark in British architecture. Morris believed that it was possible to introduce beauty into everyday life and pioneered the design of furniture and wallpaper as well as buildings. 'Have nothing in your house that you do not know to be useful,' he said, 'or believe to be beautiful.' This was his golden rule and in the Red House he applied it to his own life. He bought the plot of land before he married and had it built as a home for his new young family. His two daughters were born there.

The Victorian fashion for all things Gothic dictated that the exterior of the house was red brick, but influenced by the designs of medieval architecture. Inside a variety of colours and patterns were used in the tiles, stained glass, textiles and paintwork. Morris's friend, Dante Gabriel Rossetti, called it 'more a poem than a house ... but an admirable place to live in too'. Unfortunately its creator was only able to live in it for five years. Financial strains, combined with the tedium of the daily journey from Bexleyheath to his company in London, which he had set up to manufacture his designs, forced him to sell up in 1865. He resolved never to return. The sight of the house was more than he could bear.

William Morris was one of the most influential of Victorian artists. He was one of the founders of the Pre-Raphaelite movement as well as a poet, novelist and painter. He was also a committed socialist and wanted to see ordinary craftsmen and artisans raised to the status of artists. His wife, Janey Burden, was a stableman's daughter who had sat for him as a model for his paintings. It is for his work in the area of domestic life that he is best remembered. His textile and wallpaper designs have remained enormously popular and are still on sale today.

CHAPTER 7

The Publication of Charles Darwin's
On the Origin of Species
1859

In 1859 Charles Darwin published *On the Origin of Species by Means of Natural Selection* in which he proved the process of evolution. It was one of the most important books ever written.

In June 1860, the British Association for the Advancement of Science held a historic meeting. The greatest scientific minds of the day gathered in the newly completed Museum of Natural History at Oxford, a neo-Gothic masterpiece which brought under one roof the university collection of natural history and anatomical specimens. The new building was actually rather less important than the new idea which Britain's scientists had assembled to discuss. Seven months before, Charles Darwin had published his book *On the Origin of Species by Means of Natural Selection*. Darwin himself was not at the meeting. Stress made him ill and brought on stomach pains and vomiting: he preferred the calmness of a clinic to the vigour of debate, particularly if his own work was at the centre of the argument. Several of his supporters were there, but so were many of his opponents, including Samuel Wilberforce – Lord Bishop of Oxford and a magnificent example of Victorian grandiloquence.

Wilberforce – known to his contemporaries as 'Soapy Sam' – was the third son of the anti-slavery campaigner, William Wilberforce, and like his father had a national reputation for eloquence. On the second day of the meeting, he got to his feet and began to attack Darwin's theory of natural selection. What he then said has become a matter of debate almost as intense as that surrounding Darwin's book. Turning to T. H. Huxley, a distinguished supporter of Darwin, Wilberforce is supposed to have asked him whether it was through his grandfather or grandmother that he claimed descent from a monkey. Huxley, small, slight and serious, is reported to have replied that he was not ashamed to have a monkey for an ancestor, but would be ashamed to be connected with a man who used his great gifts to obscure the truth. Wilberforce's sneering question vanquished by Huxley's poised response has become a legendary episode in the controversy generated by *The Origin of Species* in Victorian Britain: the haughty intransigence of the Church defeated by the forensic skills of science. Almost certainly, it was not quite like that. Wilberforce was not so arrogant, although he probably overstepped the mark, and Huxley not so sharp, although he seems to have rebuffed the bishop very well. The episode is interesting not for what was actually said, but for what people realised Darwin's book meant. *The Origin of Species* was about to change the world.

Charles Darwin was born in Shrewsbury in 1809. He was the son of a wealthy doctor and financier. His paternal grandfather was Erasmus Darwin, the distinguished philosopher, inventor and poet; on his mother's side his grandfather was Josiah Wedgwood, the pottery manufacturer and social reformer. These two men had known each other when, as members of the Lunar Society in Birmingham, they had met to discuss the great ideas of the day. Charles Darwin went to Edinburgh University to study medicine, but the brutality of surgery was not to his taste and he found himself drawn towards natural history. In this he was not unlike many other nineteenth-century gentlemen of the time. A growing knowledge of the world around them encouraged their interest in fossils, beetles and butterflies, and the chalk cliffs and shoreline of Britain played host to an army of determined and intelligent collectors, capturing, fishing, sifting and scraping in search of the secrets of creation. Darwin's father, worried that his son was being too easily diverted, sent him to Cambridge University to learn that other discipline then popular with well-heeled gentlemen – studying to become a clergyman. But Darwin had taken to natural history in a way that was altogether too serious to be put aside. At Cambridge he became friends with the Professor of Botany, John Henslow, who suggested to the captain of HMS *Beagle* that Darwin would be the ideal naturalist to fill the position of unpaid gentleman's companion during a two-year voyage to chart the coastline o f South America. Darwin overcame his father's opposition to the scheme and on 27th December 1831 set sail from Plymouth.

HMS *Beagle* took nearly five years to complete its voyage. By the time it finally returned to Britain in 1836, Charles Darwin was a scientific celebrity. When he joined the ship he seemed to think of himself as a simple assistant, someone who had been sent off to collect specimens on behalf of the distinguished scientific community back at home. In a journey that took him across the Atlantic to South America, round Cape Horn and into the Galapagos Islands, then across the Pacific to Tahiti, New Zealand and Australia; and finally to Mauritius and South Africa with a further stop on the coast of South America before the final return home, Charles Darwin was transformed from amateur specimen hunter and carefree young undergraduate into a serious naturalist. All thoughts of a career in the Church, if they had ever seriously existed, were abandoned. While he was away, he actually spent most of his time on land, observing and collecting specimens and examples. His findings were published in 1839 as a *Journal and Remarks* to accompany the captain of the *Beagle*'s own account, but they soon developed a separate and very popular life of their own. They contained some of his early thoughts about evolution and the natural world, which were then not completely formed. Darwin's family wealth meant that he did not need to find a job, and he spent the next few years lecturing, writing up his notebooks and developing the ideas he had begun to develop on his worldwide voyage. Before long these had taken the shape of certainty. Mankind had not been created by a single Godly act. It had evolved.

Darwin moved to Kent where he lived happily with his family –

he was a devoted husband and father, and was deeply distressed by the death of his eldest daughter, Annie, in 1851 – but did not publish his ideas about evolution. For nearly twenty years one of the most important scientific theories in the whole history of mankind remained locked in his home in Kent, the only written evidence of its existence contained in a manuscript nearly 200 pages long, which Darwin had had carefully copied and kept in his study with instructions to his wife, Emma, to publish in case of his sudden death. On a purely domestic level, he did not want to upset his wife's religious beliefs. More widely, he knew that what he had discovered would shake Victorian Britain to its foundations. Charles Darwin studied barnacles, while the world remained in ignorance of its origins.

All human beings, however noble and however kind, have egos – and Charles Darwin was no exception. In 1858 he discovered that his was the better part of discretion when out of the blue he received a paper from a naturalist called Alfred Russel Wallace. It was entitled 'On the Tendency of Variations to Depart Indefinitely from the Original Type'. Darwin had only met Wallace once, but the two men enjoyed a professional correspondence. Here, in the latest manuscript to be sent to him from the Malay Archipelago where Wallace had been working, Darwin recognised some, although not all, of his own ideas. Darwin agonised, then sat down and wrote. In December 1859 his book went on sale.

He knew that what he had discovered would shake Victorian Britain to its foundations.

In an essay written for the hundredth anniversary of the publication of *The Origin of Species*, the distinguished British scientist, Sir Julian Huxley, himself descended from Darwin's friend, T. H Huxley, said this:

Charles Darwin is and will always remain one of the pre-eminent figures in human history. He rendered evolution inescapable as a fact, comprehensible as a process, all-embracing as a concept. After Darwin it became necessary to think of the phenomenal world in terms of process, not merely in terms of mechanisms, and eventually to grasp that the whole of reality is a single process of evolution.

That is a tremendous statement. To call someone 'one of the pre-eminent figures in human history' is to afford them a status to which very few, certainly no more than a handful, can lay claim. But Darwin is entitled to the accolade, not because of what he was but because of what he discovered. In one book he threw the biblical laws of creation out of the window and demolished beliefs about human existence which had governed Western society for thousands of years. Darwin stated that all the species that have ever lived on earth may form a single tree of life. He had first drawn a sketch of an evolutionary tree after the end of the *Beagle* voyage in 1837. He went on to say that any group of a similar species – such as a type of bird – was descended from a single, common ancestor and all birds, of all types, were also descended from a single ancestor from an earlier time. All animal and plant species could share a common ancestry if they were traced back far enough. Darwin then explained the process by which this ancestral development had been driven – natural selection. Species diverged as they evolved from their single ancestor; they adapted to their changing needs – flying, swimming, burrowing and so on; and they progressed in their development so that higher creatures had sophisticated mechanisms – arms and legs, mouths and ears – while lower ones moved and reacted in a more cumbersome manner. In other words Darwin said that all human beings and all animals evolved from common species which may themselves have evolved from one single root; and that in the process of evolving, natural selection – the survival of the fittest – determined which species lived on and which did not. All of his subsequent works were to a large extent a further discussion of these fundamental ideas and built and expanded upon them.

One of the most interesting aspects of the impact of Darwin's book was – and still is – on religion and religious thought. Today

Five Popular Composers

16th Century: Thomas Tallis (c.1505–1585)

Thomas Tallis survived the reigns of four Tudor monarchs and, at a time when music-making revolved almost entirely around the Church, produced some of the finest music ever composed by an Englishman. Most of his compositions were choral: one of the most famous is 'Spem in Allium' – 'There is no hope but in God' – a motet for forty voices. We do not know why or when it was written, but some scholars think it might have been for the fortieth birthday of either Mary Tudor in 1556, or Elizabeth I in 1573.

17th Century: Henry Purcell (c.1659–1695)

Many people believe that Henry Purcell was the greatest of all British composers. He wrote music both for the Church and the theatre, holding the posts of organist of Westminster Abbey from 1679 and of the Chapel Royal from 1682. His most celebrated work is the chamber opera *Dido and Aeneas*, which introduced ideas completely new to British music of the time.

18th Century: George Frederick Handel (1685–1759)

Not British by birth, but probably Britain's best-loved composer, Handel dominated the London musical scene throughout the first half of the eighteenth century. He was born in Halle, Germany, where he worked briefly as a church musician before pursuing a career in opera. A natural man of the theatre, Handel abandoned opera in the Italian style in favour of oratorios when he realised these were more to the taste of his public. His most famous is *Messiah*, first performed in Dublin in 1742 and a spectacular favourite with British audiences ever since.

---

very few people would question the idea of evolution, or natural selection: they are accepted as inviolable scientific truths. The issue with which people have had to wrestle – and in the nineteenth century this was by far the biggest issue of all – was what effect did Darwin's discoveries have on a belief in God as the Almighty, the Creator and ultimate universal power? Darwin himself came from a

19th Century: Gilbert and Sullivan

The composer Arthur Sullivan (1842–1900) with his librettist
William Gilbert (1836–1911) wrote fourteen comic operas until their
acrimonious split in 1896. *The Mikado, The Pirates of Penzance, Iolanthe*
and *HMS Pinafore* – as well as many of their other operettas – remain
as popular today as they did when they were first performed in
Victorian London. Arthur Sullivan was also a serious composer while
Gilbert wrote a large number of plays and poems; but it is for their
work together that they are still remembered today.

20th Century: The Beatles

The Beatles were the most influential band of the twentieth century.
Their most famous songs – including 'Please, Please Me', 'Help',
'Hey Jude' and 'All My Loving', as well as many others – have become
some of the best-loved and most enduring popular songs ever written.
The Beatles: John Lennon (1940–80), Paul McCartney (1942–), George
Harrison (1943–2001) and Ringo Starr (1940–) recorded together for
the first time in 1962, and for the last in 1969. They have sold more
records than any other group or artist.

strong Nonconformist background and although he stopped going
to church, he never described himself as an atheist. He preferred
the term 'agnostic', a word invented by T. H. Huxley to describe
the thinking of people like him whose faith had been tempered
by science. In a lecture he gave at the beginning of the year in
which *The Origin of Species* was published, Huxley declared: 'Science,

and the methods of science, are the masters of the world.' But, he added, 'True science and true religion are twin-sisters, and the separation of either from the other is sure to prove the death of both.' He urged people to desert the two extremes of each – 'bigoted orthodoxy' in religion, and 'conceited scepticism' in science. This liberal-minded, middle way was not to everyone's taste. The naturalist Philip Gosse, whose popular books about the seashore helped give birth to the Victorian fashion for aquariums, remained a fundamental Christian throughout his life despite his detailed knowledge of sea anemones and orchids. (These attitudes are described by his son, Edmund, in his book, *Father And Son*, about life with his fanatically religious father as they went hunting together for specimens along the coast of Devon.) In the middle of the nineteenth century the Victorian world turned to nature to find the answers to existence. It raided rock pools, pinioned butter-flies and chipped out fossils in its search for truth. For men like Philip Gosse – or even Bishop Wilberforce – scientific endeavour was just further proof of the existence of God. But for men like Huxley the discoveries of science meant that the old biblical laws of religion had to be treated with scepticism. Faith was fine, but theology profoundly unscientific.

The man who discovered the actual truth stayed apart from the great debate, professing illness when it grew too close, preferring simply to deliver his conclusions than debate their consequences. Charles Darwin was a messenger – one who knew all too well that his message, like the message from Palestine 1,800 years before, would change forever how people thought about their world.

CHAPTER 8

The Football Association Publishes 'The Laws of Football' 1863

In 1863 the newly formed Football Association published 'The Laws of Football'. Britain had been given the rules for a national obsession.

The football manager, Bill Shankly, is supposed to have said that 'some people think football is a matter of life and death – but it's more important than that'. True or not, the remark is a witty embodiment of the British attitude to the country's favourite game. Shankly himself was the perfect representative of its love affair with football. Born in a poor Ayrshire mining community, he became a distinguished player for Preston North End and Scotland, but the Second World War interrupted his career and in 1949 he became a club manager, first for Carlisle then for Grimsby, Workington, Huddersfield and finally – and most memorably – for Liverpool. At Liverpool, which he managed from 1959 to 1974, he took the club from the bottom of the Second Division to the top of the First – the Premier League did not then exist – and to two victories in the FA Cup. The fans loved him, and he returned their affection. He knew instinctively why football was important to them and how much the success of their club mattered. Liverpool's football stadium in Anfield – whose famous stand 'The Kop', is named after a Boer War battle where many Liverpudlian soldiers lost their lives – has gates dedicated to Bill Shankly. Above them is a quotation from the club's anthem, a popular song from a Broadway musical, 'You'll Never Walk Alone'. History and popular culture combine to evoke the spirit of football – and pay tribute to its heroes like Bill Shankly.

The British have been kicking a ball around since the twelfth century – and probably before then. Medieval kings were often worried about the distractions of the game because it took young men away from the far more important task of practising the longbow. Edward IV passed a law in 1477 stating that 'no person shall practise any unlawful games such as dice, quoits, football and such games', ordering them to practise archery instead. No doubt the King was also concerned about the nature of the game which was rather less organised than it is today. Young craftsmen and apprentices divided into two teams – often just large crowds – and threw, kicked and chased an inflated animal bladder from one town to the next. It was rough, noisy and violent. In Wales in 1550, a contemporary report described 'a thousand or fifteen hundred men' chasing one ball, and this anarchic approach to the game seems to have persisted until the seventeenth century. Oliver Cromwell viewed football in the same light as cock-fighting and bear-baiting, and ordered its suppression.

By the end of the eighteenth century the game had developed into a more coherent form. In 1801 Joseph Strutt included a description of it in his book *The Sports and Pastimes of the People of England*. He wrote about it in a section devoted to 'Rural Exercises Practised by Persons of Rank', observing that the game had been 'formerly much in vogue among the common people of England' but was now being revived 'in our great public schools'. The upper classes had spotted the game's value and were busy refining it into something they wanted to play. This process was encouraged by educational reforms. In the first half of the nineteenth century the public schools of England, led by Rugby where Thomas Arnold had become headmaster in 1828, began to promote sport as an important part of education. Arnold was one of Britain's greatest educational reformers. He introduced subjects such as modern history and modern languages into his school's curriculum, but he believed that education was not just about learning, but about the development of character as well. Sport helped that process. Each school played football by its own rules. Some used both hands and feet, others – particularly Eton and Harrow which owned big, open playing fields – concentrated on kicking the ball long distances. Because the schools played different games they could not play against each other. In 1848 they met in Cambridge and after an eight-hour meeting produced the first set of formal rules for the game they called 'association football'. But variations still persisted. One of the convenors of the Cambridge meeting, a teacher called J. C. Thring, later published what he called 'Rules for the Simplest Game', which contained instructions such as: 'Kicks must be aimed only at the ball', and 'No tripping up or heel kicking allowed'. The riotous and disorganised assemblies of Britain's working towns-people were being brought under the patrician control of men with a more refined outlook on life.

At the same time the new game of association football was beginning to spread from the playing fields of Eton and other public schools to Britain's towns and cities. A club was established in Sheffield in 1857 and five years later Notts County, the oldest club still existing in the Football League, was founded. The need for clear rules to govern the game, and an organisation to adminis-ter them was pressing. In 1863 a group of representatives met at the Freemason's Tavern in Great Queen Street, London and, having formed the Football Association, issued the 'The Laws of Football'. A game which would eventually embody the hopes and passions of a whole nation had been born.

'The Laws of Football' of 1863 set out, among other things, the size of the pitch, the rules governing free kicks, the rules about handling the ball and the rules against tripping and pushing an opponent. Eight years later the Football Association set up a Challenge Cup so that member clubs could compete against one another and the game grew rapidly in popularity. By the end of the nineteenth century much of the apparatus of the sport we recognise today was in place. Each game had a neutral referee, the goals had crossbars and nets, and players were starting to get paid.

It was played in state schools – it was considered more suitable for frail, sometimes undernourished children than rugby – and was seen as a healthy, responsible pastime. Sir Watkin Williams-Wynne, the MP for Denbighshire was of the opinion that 'after playing a good game of football ... young men are more glad to go to bed than visiting the public house'. Charles Alcock, the first Secretary of the Football Association and the driving force behind the development of the sport in its early years, went further. Football, he observed, had become 'the pursuit of thousands ... almost magnified into a profession'. The game was quickly slipping away from the representatives of the public schools who had organised it. It had been adopted by the country at large and was becoming enormously popular in Britain's industrial towns. The creation of the Football League in 1888 contributed to this. Twelve clubs, all from the Midlands and the North of England, formed themselves into a league to play matches against one another. Preston North End – the 'Old Invincibles' – carried off the honours.

It is not difficult to see why football became so popular so quickly. It was easy to play and could be practised on open ground almost anywhere. It was not expensive. It did not require much equipment. All these factors made it the ideal sport for working men from Britain's industrial towns who stood little chance of being able to play golf, tennis or even cricket – and no chance whatsoever of going hunting or shooting. Football was something they could make their own, in the park, in the street or on a stretch of waste land. The ugliest patch of earth could be converted with a little imagination into the grandest stadium: street cries became the roar of the crowd. The creation of local teams helped build loyalty and generate excitement. The 'simple game' which a public school master had described rather tersely in 1862, had, by the end of the century, become a cultural and social phenomenon, and has remained so ever since.

At the end of the nineteenth century a professional football player called Archie Hunter described his early years in the game, when it was just beginning to take off in Britain. 'We went in for the new game with enthusiasm,' he said. 'Every night saw us in hard training and we learned the art of working well together. Good combination ... is greatly to be preferred to the muscular powers of one or two ... Strength has got very little chance against science.' The team and team loyalty had entered the bloodstream of the British way of life. One team that would have needed to dig deep on its reserves of loyalty in the first days of football was a side named Bon Accord from Aberdeen. In 1885 they were drawn to play against Arbroath in a first-round match of the Scottish Cup, a competition which had been invented two years after its English counterpart. Their name was taken from the watchword that was used to announce the beginning of the storming of Aberdeen Castle during the Scottish War of Independence. Unfortunately they were not capable of any storming at all on the wet September day they faced Arbroath. They lost 36–0. The Arbroath centre forward, John Petrie, scored thirteen goals, a record which still stands today. The Arbroath goalkeeper had so little to do that he borrowed an umbrella from one of the spectators to try to keep dry.

Today Arbroath is in the Third Division of the Scottish League. But the club still remembers with pride the day it beat Bon Accord so handsomely. In football, then and now, the team's the thing.

CHAPTER 9

The Foundation of the BBC
1927

In 1927 the British government created the British
Broadcasting Corporation, the BBC. It was the first
public service broadcaster in the world. Since its
foundation it has grown into a central part of British
life and a worldwide example of impartial broadcasting.

I worked for the BBC for many years. I joined in the late 1960s
when it was still organised in a similar manner to the Civil Service.
Heads of departments did not have names, but initials – the Head
of Television Current Affairs, for instance, was known as and
referred to as H.C.A Tel – and every member of staff had a final
salary pension. When I first left in 1990 it had changed completely,
and was about to change even more. It was no longer a 'cradle-to-
grave' employer. Most people worked on contracts, and very short
contracts at that. Everybody knew everybody else by their Christian
names. Nobody wore a tie. The BBC had transformed itself from
a rather grand, aloof institution into a modern media beehive.
Of all the many extraordinary talents which it possesses, its ability
to survive is one of its most impressive. It is an organisational
chameleon, sometimes seemingly inert but always waiting and
watching ready to adapt to necessary change.

The BBC, like many other things in Britain, was born out of
commercial enterprise. In 1922 a company known as the British
Broadcasting Company was established to provide a national broadcasting service from the network of radio transmitters operated by
the six big engineering concerns which owned it. They included
Marconi, Metropolitan-Vickers and General Electric, the last two of
which had ties to sister companies in America. The company hired

a Scottish engineer called John Reith to run their business and got down to work. In August 1923 it broadcast its first national news bulletin and the following month published the first edition of the *Radio Times*. By the end of 1925 it had more than 650 employees, upon whom John Reith had begun to impose his stern code of behaviour. Radio announcers, for instance, had to wear dinner jackets when reading the news. All this activity was exciting, but also concerning. The idea of a national broadcasting system entirely in private hands was not something which the government viewed with equanimity and in 1925 set up a parliamentary committee to look into it. The committee, under Lord Crawford, recommended the estab-

The BBC had transformed itself from a rather grand, aloof institution into a modern media beehive.

lishment of a public corporation funded by a licence fee. It declared that the content of the new national network should contain a higher proportion of educational content and that 'every effort should be made to raise the standard of style and performance ... particularly in music'. It added loftily 'that a moderate amount of controversial matter should be broadcast, provided that the material is of high quality and distributed with scrupulous fairness'. This, as the historian A. J. P. Taylor remarked, 'endorsed the moral case for monopoly'. Public service broadcasting in Britain began life as a splendid imposition. The theatre, the music hall, books and art were all allowed to flourish as they wished, albeit moderated occasionally by the interference of the Lord Chamberlain who acted as a guardian of public decency. Broadcasting was not to be afforded such luxury. The population could not be trusted to enjoy un-regulated material pumped into their homes through their wireless sets: it had to be controlled.

The government recognised that this could not be done directly by the machinery of the state and followed the recommendations of Lord Crawford's committee by setting up a Board of Governors to act as the public trustees of the new corporation. The governors,

British Humour

The British love a good joke. Their ability to laugh at themselves is one of their most endearing qualities. The growth in the popularity of radio and then television from the end of the Second World War gave birth to a constant stream of comedians with whom the nation laughed with affectionate happiness. Here are ten of the most famous with some of their catchphrases and characters.

ITMA (It's That Man Again) (1939–1949, Radio)

Tommy Handley led the cast in the most popular radio show of the wartime years, playing such characters as the Minister of Aggravation and Mysteries in the Office of Twerps. The title was taken from a contemporary newspaper headline about Hitler.

Catchphrase, said by Mrs Mop the charlady as she announced her arrival in Tommy Handley's office: 'Can I do you now sir?'

TIFH, Take It From Here (1948–1960, Radio)

TIFH introduced the everyday story of the Glum family, starring Jimmy Edwards as Mr Glum with Dick Bentley as his moronic son, Ron Glum, and June Whitfield as Ron's frustrated fiancée Eth'. Their comic interludes always began with Eth' wheedling her way into Ron's foggy mind:

'R... oooo... nnn?'

'Yes Eth'?'

Hancock's Half-Hour (1954–1961, Radio and Television, later simply Hancock)

Written by Alan Simpson and Ray Galton, the character of Anthony Aloysius St John Hancock was one of the great comic creations of the post-war years. His mixture of bravado and confusion was never on better display than in the famous 'Blood Donor' episode. Hancock is shocked to discover he has to give a whole pint before he gets his free cup of tea: 'A pint? That's very nearly an armful!'

Steptoe and Son (1962–1974, Television)

Simpson and Galton also created the characters of the rag-and-bone man Albert Steptoe and his son Harold. Wilfred Brambell and Harry H. Corbett (he added the 'H' to distinguish himself from Sooty's puppetmaster) played the much-loved characters. The son, desperately trying to raise standards in the Steptoe household, would frequently admonish his father: '*You dirty old man!*'

Round the Horne (1965–1968, Radio)
One of the greatest radio sketch shows, starring a variety of wonderful characters presided over by straight man, Kenneth Horne. Two of the most popular were the camp duo Julian and Sandy, played by Hugh Paddick and Kenneth Williams, at work in a variety of 'bona' businesses. '*Hello, I'm Julian and this is my friend Sandy!*'

The Benny Hill Show (1969–1989, Television)
Benny Hill's sketch show was one of the few British comedies to be a hit in America as well as Britain. It featured a heavy dose of slapstick and *double entendres*, and often ended with a speeded-up scene of Benny chasing, or being chased by, a gaggle of scantily clad women.

The Morecambe and Wise Show (1968–1983, Television)
The most popular television comedy show of its time starred Eric Morecambe and Ernie Wise. It often featured celebrity cameos in which Ernie would invite a famous personality to join the show – and Eric would then mess it up. Eric would turn to the audience and say: '*What do you think of it so far? . . .*'

The Two Ronnies (1971–1987, Television)
Ronnie Barker and Ronnie Corbett were the stars of this popular show. Many of the sketches were written by Ronnie Barker under a pseudonym: to begin with even his partner did not know that he was the author. 'Four Candles' – set in a DIY store – is one of its best-known sketches in which Ronnie Corbett plays the owner of a hardware store and Ronnie Barker is his customer:

Barker: '*Four candles!*'
Corbett: '*Four candles? There you are, four candles.*'
Barker: '*No, four candles!*'
Corbett: '*Well there you are: four candles!*'
Barker: '*No, fork 'andles! 'Andles for forks!*'

Yes Minister (1980–1984, Television)
In this excruciatingly accurate parody of life in the corridors of power, Nigel Hawthorne played the scheming Permanent Secretary,

Sir Humphrey Appleby, and Paul Eddington the bumbling Minister, Jim Hacker. 'Sir Humphrey' has become a British description for all obstinate bureaucrats.

Monty Python's Flying Circus (1969–1974, Television)

Graham Chapman, John Cleese, Terry Gilliam, Eric Idle, Terry Jones, and Michael Palin took British comedy to new heights in a programme of sustained absurdity. *Monty Python* was a completely new type of humour which rapidly established itself with British audiences. The dead parrot sketch starring John Cleese and Michael Palin is one of its immortal moments. Cleese is returning a parrot to a pet shop because the creature has died. The pet shop owner, played by Palin, claims it's not dead, just 'pining'.

'It's not "pinin'!" It's passed on! This parrot is no more! It has ceased to be! It's expired and gone to meet its maker! This is a late parrot! It's a stiff! Bereft of life, it rests in peace! If you hadn't nailed it to the perch it would be pushin' up the daisies! It's rung down the curtain and joined the choir invisible! THIS IS AN EX-PARROT!'

The Office (2001–2003, Television)

Ricky Gervais played David Brent in this frighteningly observant comedy series about life in an office in Slough. Brent is an office manager with no shame and no self-awareness – a comic creation who manages to make you shiver with embarrassment and roar with laughter at the same time.

---

not government ministers, were responsible for regulating its output – although the organisation remained dependent on the state for the amount of money it received through the licence fee. This arrangement was at the heart of how the BBC was supposed to work and was the cause of both its triumphs and its failures. On the one hand it was free of government interference and allowed to exercise its creativity and judgement as it saw fit. On the other, once it offended the government – which naturally presented its concerns as representing public opinion – it ran the danger of being reduced through financial starvation. The history of the BBC is the history of an organisation trying to keep the favour of the government without appearing to do so.

Radio was simply the first frontier. It expanded overseas when the BBC set up the Empire Service in 1932, a title later modified to the Overseas Service (now the World Service) to suit Britain's post-imperial status. But it was television which created the greatest change of all. By the mid-1930s, transmissions from Alexandra Palace in North London, watched by only a few thousand people, had covered Wimbledon, the FA Cup Final and the Coronation of King George VI. John Reith was sceptical about the appeal of this new system of broadcasting and, anxious for new opportunities, resigned. He left behind his Calvinistic concept of a BBC designed 'to educate, inform and entertain' – in that order – and an organisation on the brink of the most important cultural breakthrough in the history of the twentieth century.

The outbreak of the Second World War delayed the development of the BBC's television services, but greatly enhanced its reputation as a reliable and impartial source of news and information. The BBC became the voice of Britain, clear, reassuring and imperturbable. As the war came to an end another parliamentary committee recommended that its television experiments should start up again. It argued that the educational advantages of such a service could be enormous, but added, with telling prescience, that 'it is in the televising of actual events, the ability to give the viewer a front-row seat at almost every possible kind of exciting or memorable spectacle, that Television will perform its greatest service'. When the BBC provided television coverage of Queen Elizabeth II's coronation in 1953, an estimated 20 million people saw it. The foggy pictures first peered at by excited engineers only twenty-four years before were now the lifeline of a nation. The age of television had dawned.

The BBC was not allowed to have the field to itself. In 1955 Independent Television was created on the basis of a regional system of commercial franchises providing both local and national programmes. Just as the BBC had recruited a stern Scottish moralist,

John Reith, to manage its affairs in its early years, so the new Independent Television Authority recruited an urbane and distinguished scholar, Kenneth Clark, to be its first chairman. Television companies have always relied on the great and the good to protect themselves from accusations of pandering to populism. The invention of ITV radically changed the nature of British broadcasting. The BBC was forced to compete and, worried lest its viewing figures declined to a point where it would no longer be able to justify its income from the licence fee, moved the concept of entertainment higher in its list of priorities. While it still professed to subscribe to the 'Reithian' trio of education, information and entertainment, it had to rely principally on its ability as an entertainer in order to survive.

This set the pattern for broadcasting in the years which followed. In 1962 the Pilkington Report on Broadcasting lambasted ITV for the low quality of its programmes; fifteen years later another report, chaired by Lord Annan, tackled the issues raised by the BBC's policy of beginning to produce iconoclastic and satirical programmes such as *That Was the Week That Was*. Television had sprung out of its box to become the main source of entertainment in people's homes. They watched with delight whatever they were given – nightly dramas such as *Coronation Street*, comedy shows such as *Hancock*, or *Steptoe and Son*, and informative documentaries like *Civilisation* (presented on the BBC by the former chairman of the ITA, Kenneth Clark). In this environment, turning back to the original concept of public service broadcasting, which had been invented essentially as a means of controlling public taste, was interesting but fruitless. The sheer power of television, combined with constantly developing technology – colour television began in the late 1960s – meant that the definitions upon which broadcasting had been founded were probably ripe for change.

It was in nobody's interest to make any revisions. The BBC, dependent on the secure revenue from the licence fee, argued that there was no better way to pay for its services. ITV, dependent on revenue from advertising, had no desire to see the BBC sharing its money and so supported its rival's arguments. In the 1980s the Conservative government under Margaret Thatcher explored ways of separating the BBC from the licence fee as part of its economic reforms. Mrs Thatcher found the concept of the licence fee – a universal household tax – an undemocratic method of raising the money for a broadcasting service which, given the expansion of the television industry, could no longer be regarded as purely national. She failed. The shape and structure of British public service broadcasting, built around a central public corporation which receives money from nearly every citizen through the licence fee, has remained largely unaltered since long before television itself was invented. New systems of communication – initially just rival commercial stations, but latterly satellite and other services, including those provided over the internet – have not managed to budge the BBC from its central, deep-rooted position at the heart of Britain's cultural life. It has successfully adapted the concept of public service broadcasting to suit its changing needs. The idea began as a way of leading and influencing public taste by conviction and example: it has come to mean providing all sections of the British community with something they can understand and enjoy. It no longer imposes, it reflects and the stern morality of John Reith has been diluted into something more cosy. In this way the BBC has managed to maintain its connection with the people it has an obligation to serve.

The resolute permanence of the BBC is due to three things – the quality of its programmes, its political skill and the impossibility of making any serious change to its funding following the invention of commercial television more than fifty years ago. One of my last jobs for it was being part of the team which set up an international television channel, 'BBC World', based on the output of World Service Radio. The BBC had hoped that Mrs Thatcher's administration would allow it to create this out of the licence fee, but she disappointed them. It was forced to raise the money commercially and we travelled to many different parts of the world in search of possible partners. Everywhere we went the name of the BBC opened doors. In India, the Far East, Europe and even America mention of the BBC was met with respect and admiration. As a toughened television executive I found this both surprising and heart-warming. The BBC, I realised, is one of the things about Britain which people abroad most admire. Here at home the concept of public service broadcasting often seems to be little more than a convenient mantra – a useful phrase to justify activities which in almost any other circumstances would never attract a penny of public money. But somehow, in a uniquely British way, it has built something of lasting value. The British may not all love the BBC, but most of them admire it, and hardly any of them would like to see it go. It has crept into every corner of their lives and settled there, sometimes a source of irritation, often a means of comfort but always above all the representative of continuity.

CHAPTER 10

Frank Whittle Designs the First Turbo Jet Engine
1930

In 1930 a British engineer called Frank Whittle
designed the world's first jet engine. The age of
worldwide air travel was born.

In the autumn of 1870 Paris was under siege. A Prussian army had
swept through Eastern France and was waiting to capture the
French capital. The Franco-Prussian War was one of the most
shocking and horrifying episodes in the history of nineteenth-
century Europe. The Second Empire of Napoleon III collapsed like
a little wicker fence before the advancing might of the Prussian
military machine under the ultimate command of the Kaiser,
Wilhelm I, and his all-powerful Chancellor, Otto von Bismarck.
Trapped inside Paris with the rest of the population was Leon
Gambetta, the Minister of the Interior in the new, hastily created
French government. As the siege continued he realised that he
needed to join his colleagues who were trying to organise resistance
from the city of Tours in the Loire.

The only way out was by air, and on 7th October Gambetta
climbed aboard the only means of flight then available to man – a
balloon. The big contraption soared up above the streets of Paris
and out over the city gates where Prussian troops began to fire on it.
The pilot, who was not used to taking the balloon on long journeys,
lost control and it began to descend rapidly near the town of
Chantilly. It landed safely and, after ballast had been thrown over-
board, ascended once more to the accompaniment of further
enemy fire. Gambetta's hand was grazed, but the balloon flew on

until suddenly another shot pierced the material which housed its gas. Gambetta could hear the sound of Prussian drums on the ground below and urged his inexperienced pilot to land on the far side of a river, as far away from the enemy as possible. The balloon had just enough power to achieve this and after scraping a large oak tree the pilot finally brought it in to land. Gambetta escaped and reached Tours safely to become in later life one of the most distinguished leaders of the Third French Republic. The oak tree which the balloon hit as it landed was cut down. Its owner was a royalist who disapproved of the fact that it became a destination for visitors wanting to see where one of the country's foremost republicans had so narrowly escaped.

Gambetta's escape from Paris came at a crucial period in the history of flight. Only sixty years separates his unwieldy and dangerous journey in a balloon from the invention of the jet engine; barely thirty from the world's first aeroplane. The balloon had first thrilled the world in 1783 when the Montgolfier brothers lifted theirs to a height of 6,500 feet above their home town of Annonay in France. Floating upwards and then relying on wind currents was the only method of flying which mankind could make work. A Yorkshireman called Sir George Cayley researched and discovered the theoretical principles of flight at the beginning of the nineteenth century. Around 1799 he drew sketches of something not unlike the aeroplane which would be invented a hundred years later. In 1849 he built a glider which successfully carried the son of one of his servants a short distance. Four years later his coachman was propelled 900 feet across Brompton Dale in North Yorkshire in a glider with three horizontal wing structures. After it crashed the coachman is reported to have told his master that he wished to give in his notice. 'I was hired to drive, Sir,' he said, 'not to fly.' Cayley understood that flying required lift and thrust and that manned flight would not be possible until a suitable engine had been built. His ideas did not receive widespread acknowledgement: they were admired for their theoretical value rather than their practical application. In the middle of the nineteenth century, steam was still the only method of generating power, but coal fired engines were soon proved to be too heavy for use in the air.

The invention of the petrol engine towards the end of the nineteenth century provided the early aviators with the lightweight method of propulsion they needed. Orville and Wilbur Wright built an engine to their own design when, in December 1903, Orville flew their first aircraft for twelve seconds. Although they did not actually invent the first aircraft, the Wright brothers carried out the world's first manned, powered, sustained and controlled flight by an aircraft which was heavier than air. Their detailed aeronautical experiments meant that they were able to put knowledge into practice. Man had finally brought the power of flight under his control.

The story of Frank Whittle bears several similarities to that of another great British pioneer of power, James Watt. Like Watt, Whittle had to struggle to get his ideas accepted and was forced to rely on private enterprise to have them developed. Both men had to stay in their ordinary jobs because they could not afford to leave and work full time on their revolutionary ideas. Whittle was born in Coventry in 1907 and joined the RAF in 1923 where his skills so impressed his commanding officer that he was recommended for the Officer Training College at Cranwell – a rare honour for someone from an ordinary working-class background. At college he worked on his ideas for jet-propelled flight and again, rather like James Watt, 150 years before, struggled with the concept of how to get his engine to provide sufficient thrust without becoming too heavy. Watt, in the age of steam, had invented the idea of a separate condenser. Whittle, in the age of oil, invented the idea of using a gas turbine. He realised that instead of having a piston engine to provide the compressed air needed for the engine's burner, a turbine could be used to extract power from its exhaust. This could then drive an actual compressor, while the rest of the exhaust could be harnessed to propel the plane. He sent his idea to the Air Ministry who did not really understand it and passed it to an engineer called A. A. Griffith, who had himself written an important paper on jet engine design. Griffith told the Air Ministry that some of Whittle's calculations were wrong. The Ministry then totally rejected Whittle's idea.

Whittle was dejected, but his friends told him to patent his idea, which he did. He went off to Cambridge and collected a first-class degree in the Mechanical Sciences tripos, but in 1935 his patent lapsed because he could not afford the £5 to have it renewed. It was at this moment that private enterprise came to the rescue. Two former RAF men approached him with the idea of setting up a company to continue work on his jet engine. Together the three men, funded by a loan of £2,000, formed 'Power Jets Limited' and began working out of a factory in Rugby. The RAF, which still did not believe in Whittle's ideas, allowed him to work on the project for six hours a week. In April 1937 the company ran a successful test of the engine, which the Chairman of the Aeronautical Research Committee, Henry Tizard, described as 'streets ahead' of anything else he had seen. The Air Ministry now took an interest and furnished the company with a grant of £6,000 to build a flyable version. Britain was on the brink of war and the government's priority was to build Spitfires and Hurricanes. Work on Whittle's project was still subject to delay. Worse still, in Germany an engineer called Hans von Ohain had started work on a similar project in 1935 and had overtaken the British effort. German jets were getting ready to fly.

Frank Whittle had finally dragged his reluctant country into the jet age.

It was not until after the war had started in 1939 that the Air Ministry finally committed wholeheartedly to the production of Whittle's jet. His company had nearly run out of money but as the value of its invention became clear it was asked to gear up to produce 3,000 engines a month. In May 1941, four years after it had run its first successful test, the Whittle jet plane – W.1 – took off from Cranwell and flew for seventeen minutes at a speed of 340 miles an hour. It had previously flown in secret tests in the English countryside where people who saw it marvelled that a plane could fly without propellers. Frank Whittle had finally dragged his reluctant country into the jet age.

In 1944 his company, Power Jets Limited, was nationalised. Frank Whittle was given £100,000 in compensation for his shares and went to work elsewhere. In 1976 he emigrated to America and became a research professor at the American Naval Academy in Annapolis. His old rival, Hans von Ohain, also settled in the United States and the two men became friends. Whittle originally thought that von Ohain had stolen his ideas, but realised later that he had arrived at them at about the same time, but had had the good fortune to be supported by a government which recognised the value of what he had discovered.

Today the jet engine is part of all our lives. The airport is as familiar to most of us as the train station or the bus stop. We undertake huge journeys across the world with nonchalant familiarity. Frank Whittle's invention has led the world into an age of air travel which no one would have predicted when he struggled to get his ideas accepted more than seventy years ago.

Index

Picture Acknowledgements

Credits are by page number in order from left to right and top to bottom

1 – National Army Museum, London/The Bridgeman Art Library; 2 – The Crown Estate/The Bridgeman Art Library; Birmingham Museums and Art Gallery/The Bridgeman Art Library; Louie Psihoyos/Corbis; 3 – Royal Hospital Chelsea, London, UK/The Bridgeman Art Library; 4 – Ann Ronan Picture Library; Bettmann/Corbis; 5 – Getty Images; 6 – Hulton-Deutsch Collection/Corbis; Tate, London 2008; 7 – AP/PA Photos; 8 – Getty Images; Photofusion Picture Library/Alamy; 9 – Museum of London; Getty Images; 10 – English School; National Maritime Museum, Greenwich, London; Tate, London 2008; 11 – Private Collection/The Bridgeman Art Library; National Gallery, London, UK/The Bridgeman Art Library; 12 – Norwich Castle Museum and Art Gallery/The Bridgeman Art Library; Tate, London 2008; 13 – Bettmann/Corbis; 14 – Red House, Bexleyheath, UK/Ann S. Dean, Brighton/The Bridgeman Art Library; Imperial War Museum/Co802; 15 – John Tramper/Shakespeare's Globe; Getty Images; 16 – Private Collection/The Bridgeman Art Library

Text Acknowledgements

War Poet by Sidney Keyes is reprinted by permission of David Higham Associates Limited; the excerpt from 'Darwin and the Ideas of Evolution' by Julian S. Huxley from *A Book That Shook The World: Essays on Charles Darwin's 'Origin of Species'* is reprinted by permission of the University of Pittsburgh Press; the quotation from *Empire* by Niall Ferguson and the extracts from *The Canterbury Tales* by Geoffrey Chaucer translated by Nevill Coghill are reprinted by permission of Penguin Press. Material from Paula Bartley's article on Emmeline Pankhurst from the March 2003 edition of *History Review* and from Mark Goldie's article on Roger Morrice in the November 2001 edition of *History Today* is reproduced by permission of *History Today*. The quotation from Simon Schama is taken from Volume 2 of his *History of Britain* published by BBC Worldwide Limited.